FROTTAGE

SEXUAL CULTURES
General Editors: Ann Pellegrini, Tavia Nyong'o, and Joshua Chambers-Letson
Founding Editors: José Esteban Muñoz and Ann Pellegrini

Titles in the series include:

Frottage

Frictions of Intimacy across the Black Diaspora

Keguro Macharia

NEW YORK UNIVERSITY PRESS
New York

NEW YORK UNIVERSITY PRESS
New York
www.nyupress.org

© 2019 by New York University
All rights reserved

References to Internet websites (URLs) were accurate at the time of writing. Neither the author nor New York University Press is responsible for URLs that may have expired or changed since the manuscript was prepared.

Library of Congress Cataloging-in-Publication Data
Names: Macharia, Keguro, author.
Title: Frottage : frictions of intimacy across the black diaspora / Keguro Macharia.
Description: New York : New York University Press, [2019] | Series: Sexual cultures |
Includes bibliographical references and index.
Identifiers: LCCN 2019007704 | ISBN 9781479881147 (cloth) |
ISBN 9781479865017 (paperback)
Subjects: LCSH: African diaspora. | Blacks—Social conditions. | Sex. | Queer theory.
Classification: LCC DT16.5 .M26 2019 | DDC 306.7089/96—dc23
LC record available at https://lccn.loc.gov/2019007704

New York University Press books are printed on acid-free paper, and their binding materials are chosen for strength and durability. We strive to use environmentally responsible suppliers and materials to the greatest extent possible in publishing our books.

Manufactured in the United States of America

10 9 8 7 6 5 4 3 2 1

Also available as an ebook

to all my anonymous tricks

CONTENTS

Introduction

Frottage

I first read Alex Haley's *Roots* (1976) in the late 1980s, in my parents' Nairobi home. It left me with a haunting image of slavery that has guided me to this book. Following his capture, Kunta Kinte is locked in a slave hold, chained together with other men: "he very slowly and carefully explored his shackled right wrist and ankle with his left hand. . . . He pulled lightly on the chain; it seemed to be connected to the left ankle and wrist of the man he had fought with. On Kunta's left, chained to him by the ankles, lay some other man, someone who kept up a steady moaning, and they were all so close that their shoulders, arms, and legs touched if any of them moved even a little."[1] I was arrested by this image. At the time, though, I could not name what intrigued and terrified me about this enforced proximity, this monstrous intimacy.[2]

The image gains in intensity as the narrative continues. During a brutal storm, bodies rub against each other and against the ship: "each movement up and down, or from side to side, sent the chained men's naked shoulders, elbows, and buttocks—already festered and bleeding—grinding down even harder against the rough boards beneath them, grating away still more of the soft infected skin until the muscles underneath began rubbing against the boards."[3] Skin, self, body is worn away through "grinding" and "grating," as bodies are fed into slavery's maw. Haley's metaphors combine images from food and sex cultures, gesturing to the roles enslaved Africans would play within food and sex economies as producers and products. Ironically, these images of food and sex—now so central to how we imagine care and pleasure—register the obscene labor of how humans are transformed into objects. The body-abrading taking place in the hold through a process of sustained rubbing accompanies the commodification taking place through ship ledgers that record weight and monetary value instead of names, religious affiliations, geohistorical origins, or philosophical orientations. In fact, several kinds of rubbing are taking place: bodies against each other; bodies against the ship; writing implements against ledgers; and the rubbing in the slave holds against the writing in the ledgers. I use the term *frottage* to figure these violent rubbings and to foreground the bodily histories and sensations that subtend the arguments I pursue.

Although I take the slave hold as my point of departure, I dare not linger there.

One can depart from the slave ship in many ways, so let me describe the argument that *Frottage* pursues. Within black diaspora studies, scholars have insisted that while slavery was intended to dehumanize captured Africans, it did not succeed. Thus, much scholarship and creative writing has been devoted to proving that the enslaved were human, primarily by foregrounding their kinship ties: they nurtured, they loved, they reproduced.[4] A powerful, if less followed, line of thinking has pursued the problem of how slavery produced "thinghood." Describing the effects of enslavement, Cedric Robinson writes, "African workers had been transmuted by the perverse canons of mercantile capitalism into property."[5] Based on her examination of ship ledgers, Hortense Spillers writes, "Expecting to find direct and amplified reference to African women during the opening years of the [slave] Trade, the observer is disappointed time and again that this cultural subject is concealed beneath the mighty debris of the itemized account, between the lines of the massive logs of commercial enterprise."[6] Those ledgers do not record names; instead, they document the process of turning humans into commodities. In a more recent assessment of ledgers from slave ships, Katherine McKittrick finds,

> Breathless, archival numerical evidence puts pressure on our present system of knowledge by affirming the knowable (black objecthood) and disguising the untold (black human being). The slave's status as object-commodity, or purely economic cargo, reveals that a black archival presence not only enumerates the dead and dying, but also acts as an origin story. This is where we begin, this is where historic blackness comes from: the list, the breathless numbers, the absolutely economic, the mathematics of the unliving.[7]

I approach the problem of blackness and queerness from this "historic blackness." This origin story removes the enslaved from the domain of the human as that figure was theorized during modernity. Taking "thinghood" as a point of departure to elaborate black diaspora histories grapples with the difficulty of how to think about those considered not-quite-human and, at times, unhuman.[8] I focus on the speculative ways that black diaspora thinkers and artists imagined they could create usable histories and livable lives: Frantz Fanon formally and conceptually disrupts European philosophy and psychoanalysis to locate the black person that these disciplines cannot imagine; René Maran uses the resources of the ethnographic novel to create a temporal rapprochement between colonial Central Africa and an Africa before the ravages of the Middle Passage; Jomo Kenyatta uses myth and fabulation to usurp the authority of colonial anthropology to describe Kikuyu lives; and Claude McKay demonstrates in poetry and prose how Jamaicans innovated intimate practices of world-making, producing spaces where queer radicals might belong. As I shift across geohistories, I do not tell a single story—such a story is impossible. Instead, I map the innovative ways black thinkers and artists have created possibilities for black being and belonging, and I argue that the intimate, especially the sexual, is central to how these figures imagined and theorized black being and belonging.

The four figures I engage—Frantz Fanon, René Maran, Jomo Kenyatta, and Claude McKay—wrote as colonial subjects in the first half of the twentieth century. As many of these figures entered the academy through postcolonial studies, their work and subjectivity is often treated as anticolonial and postcolonial, geared toward forms of freedom incarnated in the independent nation-state. As necessary as these approaches have been, they have tended to lose the specificity of what colonial subjects might have desired, the forms of livability they imagined and invented that pursue freedom, but not by privileging the nation-state. Simultaneously, focusing on these figures as anticolonial and postcolonial also risks losing how their status as colonial subjects emerges from and is part of the "afterlife of slavery": "skewed life chances, limited access to health and education, premature death, incarceration, and impoverishment."[9] It is within these conditions that these figures wrote, producing varied models for how black life could be imagined and invented as free.

This book begins from the premise that the black diaspora poses a historical and conceptual challenge to dominant histories and theories of sexuality in queer studies, which have tended to privilege white Euro-American experiences. I depart from the more familiar Euro-American genealogy of queer studies offered by scholars in fields as diverse as the classics (David Halperin), religion (John Bosworth), philosophy (Michel Foucault), history (Martha Vicinus, George Chauncey), and literary studies (Eve Kosofsky Sedgwick). Starting from the black diaspora requires rethinking not only the historical and theoretical utility of identity categories such as gay, lesbian, and bisexual, but also, arguably, more foundational categories such as normative and non-normative, human and nonhuman While I complicate queer theory's conceptual and historical assumptions, this project is not an extended "writing back" to a predominantly white queer studies: writing back recenters white queer studies as the point of departure.[10] Instead, I start with the slave ship, the place that will produce most forcefully and consistently what Toni Morrison describes as an "Africanist presence": the denotative and connotative languages and figures through which blackness is apprehended within modernity.[11]

Theorizing Frottage

I use frottage, a relation of proximity, to figure the black diaspora, for doing so unsettles the heteronormative tropes through which the black diaspora has been imagined and idealized. Frottage captures the aesthetic (as a term of artistic practice) and the libidinal (as a term of sex practice), and so gestures to the creative ways the sexual can be used to imagine and create worlds. The artist Max Ernst is formally credited with the process of inventing frottage, which consists of laying paper over a surface (a floor or desk, say), and using charcoal or pencil to rub over the paper to reveal the traces history has left on that surface. Frottage does not provide a complete narrative or even signal where the researcher should look; at best, its traces demonstrate that someone or something has passed through a space and left some kind of evidence. Within the African and Afro-diasporic archives I explore, the figure of the homosexual appears rarely and often as a fragment—as scattered sentences in Fanon's *Black Skin, White Masks* and as a single sentence in Kenyatta's *Facing Mount Kenya*. I linger at these fragments to pursue a broader reparative goal: to find "sustenance" where it has often been deemed absent or scarce.[12] The evidence frottage provides creates the grounds for speculation, and takes seriously the work speculation does in enlarging our apprehension of the world and our possibilities for being in the world.[13] Moreover, I wanted a term that keeps the body seeking sexual pleasure in view. Frottage *feels* less freighted than terms like fucking and sucking and fisting, terms that, as they have circulated within queer studies, have become identified as gay male sex practices, even when, as with fisting, they have the power to disrupt gendered and sexed positions. Finally, I wanted an awkward term, one that hinted at strangers rubbing themselves against others in public spaces, at the ways the public pursuit of pleasure can often be uncomfortable and coercive. I do not think black and queer play well together. I think they often inhabit the same spaces, and even the same bodies, in uncomfortable ways, and I want to foreground their ongoing rubbing, leading, at times, to pleasure, and, at other times, to irritation, and even possibly to pain.

As a conceptual strategy, frottage lingers on a critical and historical desire to name the black diaspora as a singular formation, the desire of that definite article "the." I do not dismiss this desire. Instead, I use frottage to foreground this intense longing for intimacy. By foregrounding desire and longing, I depart from genealogical models that anchor that definite article within a logic of kinship, whether that be biogenetic or fictive kinship. More precisely, I explore how blackness emerges and what it comes to mean without anchoring it to a genealogical tree. Instead of searching for kinship, I privilege conceptual and affective proximity: the rubbing produced by and as blackness, which assembles into one frame multiple histories and geographies. I consider the black diaspora as affective and bodily proximity. Where Earl Lewis has theorized "overlapping diasporas," I argue that pressing and rubbing rather than overlapping might offer a richer, queerer account of how diaspora functions as intimacy.[14]

Finally, though not exhaustively, I use frottage to suggest diaspora as a multiplicity of sense-apprehensions, including recognition, disorientation, compassion, pity, disgust, condescension, lust, titillation, arousal, and exhaustion. I want to approximate as much as possible the range of bodily sensations produced by the insistent touching that is diaspora. I find especially useful Sianne Ngai's discussion of "irritation" as a "noncathartic . . . ongoingness."[15] It might be that the enforced proximity produced by the category of blackness rubs up against the desire for intimacy expressed in the definite article "the," producing irritation as the black diaspora's dominant affect. Irritation, a term that captures an emotional and corporeal response, is a helpful term for thinking about the contested nature of blackness as a shared feature of Africa and Afrodiaspora. For the history of blackness as a shared category is marked by disagreement, disavowal, and ambivalence, from those who distinguish themselves as "African, not black," to those who police blackness as a product of Atlantic slavery and thus unavailable to other populations, to those who claim a nativist distinction between U.S. southern descendants and Afro-Caribbean and African descendants. Yet the visual logic of blackness, which is modernity's legacy, does not care for such fine distinctions. In using frottage, I highlight the affective conflicts and practices of difference that suture the black diaspora.

I arrived at frottage through a series of conceptual and historical impasses—as part of theorizing the term, I narrate those impasses. When I started this project in 2005, my keyword was "kinship." It was central to African studies, primarily in anthropology, but also in the other two disciplines that dominate African studies—political science and history. It was also central to the broad field of black diaspora studies, whether one followed the Herskovitz line of African survivals or embraced the Frazier model where Africans in the New World invented new ways of being.[16] In scholarship by Carol Stack, novels by Gloria Naylor, Toni Morrison, and Alice Walker, and poetry by Ntozake Shange and Audre Lorde, fictive kinship—kinship that does not rely on a blood relationship—became as important as blood kinship. Gay and lesbian studies affirmed the importance of kinship: Kath Weston's *Families We Choose* (1991) powerfully demonstrated how gays and lesbians created and innovated within kinship structures, changing the meaning of kinship. Yet, kinship remained vulnerable to queer critiques of heteronormativity (a "sense of rightness," as Lauren Berlant and Michael Warner describe), the dominance of the couple form, and the foundational place of the child (and reproduction) as the heart of kinship.[17] Kinship seemed too important a concept to jettison, but I could not figure out how to write about it. I remain convinced that kinship refuses forms of intimate innovation, but I do not know how to stage that argument.

From kinship, I moved on to "deracination," a term that captures the violence of the Middle Passage and figures queering as a violent ejection from the social. Deracination spoke not just to black and queer pasts—some of them black, some of them queer, some of them black and queer—but to black and queer presents as well, capturing the violence of gentrification elaborated by Samuel Delany and Christina Hanhardt, the ravages of exile and immigration discussed by Eithne Luibhéid and Chandan Reddy, and the quotidian moments of exclusion captured by "No Fats, No Femmes, No Blacks, No Asians" on hook-up apps.[18] Deracination, a word that captures being uprooted and losing place and being, described the unmaking work of the Middle Passage: how the enslaved were ejected from the status of human through commodification and punishment. Deracination remains central to this book, but I needed a term that spoke more directly to *intra*-racial concerns. I fear that deracination focuses on the strategies through which white supremacy produces blackness, and I did not want to write that book: a black queer studies that constantly imagines itself as a response to a white queer studies is debilitating.

Frottage tries to grasp the quotidian experiences of intra-racial experience, the frictions and irritations and translations and mistranslations, the moments when blackness coalesces through pleasure and play and also by resistance to antiblackness. More than simply proximity, it is the active and dynamic ways blackness is produced and contested and celebrated and lamented as a shared object. It is bodies rubbing against and along bodies. Histories rubbing along and against histories. It is the shared moments of black joy and black mourning. It is what is known on Twitter as #diasporawars, when Afro-Europeans and Afro-Caribbeans and Afro-Americans and Africans gather, often angrily, to work through difference. At such moments, little is taken for granted. Except we know that the difficult work of working through difference is necessary for our survival and our pleasure. Taking nothing for granted, we explore and create new ways to imagine and be with each other.

The Genealogical Imperative

Frottage thinks alongside and beyond the dominant frame in black diaspora cultures and studies: the structure of blood descent that I describe as a genealogical imperative. Alexander Crummell's famous 1888 statement, "a race *is* a family," has had a vibrant, ongoing life in black diasporic cultural and intellectual production.[19] Although this genealogical imperative can be traced across multiple black diasporic geohistories, in what follows I turn to African American histories to illustrate how it has functioned as a scholarly and aesthetic injunction.

Following the publication of the Moynihan Report (1965) in the United States, which blamed slavery for destroying black families and creating a "tangle of pathology," scholars mounted a sustained campaign to refute those claims. Influential studies including Carol Stack's *All Our Kin: Strategies for Survival in a Black Community* (1974), Herbert Gutman's *The Black Family in Slavery and in Freedom, 1750–1925* (1974), Richard Price and Sidney Mintz's *The Birth of African-American Culture: An Anthropological Perspective* (1976), and John Blassingame's *The Slave Community: Plantation Life in the Antebellum South* (1979) emphasized the enduring strength and longevity of heterosexual kinship bonds, in slavery and in freedom.

Here, let me tread carefully: these studies did not reify the black family in any singular way. Many criticized Moynihan for seeing black community relations through the lens of a white nuclear family. For instance, drawing on Stack, Mintz and Price write, "One of the problems with traditional studies of the black family . . . was a tendency to reify the concept of 'family' itself. . . . [I]n Afro-America, the 'household' unit need by no means correspond to 'the family,' however defined."[20] They follow this correction by focusing on the historical role of kinship during slavery, asking, "What, if anything, might have constituted a set of broadly shared ideas brought from Africa in the realm of kinship?"[21] Their speculative answer is instructive for understanding the role of kinship in black studies:

> Tentatively and provisionally, we would suggest that there might have been certain widespread fundamental ideas and assumptions about kinship in West and Central Africa. Among these, we might single out the

sheer importance of kinship in structuring interpersonal relations and in defining an individual's place in society; the emphasis on unilineal descent, and the importance to each individual of the resulting lines of kinsmen, living and dead, stretching backward and forward through time, or, on a more abstract level, the use of land as a means of defining both time and descent, with ancestors venerated *locally*, and with history and genealogy both being particularized in specific pieces of ground. The aggregate of newly arrived slaves, though they had been torn from their own local kinship networks, would have continued to view kinship as the normal idiom of social relations. Faced with an absence of real kinsmen, they nevertheless modeled their new social ties upon those of kinship.[22]

This rich passage describes how kinship and genealogy subtend racial alliances: "kinship" provides a "shared" vocabulary that mitigates geohistorical differences. "Shared ideas" of kinship and genealogy enable intra-racial collectivity by "defining an individual's place in society." Kinship provides social legibility and structures social relations, allowing individuals to be recognizable through their real and imagined relationships to others. But while the change from "family" to "kinship" critiques and displaces the nuclear family and the couple form as privileged models, the reliance on genealogical models to generate social and cultural legibility privileges reproductive heteronormativity.

Mintz and Price reveal how the standard queer critique of the heteronormative couple cannot account for black diasporic and African modes of creating normativity. Take, for instance, Lauren Berlant and Michael Warner's field-defining "Sex in Public," which positions queerness against "the heterosexual couple," imagined as "the privileged example of sexual culture."[23] That queerness challenges and disrupts coupled heterosexuality is now taken as common sense within queer studies, in a way that attending to other geohistories must complicate. Consider, for instance, this description of African family structures from philosopher Nkiru Nzegwu:

[*Family Matters*] deals with different forms of family relationships, notably consanguineal, nuclear, mixtures of the two, polygamous, matrilineal, patrilineal, dual-descent, matrifocal, patrifocal, patriarchal, and matriarchal. A consanguineal family construes the family as composed of kin, while the nuclear treats the family as composed of a man and his wife and children. Polygamous families are made up of a male or female husband with multiple wives. A matrilineal family traces descent through the mother, while a patrilineal one traces descent through the father, and a dual-descent family traces descent through both the mother and the father. Matrifocality describes a family that is based or focused on the mother, whereas a patrifocal family is centered on the father. A patriarchal family is one in which the father has the dominant power in the family, and a matriarchal family is one which in the mother has the dominant power in the family.[24]

Even though Nzegwu uses "family relationships" as opposed to Berlant and Warner's "sexual culture," anthropological traditions instruct us that such family relationships indicate allowable and taboo sexual proximities. Focusing on the heterosexual couple misses how African and Afro-diasporic intimate structures and traditions generate their own forms of normativity and queerness. If, instead, we focus on the multiple ways heteronormativity functions within a broadly conceived genealogical imperative, we might ask with Elizabeth Povinelli, "Why does the recognition of peoples' worth, of their human and civil rights, always seem to be hanging on the more or less fragile branches of a family tree? Why must we be held by these limbs?"[25] Learning from Povinelli, we can question the genealogical imperative in Afro-diasporic and African scholarship.

It is, perhaps, easier to acknowledge how the genealogical imperative has shaped scholarship in anthropology and history, fields marked by their interests in kinship and community, on the one hand, and change over time, on the other. But the genealogical imperative has also guided aesthetic criticism, and a particularly fine example can be found in Houston Baker's *Modernism and the Harlem Renaissance*. In a telling passage, Baker weds Afro-diasporic scholarship to the genealogical imperative:

The family signature is always a renewing renaissancism that ensures generation, generations, the mastery of form and the deformation of mastery. What I *have* said is that the family *must* explore its own geographies. . . . Renaissancism's contemporary fate is our responsibility, demanding a hard and ofttimes painful journey back to ancestral wisdom in order to achieve a traditional (family) goal. That goal is the discovery of our successful voices as the always already blues script . . . in which a new world's future will be sounded.[26]

Baker's intricately constructed prose allows no separation between the aesthetic and the biological, the artistic and the historical, the culturally productive and the biologically reproductive. The repeated "renaissancism" formally enacts his injunction to re-create and procreate, especially as renaissance refers to rebirth. To write with the "family signature" is to produce and reproduce, to affirm, always, the hetero-temporalities that connect the ancestors to the future. The task of Afro-diasporic scholarship, then, if one follows Baker, is always genealogical. In fact, Baker's italicized *"must"* demonstrates what I'm calling an imperative, and, more broadly, becomes a mode of aesthetic evaluation. Truly valuable aesthetic work must follow and value the genealogical imperative.

Lest this focus on the family be understood as an exclusively African American affair, scholarship in the broader range of the black diaspora similarly understands experience through hetero-kinship tropes. For instance, introducing a major anthology of black diaspora scholarship, Isidore Okpewho acknowledges the impossibility of encompassing black diasporic diversity. But this diversity is subsequently managed through hetero-kinship tropes, as the black diaspora is marked by its relationship to "the mother continent" and those scattered are re-collected as "sons and daughters."[27] These are small, and, arguably, casual moments in Okpewho's argument, but this very casualness demonstrates the ease with which hetero-kinship is taken for granted as an operational principle of black diaspora scholarship.[28] I draw attention to them because of how they manage black diasporic geohistorical diversity under the rubric of hetero-kinship figured as genealogical descent. While African and Afro-diasporic scholars might not all agree on racialization, politics, religion, ethnicity, economics, or culture, hetero-kinship is consistently reinforced as a capacious category that manages all difference. It is precisely the casual, unremarked way that hetero-kinship tropes lubricate difference that interests me.

The term "diaspora" combines two terms, *dia* (across) and *sperein* (scatter), and invokes the labor of spores as they spread to germinate.

Although scholars have focused on diaspora as dispersal, the often un-named critical hope is that such scattering results in communities: what Brent Hayes Edwards has termed the "futures of diaspora" takes place on the grounds of hetero-genealogy.[29] However, I argue that another black diaspora is possible. *Frottage* tracks the uneven traces of dispersal and scattering associated with diaspora, attempting to arrest the heteronor-mative inevitability that would conflate dispersal with hetero-futurity. The geohistorical range of my archive—Fanon's Martinique and France, Maran's Central Africa, Kenyatta's Kenya and England, and McKay's Jamaica—attempts to disrupt the inevitability of hetero-insemination by multiplying dispersion. Moreover, I hope that this geohistorical range will arrest a genealogical impulse that often takes root when one geo-historical location is made the center. Simultaneously, in juxtaposing these geohistories and the various genres that represent them—McKay's poetry and fiction, Kenyatta's ethnography, Maran's ethnographic fic-tion, and Fanon's philosophy—I figure the black diaspora as proximity and rubbing rather than descent. These authors and works often speak past, over, and through each other, producing not a unified or unifying chorus, but dissonant voices that, every so often, come together in their shared quests for freedom. Here is the black diaspora not as kinship, but as dissonant, freedom-seeking intimacy.

The remainder of this introduction outlines key concepts that recur throughout the book and that help to suture its disparate geographies and genres: the relationship between the genealogical imperative and the ethnographic imagination, which I track through the foundational black diasporic thinker Edward Wilmot Blyden; and the relationship be-tween hybridity and thinghood as they circulate within black diaspora theorizations of race and sexuality.

The Genealogical Imperative and the Ethnographic Imagination

In 1908, Liberian intellectual Edward Wilmot Blyden published *African Life and Customs*, a collection of articles that had first appeared in the *Sierra Leone Weekly News*. It was issued "with the desire, if possible, of unfolding the African, who has received unmixed European culture, to himself, through a study of the customs of his fathers, and also of assisting the European political overlord, ruling in Africa, to arrive at a proper appreciation of conditions."[30] *African Life and Customs* attempted to counter the deracinating effects of modernity by providing Afro-diasporic populations, those who had "received unmixed European culture," with a manual of how to be African. In its simplest form, *African Life and Customs* belongs to the body of antiracist discourse produced by black diasporic activists and intellectuals through the latter part of the nineteenth century and the early part of the twentieth. It shares similar aims with Frederick Douglass's multiple narratives, Frances Harper's novels, Booker T. Washington's *Up from Slavery*, and Casely Hayford's *Ethiopia Unbound*. Disparate though these works might be, they all attempt to prove the black person's humanity and capacity for civilization. In autobiographies, sermons, manifestoes, polemics, essays, and novels, Afro-diasporic activists in the nineteenth century contested racist depictions of black people as primitive and hypersexual. These works take on new life in the twentieth century, when they forge bonds among African and Afro-diasporic populations. Their focus ceases to be primarily interracial and becomes intra-racial and international—in a word, diasporic.[31] I examine *African Life and Customs* as a foundational work that weds the genealogical imperative to what I will describe as the ethnographic imagination, a wedding that animates black diasporic cultural and scholarly production throughout the twentieth century.

Blyden was, arguably, the preeminent black diaspora scholar of the late nineteenth and early twentieth centuries. He was born in 1832, in St. Thomas, Virgin Islands, then part of the Danish West Indies. Denied admission to colleges in the United States to study theology because of his race, he immigrated to Liberia, where he completed high school and was later ordained as a Presbyterian minister in 1858. An autodidact, he learned to read and write Latin, Greek, Hebrew, Spanish, French, Italian, Arabic, and a few African indigenous languages. He first rose to international prominence in the 1860s, when he traveled through the United States to recruit immigrants to Liberia, a practice that he continued for the following thirty years. Over the course of a lengthy career, he served as a professor of classics at Liberia College (1862–71), secretary of state (1864–66), Liberia's first ambassador to Britain (1877–78), president of Liberia College (1880–84), and ran for president of Liberia in 1885. In addition to numerous articles published in venues such as *Methodist*

Quarterly Review, *Fraser's Magazine*, the *American Missionary*, and *Sierra Leone Times*, he also published books, including *Liberia's Offering* (1862), *From West Africa to Palestine* (1873), and *Christianity, Islam, and the Negro Race* (1887). He died in Liberia in 1912.[32]

I begin with Blyden because I read his *African Life and Customs* as a methodological forerunner to Afro-diasporic cultural and intellectual production over the twentieth century. He provides a method for Afro-diasporic populations to reconnect with their past: they can "study" the "customs" of their "fathers." Blyden's emphasis on "study" and "customs" embeds him, broadly, within ethnographic practices, and, more specifically, within an ethnographic imagination that will be taken up by writers across the black diaspora including Jean Toomer, Claude McKay, Langston Hughes, Nella Larsen, Zora Neale Hurston, Léopold Sédar Senghor, Chinua Achebe, Flora Nwapa, and Ngugi wa Thiong'o. The phrase "ethnographic imagination" is capacious, and I use it to denote the array of fantasies, desires, and imaginations that subtend ethnographic projects in their various instantiations as armchair anthropology, fieldwork-based research, and literary and cultural production; the desire to record fading modes of living (Toomer and Hurston), to imagine past histories of living (Senghor and Nwapa), to describe emergent modes of living (McKay, Hughes), and the impulse to locate collectivity forming and collectivity fracturing within the register of the intimate (the home, the family, the community, the village). Indeed, a guiding premise for this book is that the ethnographic imagination subtends black diaspora cultural production and political imagination throughout the twentieth century.

African Life and Customs consists of fifteen short chapters that can be divided, broadly, into meditations on social, economic, and political organization. Following a short introductory chapter that surveys the existing scholarship on Africa, Blyden devotes the following four chapters (2–5) to the African family; the next five (6–10) to what he terms "industrialism," or more broadly economic structures; the next two (11–12) to political organization, or the treatment of "criminals"; and the final three (13–15) to religion. By presenting a picture of what anthropologists will later theorize as a functional society, Blyden attempts to rehabilitate the negative image of Africa in colonial accounts. In the same spirit as Crummell's statement that race is "like a family," Blyden imagines that the functional society he describes should provide a paradigm for global black collectivity.

For Blyden, this rehabilitation takes place, most urgently, on the level of the intimate. He describes "the family" as the foundation of African society:

> The facts in this African life which we shall endeavour to point out are the following:—
>
> 1st. The Family, which in Africa, as everywhere else, is the basic unit of society. Every male and female marries at the proper age. Every woman is required and expects to perform her part of the function of motherhood—to do her share in continuing the human race.[33]

He amplifies this point:

> The foundation of the African Family is plural marriage and, contrary to the general opinion, this marriage rests upon the will of the woman, and this will operates to protect from abuse the functional work of the sex, and to provide that all women shall share *normally* in this work with a view to healthy posterity and an unfailing supply of population.
>
> It is less a matter of sentiment, of feeling, of emotion, than of duty, of patriotism. Compulsory spinsterhood is unknown under the African system. *That* is a creation of the West. Its existence here is abnormal, anticlimactic, and considered a monstrosity . . . and is destined, wherever it seems to exist in practice, to disappear as an unscientific interference of good meaning foreign philanthropists with the natural conditions of the country.[34]

Blyden's discussion is predicated on an implicit contrast between Africa and the West, one marked by the two italicized terms: "*normally*" and "*That.*" African women participate "*normally*" in "the functional work of the sex." Through this "*normally*" Blyden critiques colonial works that claimed African women pursued *non*functional types of sex. As a native of the West Indies and a devoted anglophile, Blyden would, no doubt, have been aware of Edward Long's claim that African women were as "libidinous and shameless as monkies and baboons," and their "hot temperament" gave "probability to the charge of their admitting these animals frequently to their embrace."[35] Against these charges of wayward libidos, Blyden describes African women as privileging "motherhood" above all else, thus tying gendered and racial normativity to hetero-reproduction. Even though Blyden discusses hetero-reproduction as a "duty," he emphasizes that women *choose* to fulfill this duty: "marriage rests upon the will of the woman."[36] Women may not be able to choose whether or not they will marry—that is a duty—but, in Blyden's account, they can choose who they will marry, and thus make duty less onerous. And since all women participate in this duty to marry and reproduce, no single woman feels unduly burdened. Blyden's emphasis on women also recognizes that African women had borne a disproportionate share of racist representation as visible embodiments of, contradictorily, lack and excess, hyper- and hypotrophied bodies. As with other black diasporic writers from the late nineteenth and early twentieth centuries, Blyden offers alternative frames through which to consider African women's practices.

More than simply a defense of African life, *African Life and Customs* critiques European modernity for its failures, which manifest at the level of intimate life. Echoing the alarmist rhetoric that erupted because of white women's emergence into full participation in urban moder-nity—as single, unmarried, engaged in sex work—Blyden excoriates the West's failures, while arguing, "Under the African marriage system . . . [t]here are no 'women of the under world,' no 'slaves of the abyss.' Every woman is above ground protected and sheltered."[37] "African marriage system" describes an ahistorical ideal by this point in history. By 1908, urbanized women in Africa engaged in trade and sex work, redefining their social and economic landscapes. Blyden's implicit contrast, then, is not only between a decadent West and an innocent Africa, but also between a pre-urban and an urbanizing Africa. He rails against the de-racinating effects of urban modernity that threatened an Africanness he defined as hetero-reproductive.

In Blyden's estimation, Christian-advocated monogamy was a failed system; African polygamy solved real problems. He writes, "[W]e are told by English periodicals that there are a little over five millions of unmarried women in Great Britain and the number is increasing. It is stated also that in the City of London alone there are 80,000 profes-sional outcasts."[38] A slippery logic of innuendo coats these statements:

unmarried women have limited options; urban spaces present themselves as places with many options; unmarried women choose to go to urban spaces to pursue options; on arriving there, they change from being "unmarried women" to "professional outcasts." Urbanization creates professional outcasts. "Professional outcasts" elides sex workers and career women, marking both as intimate failures. In contrast, Blyden claims that Africa has no such problems: "We are quite sure that there are not so many unmarried women in the whole of Africa between the Atlantic and the Red Sea and from the Cape to the Mediterranean."[39] These expansive geographies suture Africa as a space held together by shared intimate practices.

Yet, African intimate practices are not simply natural; they are actively cultivated. Blyden argues they arise from centuries of experimentation. Africa "solved the marriage question for herself thousands of years ago. It has needed no revision and no amendment, because founded upon the law of Nature and not upon the *dictum* of any ecclesiastical hierarchy."[40] While the "law of Nature" provides a foundation, it must also be complemented by a pedagogy of intimacy: "[T]here is *among Africans* a regular process of education for male and female, for a period of at least three years, to prepare them for the [intimate] life they are to follow, and the [marriage] system under which they are to live."[41] If Afro-diasporic populations fail at intimacy, as so many Euro-American observers suggested from at least the eighteenth century, then that failure results from the deracination of diaspora, and indicates nothing inherent about African nature. In fact, complaints about black people's hypersexuality in the archives of colonial modernity register European, not African, failing. Blyden's claim about intimate pedagogy also rebukes the civilizing mission's pretension to instruct Africans in domestic and intimate matters. Such education, he insists, leads to African degeneration. At each point, Blyden emphasizes that Africans train themselves to be appropriately gendered and socialized; that their lives are structured by adhering to prolonged periods of training; that this training is learned from nature and the natural world, and is not a foreign imposition; and that if any observers want to know anything about Africans, then they should observe intimate life and intimate practices above all else.

For Blyden, one cannot claim an authentic African or Afro-diasporic identity without practicing appropriate heterosexual intimacies. Indeed, one cannot be recognized as legibly African or Afro-diasporic without embedding oneself within a heterosexual matrix. Far from being idiosyncratic, this yoking of married, reproductive heterosexuality to legibility is central to contemporary African philosophy. Kenyan-born ethnophilosopher John Mbiti codified the relationship between the genealogical imperative and social legibility in *Introduction to African Religion*, first published in 1975. "Marriage," Mbiti writes, "fulfills the obligation, the duty and the custom that every normal person should get married and bear children. . . . Failure to get married is like committing a crime against traditional beliefs and practices." Marriage, adds Mbiti, provides "completeness": "Marriage is the one experience without which a person is not considered to be complete, 'perfect', and truly a man or a woman. It makes a person really 'somebody'. It is part of the definition of who a person is according to African views about man. Without marriage, a person is only a human being minus."[42] Marriage confers proper gender, and proper gender confers full humanity. As Mbiti's argument proceeds, he raises the stakes: not only does heterosexual marriage satisfy "duty" and "custom" and "tradition," in which case those who claim to be modern can safely disavow marriage; but it also certifies one as "truly a man or a woman," as a "human." Mbiti's argument welds the genealogical imperative to gendered and human legibility, the grounds from which one can be recognized as human. Along similar lines, Ghanaian philosopher Kwasi Wiredu, drawing on Akan culture, writes,

> Being married with children well raised is part of the necessary conditions for personhood in the normative sense. A non-marrying, non-procreative person, however normal otherwise—not to talk of a Casanova equivalent—can permanently forget any prospect of this type of recognition in traditional Akan society. The only conceivable exceptions will be ones based on the noblest of alternative life commitments.[43]

Personhood, Nigerian philosopher Ifeanyi Menkiti writes, "is the sort of thing which has to be achieved, the sort of thing at which individuals could fail."[44] Marriage and reproduction are essential processes in achieving personhood. I offer this very brief survey of contemporary African philosophy to indicate the central role intimate relations play in African philosophies of personhood. At the same time, some of the most influential African philosophers of personhood either live and work in North America or Europe and publish primarily in North America and Europe.[45] Consequently, their works are more properly framed as African *and* Afro-diasporic. From Blyden through Mbiti, Wiredu, and Menkiti, African and Afro-diasporic scholars have wedded a genealogical imperative to an ethnographic imagination, producing black legibility—personhood—through this wedding.

Hybridity

Contesting a model that frames legibility through hetero-kinship, recent black diaspora scholarship has argued for more capacious models of blackness. Rinaldo Walcott provocatively argues, "[T]he diaspora by its very nature, its circumstances, is queer," adding, "the territories and perambulations of diaspora circuits, identifications, and desires are queer in their making and their expressions."[46] However, accepting the proposition that diaspora "is" queer risks glossing over multiple, conflicting histories of intimate discipline and dissent. How, exactly, does queering happen in the black diaspora? As I have already argued, the genealogical imperative in black diasporic scholarship arrests the deracinating, queer act of dissemination in the term "diaspora," which refers to scattering or sowing, by foregrounding insemination and fertilization as the inevitable end-point. Restoring the queer potential of diaspora requires making visible the normalizing, genealogical imperatives in current scholarship on the diaspora. To understand the stakes of disrupting diaspora's genealogical imperative, this section examines the concept of hybridity, which has become central to contemporary black diaspora studies. Hybridity is most often used to contest notions of racial and ethnic purity and, in a more extended conceptual vein, to contest all ideas of purity that police human and cultural diversity. Yet, I worry that the good the term does in fighting against violent exclusions depends on unexamined notions of gender and sexuality. I trace a brief genealogy of the term's migration from black British studies to the United States, to highlight a moment of what Brent Edwards might describe as the problem of translation across geohistories.[47] In tracing this history, I demonstrate the tenacious hold of the genealogical imperative on black diaspora scholarship, a hold that, I will argue, attempts to manage geohistorical disruption by privileging intimate normativity.

Within literary and cultural studies, the most prominent model of the black diaspora stems from the black British school of thinkers, which includes Stuart Hall, Kobena Mercer, Hazel Carby, and Paul Gilroy. These scholars sought to challenge the too-easy suture between race and nation that imagined Britain as a white nation. Against models of racial and ethnic purity, these thinkers embraced the possibilities of post-identitarian models of affiliation. The migration of these scholars and their thinking to the U.S. academy, and their encounters with African American studies, broadened their critiques of ethno-racial essentialisms. Thus, Carby's contribution to the 1985 special issue of *Critical Inquiry*, "Race, Writing, and Difference," shifted the terrain of black feminist critique from nation to empire, embedding a genealogy of black feminist theorizing within a history of colonialism.[48] Her *Reconstructing Womanhood* (1987) critiqued a U.S. black feminism that rooted itself in the South. Invoking a diasporic critique, she urged black feminists to look beyond a race-nation suture grounded in southern rurality, and encouraged them to consider the varieties of blackness produced in urban spaces by practices of migration and immigration.

The urban promiscuities enabled by migration and immigration, through histories of slavery and colonialism, and in the postcolonial and postslavery moment in Britain, subtended Hall's theorization of blackness and diaspora. In "New Ethnicities," Hall emphasizes that in Britain, "the term 'black' was coined" to describe a "common experience of racism and marginalization" and to "provide the organizing category of a new politics of resistance, among groups and communities with, in fact, very different histories, traditions, and ethnic identities."[49] Its emergence as a category of organization was "rooted in the politics of anti-racism and the post-war black experience in Britain."[50] Framed as a strategy of affiliation rather than as evidence of filiation, that is, as a political category rather than a genealogical one based on blood descent and phenotype, "black" could enable a politics that recognized the weight assumed by blackness under colonial modernity as a master signifier of negation. Embracing "black" as a category also recognized, and contested, the color hierarchies across Africa and Afro-diaspora that distinguished between "colored" and "black," promising social mobility to those who rejected blackness. As Hall emphasizes, "black" was used to "build forms of solidarity and identification which make common struggle and resistance possible but without suppressing the real heterogeneity of interests and identities."[51] At a crucial moment in "New Ethnicities," Hall points to the queer implications of his work: "a great deal of black politics . . . has been predicated on the assumption that the categories of gender and sexuality would stay the same and remain fixed and secured."[52] This brief moment further anchors Hall's emphasis that "black" is not a hetero-reproductive category of sameness, but a strategic coalition of diverse interests.

This framework of blackness as spatially constructed through postwar immigration and politically framed as an antiracist strategy of coalition grounds Hall's concept of diaspora. Toward the end of "New Ethnicities," Hall describes "the black experience as a *diaspora* experience," turning toward languages of cultural mixing: "the process of unsettling, recombination, hybridization, and 'cut-and-mix'—in short the process of cultural *diaspora-ization*."[53] Metaphors of rupture and deracination ("unsettling") sit uneasily alongside those of biogenetic manipulation ("recombination," "hybridization"), as these, cumulatively, are routed through musical styles of "cut-and-mix." In moving among these metaphors drawn from spatiality, biogenetics, and musical technology, Hall figures hybridity as endlessly manipulable at multiple levels, from the social and the cultural, to the biological and the psychic, to the mechanical and the technological. It is precisely because hybridity functions at so many levels that it can be a useful concept.

When taken up in the United States, Hall's invocation of hybridity assumes a biohistorical life as a way to think about the afterlife of slavery's one-drop rule. As Tavia Nyong'o has argued, "hybridity" became a fetish that challenged U.S. racial logics by emphasizing that racial purity was a fiction.[54] Hybridity was assumed to solve the problem of race and racism because it insisted that race was a fiction that could not withstand close historical and biological scrutiny. Within the U.S. academy, hybridity loses the complex interaction among the spatial, the biogenetic, and the technological, and is restricted to the biogenetic: the black British turn to culture, envisioned as a way beyond the biohistorical, is reembedded within the biohistorical in the U.S. academy. The haunting of hetero-reproduction within black British thinking on hybridity assumes a more fleshly configuration as that thought is taken up in the United States.

This cultural and biohistorical problematic finds its apogee in Gilroy's *The Black Atlantic: Modernity and Double Consciousness*. I turn to Gilroy's book because since its publication in 1993, it has become foundational to theorizations of blackness, whether these are located at the scale of the nation, the region, or the transnational. More explicitly than any of the other black British contingent, Gilroy stages his work as an encounter between black British (or "black European") and U.S. models of racialization; *The Black Atlantic* attempts to metonymize black British experiences of immigration to consider transnational racialization. Gilroy argues that intellectual, cultural, and social forms of hybridity can unsettle exclusionary and dangerous forms of ethnonationalism. Positioning himself as against frames that align race with culture and privilege the nation as the site of racialized expression, he urges, instead, "the theorization of creolisation, métissage, mestizaje, and hybridity," terms that name "the processes of cultural mutation and restless (dis)continuity that exceed racial discourse and avoid capture by its agents."[55] These terms, however, are "rather unsatisfactory": as biogenetic metaphors of mixing, they risk reproducing a "racial essentialism" grounded in heteropatriarchal norms.[56] Gilroy attempts to manage this risk by turning to music as a metaphor for how black Atlantic interactions can transcend the race-culture suture, on the one hand, and heteropatriarchal norms, on the other.

Gilroy's turn to music follows a metaleptic logic: black expressive culture, he argues, does not confirm a pregiven black identity but actively constitutes and contests ideas of blackness. Black cultural expression becomes the grounds for a new anti-essentialist black ontology: "The syncretic complexity of black expressive cultures alone supplies powerful reasons for resisting the idea that an untouched, pristine Africanity resides inside these forms, working a powerful magic of alterity in order to trigger repeatedly the perception of absolute identity."[57] In privileging music, Gilroy seems to be about as far away from biology as possible, and certainly nowhere near the realm of the genealogical imperative. Music, however, as he admits, can also be used to ground racial authenticity. Forms such as the spirituals, folk songs, the blues, ska, reggae, and rap can be adduced as expressing blackness. He notes, for instance, that Zora Neale Hurston distinguished between the inauthentic spirituals performed by the Fisk University Singers and real spirituals.[58] Against this policing of black expression, Gilroy privileges "the globalisation of vernacular forms."[59] As forms travel and are adapted across multiple spaces—think of U.S. jazz forms being adapted by Nigerian highlife musicians, for instance—music no longer suggests an easily locatable origin, but is, instead, a site of endless remixing and reinvention.[60]

As compelling as I find Gilroy's use of music to reframe black collectivity, I find myself stuck at the banal fact of embodiment: quotidian practices of crossing the street, crossing international borders, the collection of census and biometric data, the multiple ways that black embodiment is sedimented in everyday life, within and across nations.[61] Cultural forms can travel and be remixed in ways that bodies cannot. Here, I'm not simply insisting on the stubborn "stuff" of embodiment, but also on the powerful labor of ideology. After all, the historical fact of racial mixing and blending does little to mitigate the ideological labor of racial policing.[62]

Moreover, I remain unconvinced that critiques of *racial* logics of collectivity necessarily address *intimate* arrangements of collectivity. One can be against race while defending the salvific power of reproductive heterosexuality. Indeed, hybridity promises to complicate the problem of race, but risks privileging reproductive heteronormativity. Collectivity, in this instance, is forged on the grounds of what Audre Lorde terms "heterocetera": an embedding within real and fictive hetero-kinship lineages.[63] Connectedness is not simply an abstraction or metaphor, but an affirmation of shared intimate values. Hybridity and connection turn on the genealogical tree.

"Thinghood"

Yet the branching of a family tree is not the only way to envision diaspora, and I turn to theorists of thinghood to suggest a posthybridity model for envisioning the black diaspora and framing black diasporic queerness. Hortense Spillers's classic "Mama's Baby, Papa's Maybe" offers another genealogy for the queerness of the black diaspora. Spillers theorizes the Middle Passage as a subject-obliterating, thing-making project. In doing so, she takes on the challenge of contemplating what Aimé Césaire termed "thingification."[64] This urge to humanize enslaved Africans, she contends, is motivated by our inability to imagine the thing-making project of slavery, which is "unimaginable from this distance"; but to insist on the enslaved African's humanity risks avoiding the problem of the slave as commodity. How might a queer diaspora that begins from thing-making function?

Spillers provides a tantalizing glimpse of this (im)possibility:

> [The New World] order, with its sequence written in blood, *represents* for its African and indigenous peoples a scene of actual mutilation, dismemberment, and exile. First of all, their New World, diasporic flight marked a *theft of the body*—a willful and violent (and unimaginable from this distance) severing of the captive body from its motive will, its active desire. Under these conditions, we lose at least *gender* difference *in the outcome*, and the female body and the male body become a territory of cultural and political maneuver, not at all gender-related, gender-specific. But this body, at least from the point of view of the captive community, focuses a private and particular space, at which point of convergence, biological, sexual, social, cultural, linguistic, ritualistic, and psychological fortunes join. This profound intimacy of interlocking detail, is disrupted, however, by externally imposed meanings and uses: 1) the captive body becomes the source of an irresistible, destructive sensuality; 2) at the same time—in stunning contradiction—the captive body reduces to a thing, becoming *being* for the captor; 3) in this absence *from* a subject position, the captured sexualities provide a physical and biological expression of "otherness"; 4) as a category of "otherness," the captive body translates into a potential for pornotroping and embodies sheer physical powerlessness that slides into a more general "powerlessness," resonating through various centers of human and social meaning.[65]

In positing the severing "*of the body*" from "active desire" Spillers strips away a foundation of mainstream queer studies: the role of desire, whether that be same-sex desire or desire for gender or desire for fetish-sex or aimless, polymorphous desire. It is not that one's desire is criminalized or pathologized; desire itself becomes impossible in the brutal transition of thing-making.

What did it mean for enslaved Africans to "lose . . . *gender* difference"? Building on Spillers, C. Riley Snorton has recently argued that "captive flesh figures a critical genealogy for modern transness, as chattel persons gave rise to an understanding of gender as mutable, and as an amendable form of being."[66] As compelling as I find Snorton's claim, I worry about how "modern" works in this passage. What precedes the modern in this account? To be more specific, what happens to the understandings of embodiment and sociality practiced by enslaved Africans? Are they the "immutable" transformed by and into the "modern"? In *The Invention of Women*, Nigerian scholar Oyèrónkẹ́ Oyěwùmí critiqued the "age-old somatocentricity in Western thought," arguing that it could not be applied to Yorùbá society.[67] She explains,

> I came to realize that the fundamental category "woman"—which is foundational in Western gender discourses—simply did not exist in Yorùbáland prior to its sustained contact with the West. There was no such preexisting group characterized by shared interests, desires, or social position. The cultural logic of Western social categories is based on an ideology of biological determinism: the conception that biology provides the rationale for the organization of the social world. Thus, this cultural logic is actually a "bio-logic." Social categories like "woman" are based on body-type and are elaborated in relation to and in opposition to another category: man; the presence or absence of certain organs determine social position.[68]

Oyěwùmí is critiquing the entire framework that subtends the constructionist critique of essentialism: the claim that gender is socially constructed carries little force for African communities that *already* understood gender as ritually conferred. What understandings and practices of gender did enslaved Africans have? Might focusing on gender rather than kinship, as Mintz and Price do, be more useful for those of us looking for queer and trans genealogies? One crude way to track these genealogies would be through carefully reading histories of the major ethnic groups of enslaved Africans, but I worry that such a method, moving through at least four hundred years across diverse groups, risks losing the dynamic ways gender is understood and practiced. Simply, a lot changes over centuries.

Part of my concern is that African and Afro-diasporic scholars of sex and gender rarely consider African gendering frameworks prior to colonialism as conceptually rich ways of thinking through embodiment and sociality.[69] Rituals that transition toddlers to children and those children to older children and those older children to young adults and those young adults to older adults, and so on, are more than premodern, ethnohistorical curiosities. Instead, they register how geohistorical change impresses itself on social relations and practices. Knowing, for instance, that one ethnic group adopted a form of gendering from another—the Kikuyu, for example adopted ritual circumcision from the Maasai, to mark the transition from sexually inactive older child to sexually available young adult—tells us something significant about how ideas of embodiment and gender change as different African groups encounter and interact with each other. If we take African gendering practices as theoretically significant, what might become possible in thinking through African and Afro-diasporic queer and trans politics? While the geohistorical scope of my archive does not permit a full reckoning with these provocations, I mention them here to indicate the need for conceptual conversations between African and Afro-diasporic scholars engaged in tracking queer and trans genealogies.

If we consider the loss of African gendering practices and the social legibility they conferred, then Spillers's argument about the ungendering work of slave ship ledgers provides different possibilities for trans and queer genealogies and theories. Enslaved Africans who had lost social legibility—the rituals and practices and communities that recognized social, economic, cultural, and embodied status—were forced to forge new forms of legibility. Omise'eke Tinsley writes, "[C]aptive African women created erotic bonds with other women in the sex-segregated holds, and captive African men created bonds with other men. In so doing, they resisted the commodification of their bought and sold bodies by *feeling* and *feeling for* their co-occupants on these ships."[70] I want to believe this account of erotic resistance, but I am arrested by the image with which this introduction starts, of bodies grating against each other and the hold of the ship, of the various sensations of attrition and pleasure, and of how bodies and forms of social legibility—including gender— were unmade and remade. What kind of social legibilities were forged as those across different age groups and ritual status engaged each other? To amend Spillers's question, what forms of *difference* were lost and what forms of difference emerged through the frottage of the hold? And how might "thinghood" name not simply how the slave ledgers produced enslaved Africans, but also how enslaved Africans experienced themselves, as they tried to process lost social legibilities while trying to create new ones?

But the story becomes even more complicated, for the same process that produces the slave as "thing" simultaneously inflects the slave's thingness with "sensuality." Although Spillers elaborates a four-stage process that seems to proceed in a linear fashion, it might be more useful to understand this step-making as a strategic fiction that attempts to render partial, recursive, fractured, and synchronous stages: the "captive body" is at once as densely saturated with the power to elicit "sensuality" as it is excluded by its thingness from gaining agency through that sensuality. If, as a thought experiment, one takes Spillers's sequence in a linear fashion, then one ends up with a move from a "captive body," severed from its "active desire," which acts as a "thing," and through that process of thingification, becomes a "captive sexuality." Sexuality, therefore, would not name the place of subjectification, as it has in queer studies. Instead, it would name theft and commodification, thing-making and gender-undifferentiation. The queerness of the black diaspora, then, would stem from an effort to describe this figuration, which is unaccounted for in sexology's archives: the thing "severed" from its "active desire."

Within colonial modernity, blackness figures as perverse sexuality, as its potential and realization. What Spillers marks as "captured sexualities" hints at the taxonomic logic that drives sexology's will to know and ability to organize itself. If, as Foucault demonstrates, sexology is a strategy for cataloguing and managing sexual, that is, human, difference, its formal strategy can be aligned with, if not derived from, the slave catalogues that recorded color, weight, and size, not merely managing human cargo, but actively transforming humans into commodities. It is precisely the "captured sexualities" of the "thing" of "blackness" that haunts sexology, as its necessary underside, as its Africanist presence. Yet, the thinghood of blackness also renders it difficult to apprehend within a genealogy that takes sexuality as subjectifying. Here, I am marking a deep cleavage between black diaspora studies and queer studies: sexuality represents a vexed meeting ground, the place where a blackness haunted by thinghood encounters a nonblackness haunted by subjectification. We are not on shared ground.

Frottage will name this encounter between queer studies and black diaspora studies, this persistent meeting, this lingering over, this site of stimulation and frustration. But I will swerve from the too-familiar site of the interracial to focus on the intra-racial, swerve to complicate the intimacy suggested by the definite article of "the" black diaspora. Against genealogical models that invoke the definite article to claim fictive kinship grounded in a hetero-reproductive imagination, I explore the possibility of using frottage as an uneven relationship of proximity, a persistent, recurring meeting of bodies in space, an attempt to forge aesthetics and culture and politics and history from the shared "capture" of blackness.

Movement

Frottage does not focus on works primarily concerned with explicitly homosexual, bisexual, transsexual, or transgender figures. Instead, as I shift across multiple geohistories and genres, I consider a range of practices that queer different figures: the process of thingification in slave histories; the loss of erotic diversity in colonial spaces; ethno-nationalist discourses in Kenyan ethnography; and labor and punishment in Jamaican histories. Tracking the black diaspora as dispersal and dissonant intimacy, *Frottage* moves from Frantz Fanon's *Black Skin, White Masks* (1952), written in France, and drawing from residence in Martinique and Algeria; to René Maran's ethnographic novel *Batouala* (1921), written and set in Central Africa and published in France; to Jomo Kenyatta's ethnography *Facing Mount Kenya: The Tribal Life of the Gikuyu* (1938), set in Kenya and written in London; and finally to Claude McKay's Jamaica represented in the poetry collection *Constab Ballads* (1911), written in Jamaica and published in London, and the novel *Banana Bottom* (1933), written in Morocco and published in the United States. This a-chronological movement pushes against the linear, genealogical logics followed by mainstream black diaspora work. I juxtapose texts traditionally considered diasporic—Maran's and Fanon's—with those considered too local to be diasporic—McKay's and Kenyatta's—to expand diaspora's geohistories.

Each figure I consider is foundational in some way, anchoring an intervention into a field or discipline, asking what happens to that field or discipline when it must consider black being. I start with Fanon because his work poses the question of black being so persistently, especially for those of us who work at the seams of black studies, black diaspora studies, African studies, and postcolonial studies. I follow his antimethod, to the extent that an antimethod can be followed, to find resources to imagine the queer and trans figures he could not imagine. From Fanon, I move to Maran to track how Afro-diaspora and Africa can imagine and encounter each other on the grounds of the erotic, grounds that Fanon did not know how to imagine. The last two chapters, on Kenyatta and McKay, are more densely historical, demonstrating how colonial figures imagined freedom, and how the intimate and the erotic were central to those imaginations. Instead of pursuing explicitly queer or trans figures, each chapter mines the resources of the erotic to imagine freedom.

In the decades that bracket this book, from 1900 to 1960, representations of and debates about black diasporic intimacy intensified within national and transnational contexts. The literary sites of such representations include Pauline Hopkins's incestuous romance *Of One Blood* (1903); Casely Hayford's pan-African romance *Ethiopia Unbound* (1911); the lesbian poetries of Angelina Weld Grimké and Gladys Casely-Hayford; the queer poetics of Langston Hughes, Countee Cullen, and Richard Bruce Nugent; the vagabond erotics of Claude McKay's *Home to Harlem* (1928) and *Banjo* (1929); the radical feminisms of Nella Larsen's *Quicksand* (1928) and Jessie Fauset's *Plum Bun* (1929); the ethnographic romance of Zora Neale Hurston's *Their Eyes Were Watching God* (1937); the queer Négritude of Aimé Césaire's *Notebook of a Return to My Native Land* (1947) juxtaposed against the heteronormative erotics of Léopold Sédar Senghor's poetry; the charged interracial antagonisms of Mayotte Capécia's *Je Suis Martiniquaise* (1948); the infanticidal imagination of Amos Tutuola's *Palm Wine Drinkard* (1952); and the immigrant promiscuities of Samuel Selvon's *Lonely Londoners* (1956). I mark these sites to indicate the scope and richness of this temporal period, and to suggest possibilities for further scholarship. I can do no better than to paraphrase Cedric Robinson: it is not my purpose to exhaust this subject, only to suggest that it is there.[71]

I invite you to imagine with me.

1

Frantz Fanon's Homosexual Territories

Homosexuality appears in strange ways in Frantz Fanon's *Black Skin, White Masks*: metonymically, as "an attempt at rape" and an "attempt at fellatio"; as a symptom and evidence of "Negrophobia"; as white masochism; as a footnote on "anti-semitic psychoses"; as geographical absence in Martinique; as sex work in Europe; as affect—"Fault, Guilt, refusal of guilt, paranoia"; and as psychic "territory."[1] Homosexuality appears as actions (failed and realized), as textual elaboration and diversion, as labor, and as space (psychic and geographic). Of all the works examined in this book, Fanon's *Black Skin* has the most insistent, if inconsistent, treatment of homosexuality. Although other scholarship on Fanon proceeds as though Fanon exiles the homosexual from the black political imagination, I pursue the possibility that the homosexual instead haunts Fanon's theory of colonial modernity. And, revising the genealogy of the white homosexual offered by Michel Foucault, I argue that the homosexual in colonial modernity cannot be imagined without the black body.

A possible subtitle for this chapter might be "Beyond Chapter Six." Although Fanon writes about sex and sexuality throughout *Black Skin, White Masks*, his comments on homosexuality live in chapter 6, and this chapter has been the focus of queer critique. Titled "The Negro and Psychopathology" (trans. Markmann) or "The Black Man and Psychopathology" (trans. Philcox), the chapter's engagement with psychoanalysis made it especially intriguing for gay and lesbian scholars whose work was embedded within psychoanalytic paradigms.[2] However, focusing primarily on chapter 6 isolated the homosexual figure from Fanon's other discussions of sex, sexuality, and blackness. By the mid-1990s, as queer studies was consolidating into a field, a critical consensus had emerged that while the Fanon of *Black Skin, White Masks* was indispensable for thinking about blackness, and race more generally, he was too homophobic to be considered a foundational theorist of sexuality. This position was articulated by Kobena Mercer in the 1996 article, "Decolonisation and Disappointment: Reading Fanon's Sexual Politics": "Lesbians and gay critics have reaffirmed a commitment to working with Fanon by using his analysis of negrophobia to open up the issue of homophobia both in Fanon's own text and in broader narratives of nationalism as a whole."[3] Fanon's method could be mined by lesbian and gay critics, and his insights on blackness made useful, but he could not be used to think about sexuality. His homophobia barred him from the role of sexuality scholar. Mercer's status as the most prominent black gay cultural critic at the time authorized this approach to Fanon as a theorist of race, not sexuality, and most certainly not homosexuality. Scholarly work continues to live in the shadow of this divide between blackness and sexuality. To be more explicit, I am not arguing that histories and experiences of blackness should be *added* to sexuality studies, a position that is well established by now. I am arguing that sexuality studies cannot be imagined and theorized without blackness.

In broad strokes, this chapter stages a series of encounters—tricks, perhaps—with two key Fanonian terms: homosexual and desire. Tricking is risky: the public park where you cruise might be empty or the public toilet subject to a police sting; the trick you pick up online might arrive at your doorstep, look at you, and then turn around and leave; the hot guy you fuck raw might be carrying drug-resistant gonorrhea; the drugs you've taken to heighten your sexual pleasure might wear off in the middle of your encounter, and leave you realizing that you are having mediocre sex; you might, in the middle of sex, lose interest; you might fall in love with a stranger's tenderness; you might be undone by the smell of a familiar perfume or cigarette or spice; the online stranger might turn out to be your cousin. To trick with Fanon's homosexual and desire is to risk being left undone, unsatisfied, wanting more, and frightened. To trick is to risk proximity, to risk rubbing with and against the familiar and the strange, to risk becoming strange as a stranger's scent lingers on your skin after an encounter. To trick with Fanon's homosexual and desire is to risk having that encounter unsettle you, mark you.

Fred Moten writes, "Fanon's texts continually demand that we read them—again or, deeper still, not or against again, but for the first time."[4] To read with and for the homosexual and desire is to read "for the first time," to privilege terms that are not considered Fanonian keywords. To read with and against the grain. Again, or deeper still. Again, or deeper still. Again, or deeper still. For the homosexual and desire. To read for the first time is to read for one's interests—and, perhaps, survival. To seek sustenance where one has been told none might be found, to suck stones, hoping to find some life-giving moisture. Fanon teaches us how to suck stones. On the disciplining question of method, he writes, "I shall be derelict."[5] Learning from Fanon, I slip in and out of disciplinary methods, borrowing and stealing, deforming what exists while inventing what I need. But Fanon is not enough. He was unable to think about black women. We need not replicate his mistakes. This chapter thinks with Fanon and ends with Audre Lorde, because she imagined what he could not.

A black queer—sometimes diasporic—reads Fanon, and invites you—the reader, the voyeur—to participate in this encounter.

The Homosexual

As I turn to look at how the homosexual figures in *Black Skin, White Masks*, let me clarify my task. I am not interested in claiming Fanon was not homophobic.[6] While that is a conceptually interesting exercise, I'm unconvinced that it is necessary. I find the (implicit) demand that he be nonhomophobic so that queer studies can engage him a practice of racial policing that keeps the status of "theorist of sexuality" tethered to whiteness. Nor am I interested in discovering the black homosexual lurking somewhere Fanon refused to look. Indeed, given the subject-making work of "homosexual" and the thing-making work of "black" within colonial modernity, it is unclear to what "black homosexual" could refer. The "identity-constituting" and "identity-fracturing" genealogies that move from sodomite (as a legal-religious category) to homosexual (as a medical-legal-psychosocial category) to gay (as an activist-cultural-legal category) to queer (as an ostensibly post-identitarian activist-academic category) have taken the white human as the subject-object of these frames.[7] Blackness is still to be thought.

In this section, I map the conceptual terrain against which Fanon plots the homosexual, a terrain that begins with his understanding of how the black man—Fanon is androcentric—emerges in colonial modernity through sociogenesis. Another way to map the terrain would be to account for the geohistories that subtend Fanon's theorizing: his life in colonial Martinique, from his birth in 1925 through his middle-class upbringing in a family of eight children to his education under Aimé Césaire until he left home in 1944 to join the French army; his experiences aboard the *Oregon*, a ship carrying 1,000 men—at eighteen, Fanon was the youngest—that transported enlisted men from the Caribbean to "the Moroccan port of Casablanca," from where the men received basic training at the "El Hajeb camp near Meknes"; his stay at the camp, a location that was "crowded with Algerians, Moroccans and troops from the African colonies," and where a special brothel was established by the army to cater exclusively to Martiniquan soldiers, not to the white French and not to the Africans; his brief time in Algeria and then his travel to France; and his time as a student in Lyon.[8] What did Fanon experience across these different spaces and institutions? How were diverse erotics framed and practiced and understood and misunderstood? How has positioning Fanon as a *theorist* disembedded him from these geohistories, and, in the process, created a truncated understanding of how he thinks and from where he thinks? I am interested in these questions, but I do not pursue them here. I mark them to indicate the many ways scholars have yet to think about Fanon, geohistory, and sexuality.

The conceptual account that follows embeds Fanon's claims and observations about the homosexual within the terms Fanon adopts and trans*forms by routing psychoanalysis and philosophy through the experience of blackness. I learn how to think about trans*forms from Christina Sharpe:

> I want to think Trans* in a variety of ways that try to get at something *about* or *toward* the range of trans*formations enacted on and by Black bodies. The asterisk after a word functions as the wildcard, and I am thinking the trans* in that way. . . . The asterisk after the prefix "trans" holds the place open for thinking (from and into that position). It speaks, as well, to a range of embodied experiences called gender and to Euro-Western gender's dismantling, its inability to hold in/on Black flesh. The asterisk speaks to a range of configurations of Black being that take the form of translation, transatlantic, transgression, transgender, transformation, transmogrification, transcontinental, transfixed, trans-Mediterranean, transubstantiation, . . . transmigration, and more.[9]

Sharpe offers a way for us to read Fanon's questioning black body—"O my body, make of me always a man who questions"—into *Black Skin, White Masks*, as it enacts a range of trans*formations and is, in turn, implicated in the signifying chain that blackness inaugurates and interrupts. To trans*form is to ask how the black body—Fanon's body— interrupts and impedes the white thinkers he encounters, in part by naming those thinkers as white, and by noting the geohistories from and into which they write. It is to ask what happens to the black body— Fanon's body—as it rubs against those thinkers, as it experiences itself as abraded, voided, trans*fixed, and desired.

Fanon grapples with three main questions in *Black Skin, White Masks*: What does the black man want? What happens to the black man when he encounters white civilization? How can the black man pursue freedom? The second question is the major focus of the book, and it is the basis for his theory of sociogeny. Sociogeny is a slippery concept, especially since the word appears just once in *Black Skin, White Masks*:

> Reacting against the constitutionalizing trend at the end of the nine-teenth century, Freud demanded that the individual factor be taken into account in psychoanalysis. He replaced the phylogenetic theory by an ontogenic approach. We shall see that the alienation of the black man is not an individual question. Alongside phylogeny and ontogeny, there is also sociogeny.[10]

Phylogenesis refers to the development of a species and is commonly used to think about evolution whereas ontogeny refers to the development of an individual organism from the earliest stages to maturity. In Fanon's account, Freud moved from a Darwinian account of the human, which arranged groups of humans on a model embedded in scientific racism, to a model focused on interiority; from an evolutionary-historical account to a psychic-historical account that I will describe as psychoanalysis-as-ontogeny. However, Freud's innovation does not account for the black man: "neither Freud nor Adler nor even the cosmic Jung took the black man into consideration in the course of his research."[11] If, in the phylogenetic model the black man is at the bottom of the hierarchy of humans, this status is not affected by shifting to an ontogenic model. What accounts for the persistent bottom status of the black man within phylogeny and psychoanalysis-as-ontogeny? Fanon recognizes that phylogeny and psychoanalysis-as-ontogeny are dominant world-imagining, world-building theories designed to explain how life emerges and functions: they cannot simply be discarded but they cannot account for "the black man." Sociogeny interrupts and supplements the species-making and individual-forging labors of phylogeny and psychoanalysis-as-ontogeny by accounting for the *experience* of blackness. Fanon places sociogeny "alongside" phylogeny and psychoanalysis-as-ontogeny to give it equal weight: like phylogeny and psychoanalysis-as-ontogeny, sociogeny is world-imagining and world-building.

Sociogeny not only governs alongside phylogeny and psychoanalysis-as-ontogeny, but also interacts with them. Although scholars such as Homi Bhabha, Diana Fuss, and Gwen Bergner have addressed how Fanon rethinks psychoanalysis-as-ontogeny, this body of work has not placed psychoanalysis-as-ontogeny alongside sociogeny.[12] If psychoanalysis-as-ontogeny produces the individual, as theorized by psychoanalysis, it also interacts with sociogeny. Fanon addresses this interaction in chapter 6; it is the terrain against which his scattered comments on the homosexual emerge. "In Europe," he writes, "the family represents the way the world reveals itself to the child. The family structure and the national structure are closely connected."[13] Notice the scale in the first sentence, the move from Europe to family to world, a shift that not only refuses a distinction between the private and the public, but also emphasizes how colonial modernity (re)made the world so that the child raised in Europe experiences "the world" being revealed through the family. He continues, "the child leaving the family environment finds the same laws, the same principles, and the same values. A normal child brought up in a normal family will become a normal adult."[14] The parallel structure between "same" and "normal" reveals how the "normal" is produced through repetition: structures that repeat produce those habituated to them as normal. However, Fanon is not claiming that structures produce ideas of normal according to different geohistorical patterns. Rather, the world Europe has made, through phylogeny and psychoanalysis-as-ontogeny, has created ideas of the normal child and family and adult. Subsequently, he clarifies, "The white family is the guardian of a certain structure. Society is the sum of all the families. . . . The white family is the educating and training ground for entry into society."[15] In this latter formulation, "same" and "normal" have been replaced by "white." On a formal level, *Black Skin, White Masks* proceeds through repetitions with slight variations: "normal" is replaced by "white," for instance. Sociogeny, that is, how individuals inhabit and navigate family, society, nation, and Europe, is invisible, which is to say "normal," which is to say "white."

As Sylvia Wynter explains, black and white people are "socialized" "in the mode of sociogeny."[16] Sociogeny grounds ideas of family, society, and nation. More importantly, sociogeny directs how family, society, and nation are experienced. Mapping the role of experience, Wynter writes, "while the black man must experience himself as the *defect* of the white man—as must the black woman vis a vis the white woman— neither the white man or woman can experience himself/herself *in relation to the* black man/black woman in any way but as that fullness and genericity of being human, yet a genericity that must be verified by the clear evidence of the latter's *lack* of this fullness, this genericity."[17] Within the phylogeny, psychoanalysis-as-ontogeny, and sociogeny triad, white being is understood and experienced as generically human. Simultaneously, antiblackness is foundational to how (white) humanness is understood and experienced. Drawing on Wynter, Katherine McKittrick writes, "Antiblackness informs neurobiological and physiological drives, desires, and emotions—and negative feelings—because it underwrites a collective and normalized, racially coded, biocentric belief system wherein narratives of natural selection, and the dysselection of blackness, are cast as, and *reflexly* experienced as, commonsense."[18] Threading Wynter through McKittrick, the commonsense experience of whiteness is as a generic human while the commonsense experience of blackness is as defect in relation to whiteness, which is, then, defect in relation to humanness. Commonsense is not only intellectual, as it is generally understood, but also the whole ensemble of how the senses experience the world, especially how ideas and experiences of pleasure and unpleasure, beauty and ugliness, good and bad, are framed. Commonsense as aesthetic experience is marked by the fractures created by colonial modernity.[19]

Just as the human sciences produce normality by marking some characteristics as deviant, and it is through studying such deviance that ideas of normality are produced, sociogeny becomes visible by looking at what happens to the black child: "a normal black child, having grown up in a normal family, will become abnormal at the slightest contact with the white world."[20] The "world" as revealed in the black child's family does not allow the black child to function normally in the white world that is society, nation, Europe, the world conquered by Europe, and the systems of being, knowledge, and feeling—phylogeny and psychoanalysis-as-ontogeny—that subtend that world. The problem, as Fanon argues, is not "a feeling of inferiority," but "a feeling of not existing."[21] This "feeling of not existing" is based on the positions allocated to the black man within colonial modernity through the phylogeny, psychoanalysis-as-ontogeny, and sociogeny triad. Within this triad, the black man figures as the biological and as the phobic object.

"As regards the black man," argues Fanon, "everything in fact takes place at the genital level."[22] The black man is "viewed as a penis symbol," "represents the biological danger," incarnates "rape" ("whoever says rape says black man"), "symbolizes the biological," "represents the (uneducated) sexual instinct," "embodies genital power out of reach of morals and taboos," and "is genital."[23] These descriptions move between figuration ("represents," "symbolizes") and being ("embodies," "is"). The figural logic works both ways: the black man "represents the biological" and, in turn, the biological figures the black man; the black man symbolizes the genital and the genital—by which Fanon means the penis—is the black man. Lee Edelman considers the relationship of the figural to the political when he writes, "politics, construed as opposition or not, never rests on essential identities. It centers, instead, on the figurality that is always essential *to* identity, and thus on the figural relations in which social identities are always inscribed."[24] Edelman helps to illuminate the problem of the black man who is figured as biological-genital-penis. If, to take a basic premise of modernity, the political is the realm of rational debate, and if the white man represents rationality, there can be no rapprochement between the white man as reason and the black man as genital, no meeting place on shared political ground. This split is not simply between mind and body; it is also between an orderly (white) body and a sexual and sexually violent (black) body.

Within colonial modernity, the white man, "Man" in Wynter's formulation, "overrepresents itself as if it were the human itself."[25] Phylogeny and psychoanalysis-as-ontogeny are strategies for generating this overrepresentation: they generate the world that can be imagined and the human who can inhabit that world. I emphasize this point because Wynter's critique of *over*representation differs from mainstream critiques of *mis*representation. Critiques of misrepresentation assume that positive and correct representations provide black and other minoritized people with more livable lives, that the category of human can be extended through inclusion and diversity. In contrast, Wynter argues that the very conception of the human would need to be changed—the structure of overrepresentation and the strategies that generate that overrepresentation would need to be reimagined and remade. *Over*representations structure how the world is revealed to the normal, white child and direct how the black child experiences that world. Extending beyond childhood, these overrepresentations—produced through the triad of phylogeny, psychoanalysis-as-ontogeny, and sociogeny—structure society, Europe, and the world Europe imagined and made: colonial modernity. As a result, these overrepresentations dictate how the world that Europe imagined and made is experienced by white men and black men.[26] It is also within these overrepresentations that homosexuality emerges as an affair between white men and black men.

Fanon takes on the psychic role of the black man in colonial modernity when he discusses the black man as "phobogenic."[27] Let me be pedantic and note that the title of chapter 6 is "The Black Man *and* Psychopathology," not "The Black Man's Psychopathology." While Fanon describes the psychic damage suffered by black men in *Black Skin, White Masks*, he notes that the archive of psychoanalytic thought developed for the European family cannot account for the damage inflicted on the black man. He uses psychoanalytic categories such as trauma and catharsis, but always with the proviso that these must be rethought through the drama "played out every day in the colonized countries."[28] Within this drama, the black man is a phobic object *for white people and black people*, for all those trained by the phylogeny, psychoanalysis-as-ontogeny, and sociogeny triad. As theorized by Angelo Hesnard, the phobic object arouses "fear and revulsion."[29] Fanon elaborates, "the object, naturally, need not be there, it is enough that somewhere the object *exists*: it is a possibility." And adds, "In the phobic, affect has a priority that defies all rational thinking."[30] Using a sociogenic method, Fanon explores what happens when the experience of blackness is wedded to the notion

of phobia by coining the term "negrophobia." Fanon maps the (homo)
sexual economy of negrophobia: "In the majority of Negrophobic men
has there been an attempt at rape? An attempt at *fellatio*?"[31] Because the
black man is figured as rape ("whoever says rape says black man"), any
sexual violence toward any man is figured as violence *from* the black
man. It does not matter whether the sexual violence is performed by
a black man—the experience of sexual violence is racialized as black
within colonial modernity. With this example, Fanon demonstrates how
negro, as prefix, modifies the concept of phobia: it always introduces the
biological, the genital, the sexual, and the sexually violent. Because of
this figuration, the black man's role in same-sex relationships is over-
determined. This position of the black man as sexual violence leads to
his occupation in "brothels" where white men desire to be whipped by
black men.[32]

Although the relationship between negrophobia and homosexuality
is implicit in the questions Fanon asks about rape and fellatio—Fanon's
model is androcentric, so he is probably discussing sex acts between
men—the connection between negrophobia and homosexuality is made
explicit in a passage that has been scrutinized by queer critics: "the negrophobic man is a repressed homosexual."[33] The passage occurs as an
aside in a discussion of negrophobic women, and here it is in context:

> When we were in the army we were able to observe how white women
> from three or four European countries behaved in the presence of black
> men who had asked them to dance. Most of the time, the women made
> evasive, shrinking gestures, their faces expressing genuine fear. Yet even
> if they had wanted to, the black men who had invited them to dance
> would have been incapable of doing them any harm. The behaviour of
> these women is clearly understandable from the standpoint of imagina-
> tion because a negrophobic woman is in reality merely a presumed sexual
> partner—just as the negrophobic man is a repressed homosexual.[34]

Just as I have no interest in claiming that Fanon was not homophobic,
I have no interest in claiming that he was not a misogynist.[35] I take his
point to be that the white women are reacting to their *idea* of the black
man, an idea that takes precedence over the actual actions of the black
men. Fanon imagines that these white women imagine the invitation

to dance as a sexual demand in which the black men are imagining the white women as sexual partners. A lot of imagining is going on. Dancing with a black man opens one to accusations of sexual impropriety: negrophobia joins with gendered normativity to police white womanhood. As Kevin Mumford has shown, these fears were not without foundation: white women who consorted with black men in Chicago in the early twentieth century were often considered prostitutes or insane.[36] And, as Martha Hodes adds, white women who were intimate with black men during Reconstruction in the U.S. South were subject to insults and assault from members of the KKK.[37] To add to the imaginative sequence, the women may not be endangered by the black men, but they may certainly be endangered by other white women and white men. It is within this sequence of imaginary leaps that Fanon discusses the negrophobic man in an aside: "just as the negrophobic man is a repressed homosexual."

Given that Fanon does not offer a frame through which to apprehend the negrophobic man in this aside—there is no dance, no intimate occasion, no single anecdote or event to anchor his comment—it requires elaboration and speculation. What ellipses subtend this claim? What experiences and fantasies? If we track it back along the passage where it occurs and embed it within the broader geohistorical setting, the deeply homosocial world of the army, with its forced proximities that are mostly gender-segregated, takes center stage. When Fanon was enrolled in the army during World War II, the French administration provided sex workers for the men. However, it distinguished between sex workers provided for white French soldiers and those available to Martiniquan men.[38] This refusal to engage with the same sexual partners, the panic over something being transmitted through proximity to blackness, the panic over losing some element of whiteness, could be part of what Fanon interprets as repressed homosexual panic. Simultaneously, Fanon might be describing the quotidian ways that white men in the army and elsewhere disdain contact with black men—sharing accommodations, shaking hands, even walking on the same side of the street—because, on the level of the imaginary, they view black men as sexual partners and, more particularly, as sexual aggressors. Such a view accords with the common wisdom that virulently homophobic men are repressed homosexuals. Frankly, this kind of argument is uninteresting, so I won't pursue it. Little evidence exists to demonstrate that Fanon is not using "homosexual" as an insult. It is an insult. It is homophobic.

Fanon's white queer critics object to the connection he makes between negrophobia and homosexuality. Jonathan Dollimore argues that "homosexuality is itself demonized as both a cause and an effect of the demonizing psychosexual organization of racism."[39] And Edelman writes that Fanon "affirms the identity of white racism with homosexuality."[40] To my Twitter-trained ears, these objections sound like #notallwhitegaymen. More critically, these readings of negrophobia as racism and white racism misunderstand how Fanon uses negrophobia: negrophobia is not a synonym for racism. Fanon theorizes negrophobia as an effect of sociogenesis. To repeat Wynter's argument: sociogenesis shapes white people *and* black people. Translating negrophobia as racism and white racism ignores how sociogenesis generates negrophobia.

To grapple with how Fanon links negrophobia to repressed homosexuality, "We have to move slowly—that we know—but it's not easy."[41] In chapter 6, the same chapter where Fanon connects the negrophobe to the repressed homosexual, he writes, "[I]t is normal for the Antillean to be a negrophobe."[42] It is normal because "the Antillean has assimilated all the archetypes of the European."[43] Turning to the training of childhood, he writes, "I am a black man—but naturally I don't know it, because I am one. At home my mother sings me, in French, French love songs where there is never a mention of black people."[44] Because the Antillean undergoes a French education, complete with indoctrination about "our ancestors the Gauls," the Antillean experiences himself as white, so much so that the Antillean insists "the Negro lives in Africa."[45] Having been formed by the world Europe made, "it is normal for the Antillean to be a negrophobe." How do we understand this movement between "Antillean" and "black"? Introducing *Black Skin, White Masks*, Fanon writes, "As those of an Antillean, our observations and conclusions are valid only for the French Antilles—at least regarding the black man *on his home territory*."[46] A different kind of blackness is produced once the Antillean is no longer "*on his home territory*." As does a different kind of recognition: "At the start, we wanted to confine ourselves to the Antilles. But dialectics, at all cost, got the upper hand and we have been forced to *see* that the Antillean is above all a black man."[47] Yet, to read Fanon, we must hold on to the Antillean *and* the black man, noting what is synecdochic and what is not. It may be "normal" for an Antillean to be a negrophobe because of a specific geohistorical training that claims the Gauls as ancestors and that reinforces class-based colorism. This particular *experience* of blackness does not translate across many Anglo-Caribbean and Anglo-African spaces. Yet, because sociogenesis is, alongside phylogenesis and psychoanalysis-as-ontogenesis, a world-imagining and world-making structure that generates the *experience* of being human, the position of negrophobe can be occupied by white people *and* black people, by white queers *and* black queers, though it will be *experienced* differently by white people, defined as generically human, and black people, defined as defective in relation to white people.

Homosexuality (repressed and not) is an important frame for Fanon for two reasons: first, because of the figural-psychic role of the black man as genital, as penis, and as sexual aggressor within colonial modernity and, second, because Fanon figures colonial modernity as a relationship between white men and black men. Because of the relative positions occupied by white men and black men in colonial modernity, the relationship between them can never be homosocial: it makes no sense to say white *and* black men, for instance; it must always be white men and black men. This relationship is always mediated by how the black man is figured as genital and sexual aggressor by the white man. While I want to hold on to the idea that Fanon uses "repressed homosexual" as an insult, akin to how "fag" or "queer" circulate as insults, I am also arguing that alongside the insult—rubbing alongside it—is an insight into the libidinal economy that subtends relations between white men and black men, which is haunted by something that might be (mis)named "repressed homosexuality." Within the racializing logics of colonial modernity, the black man as phobic object arouses fear, revulsion, and desire. Translated into classic psychoanalytic terms, via Twitter and porn: the white father has the phallus, but black daddy will dick you down.

If the negrophobe is a repressed homosexual, what is the *unre-pressed* homosexual's relationship to the black man? Terry Goldie writes, "[T]here is no acceptable definition of the homosexual except someone who has sexual relations with another person of the same sex."[48] Although I appreciate Goldie's approach, which refuses the desexualizing ways in which homosexuality tends to be discussed in the academy, I prefer Robert Reid-Pharr's definition of queer: "[I]f there's one thing that marks us as queer, a category that is somehow different, if not altogether distinct, from the heterosexual, then it is undoubtedly our relationships to the body, particularly the expansive ways in which we utilise and combine vaginas, penises, breasts, buttocks, hands, arms, feet, stomachs, mouths and tongues in our expressions of not only intimacy, love, and lust, but also and importantly shame, contempt, despair, and hate."[49] To Reid-Pharr's expansive definition, I would add the ways such forms of contact are imagined and desired, in conscious and unconscious ways. Given the black man's role as the biological, the genital, the penis, and uneducated sexual instinct within colonial modernity, a role that is figural and psychic, it is impossible to imagine any male homosexual sex act that does not involve the figure of the black man. Fanon might be rewritten thus: whoever says sex says black man. Critical propriety has taught us to dismiss this claim as a racist fabrication, but I want to linger on it. Amending Dollimore and Edelman, I am arguing that the black man's role as genital and biological within colonial modernity means that the homosexual cannot be imagined or theorized without going through the black man: to desire sexual contact with another man is always to confront the figure of the black man who incarnates sex. Might blackness be the very core of queer desire?

While one strand of criticism has been that Fanon indicts white homosexuals, another has been that Fanon refuses the possibility of the black homosexual. Again, this is a moment when geohistory matters, and it is key not to collapse Martiniquan/Antillean and negro/black in a way that disembeds Fanon's comments from their context.[50] His comments about the possibility of the Martiniquan homosexual consist of one footnote that discusses gender-transgressive men in Martinique and non-neurotic Martiniquan homosexuals in France. The footnote occurs when Fanon is discussing an essay by Henri Baruk on "anti-Semitic psychoses." Fanon quotes Baruk, "In one of our patients the vulgarity and obscenity of his ravings transcended all that the French language could furnish and took the form of pederastic allusions with which the patient deflected his inner hatred in transferring it to the scapegoat of the Jews, calling for them to be slaughtered."[51] Perhaps the most obvious thing to note about the passage is that the words "black," "negro," "Martinique," and "Martiniquan" do not appear. If the footnote can be considered a response to a call, in the call-and-response tradition, the call in this case seems misdirected. Fanon does not footnote the entire passage— the footnote reference is placed at the word "pederastic," as though the simple act of writing that word generates a call—grounded in how black men are figured as genital and sexual aggressors—that must be answered. But the answer is strange, as it does not follow footnote conventions: it does not define the term pederast or provide additional reading material, both strategies that Fanon uses elsewhere. It shifts geohistories:

> Let us mention in passing that we have never observed the overt presence of homosexuality in Martinique, the reason being the absence of the Oedipus complex in the Antilles. The schema is well known to us. There are, nevertheless, what they call "men dressed as women" or *makoumé*. They mainly wear a jacket and skirt. But we are convinced that they lead a normal sexual life. They drink rum punch like any other guy, and are not insensitive to the charms of women, be they fishwives or vegetable sellers. In Europe, on the other hand, we have known colleagues who have become homosexuals, though always passive. But there was nothing neurotic in their homosexuality and for them it was an expedient, as pimping is for others.[52]

What compels this "mention in passing"? In French, it is "mentionnons rapidement," a rapid or quick mention.[53] And, given that it is "in passing," why isn't it simply the quick observation? What does "overt homosexuality" look like? Why does Fanon invoke a psychoanalytic frame to think about the Antilles when elsewhere he explains that psychoanalytic theorists did not think about the experience of blackness? What "schema" does Fanon know that accounts for the experience of blackness in thinking about homosexuality? Why the shift from "we have never observed" to "what they call"? Who is this "they"? What evidence grounds Fanon's observations about *makoumé*? Why should we believe Fanon because he is "convinced" *makoumé* lead "normal sex lives"? Conviction, after all, is that "sense of rightness" that Lauren Berlant and Michael Warner attribute to heteronormativity.[54] This sense of rightness—conviction—cannot be countered by evidence or argument. Does having sex with women—if that is what "not insensitive to the charms of women" means—mean that the *makoumé* do not also have sex with men? Do the *makoumé* Fanon has heard about but, seemingly, never encountered, consider themselves cis men? What other trans*formations might be at play? What does drinking rum punch have to do with gender expression, sexual practice, gender identity, or sexual identity? What does Fanon mean when he describes "colleagues who have become homosexuals"? What marked them as nonhomosexual before? How does he know they are passive? How does he know their homosexuality is not neurotic? How does he know it is expedient? Why does he compare their homosexuality to pimping?

Many other questions can be asked. I have provided this list because this footnote has assumed a disproportionate weight in queer discussions of Fanon, even though it is such a strange blend of anecdote and speculation. For instance, Kobena Mercer writes that the footnote "initially suggests that Fanon knows little about homosexuality" but then "reveals he knows all too much."[55] As my list of questions indicates, I do not share Mercer's conviction that Fanon "knows all too much." Of the various discussions of this passage, and homosexuality in Fanon more generally, I am most sympathetic to Diana Fuss's take:

> Fanon's insistence that there is no homosexuality in the Antilles may convey a more trenchant meaning than the one he in fact intended: if by "homosexuality," one understands the culturally specific social formations of same-sex desire as they are articulated in the West, then indeed homosexuality is foreign to the Antilles. Is it really possible to speak of "homosexuality," or for that matter "heterosexuality" or "bisexuality," as universal, global formations? Can one generalize from the particular forms sexuality takes under Western capitalism to sexuality as such?[56]

Sympathetic, but unconvinced. How, for instance, did black people end up in the Antilles if not because of Western capitalism as enslavement? In the world Fanon theorizes, in which colonial modernity produced and functions through the phylogeny, psychoanalysis-as-ontogeny, and sociogeny triad to produce the world as imagined and experienced, this distinction between the West and the non-West makes little sense, especially when discussing the Antilles. Fuss is right in noting that geo-history affects what is produced and understood as "culturally specific social formations of same-sex desire," but this production cannot rely on an unsustainable West and non-West binary, and most certainly not on a binary that relies on something called Western capitalism that disavows enslavement.

Perhaps, more simply, Fanon cannot imagine the possibility of the desiring black homosexual within the frames provided by colonial modernity. As a figure of interracial desire, the black homosexual would always risk falling prey to the sociogenic, negrophobic imaginary that figures him as genital and sexual aggressor. Simultaneously, given that sociogeny produces white and black imaginaries, desires, sensations, and experiences, there is no guarantee that an intra-racial relationship—a Martiniquan with another Martiniquan—would not duplicate sociogenic and negrophobic commonsense. As I conclude this section, I find myself sad that I am not able to say Fanon is not homophobic. Something in me would have liked to. But I hope I have demonstrated that one can think with and against Fanon about sexuality and the homosexual without hinging the discussion on whether or not he is homophobic.

Desire

Early in *Black Skin, White Masks* Fanon asks, "What does the black man want?"[57] Fanon answers this question in a number of ways: "The black man wants to be white"; "Black men want to prove to white men, at all costs, the richness of their thoughts, the equal value of their intellect"; he wants "to be acknowledged not as *black* but as *white*"; he wants "to go to bed with a white woman"; "That the tool never possess the man. That the enslavement of man by man cease forever. That is, of one by another. That it be possible for me to discover and to love man, wherever he is"; "I want the world to recognize, with me, the open door of every consciousness."[58] To the extent that *Black Skin, White Masks* follows a trajectory, the black man moves from wanting what colonial modernity has positioned him to want—proximity to and recognition from the white man—to seeking love and freedom beyond the "livery" prepared for him.[59] The repetition of "want" points to the active role of desire in political imagination and political action, not simply as a sensation produced by colonial modernity, but as something that rubs along and against the constraints produced by colonial modernity, and especially those constraints generated by the phylogeny, psychoanalysis-as-ontogeny, and sociogeny triad.

Fanon engages the promise and problem of desire when he writes, "As soon as I *desire* I am asking to be considered."[60] Philcox translates this passage: "I ask that I be taken into consideration on the basis of my desire."[61] In the French, "Je demande qu'on me considère à partir de mon Désir."[62] Based on the uppercase "Désir" in the French, Markmann's use of italics better approximates Fanon's tone in this sentence, a tone provided by the French visual cognate "demande." While "demande" translates as "ask," I would amend the translation to read, "As soon as I *desire*, I am *demanding* to be considered." This sentence arrives late in *Black Skin, White Masks*, in the penultimate chapter, chapter 7, after Fanon's discussion of the black woman's desire in chapter 2, the black man's desire in chapter 3, the white woman's desire in chapter 6, and the white man's desire in chapter 6. Across all these descriptions of desire, embodiment and sex are central: the black man who wants to be white attempts this transformation by having sex with a white woman, a strategy used by recent arrivals from Martinique to France; the black woman who wants to be accepted by white society enters a liaison with a white man; the black intellectual who wants white acceptance marries a white woman; the white woman who is a nymphomaniac desires sex with black men; the white colonial master asserts dominance by raping underage colonized girls; and the white man who is a masochist desires to be beaten by the black man.[63] Moreover, within the figural (conscious depictions) and psychic (unconscious apprehensions) logics of white supremacy, the black man is nothing but uncontrolled desire. By the time *desire*/Désir appears in chapter 7, Fanon has embedded it within a dense archive of embodiment, sex, and sexuality.

I dwell on the embodied, sexed, and sexualized archive of Fanon's *desire*/Désir because Fanon's most astute readers have tended to *disem*body and *desexualize Fanon's *desire*/Désir. Given the impossibly large and ever-proliferating bibliography on Fanon, I focus my discussion on scholarship by Bhabha and Gordon to track how they address desire in Fanon. In "What Does the Black Man Want?" Bhabha writes that when Fanon asks what the black man wants, he privileges "the psychic dimension," and in doing so, "he not only changes what we understand by a *political* demand but transforms the very means by which we recognize and identify its *human agency*."[64] For Bhabha, Fanon articulates "the problem of colonial cultural alienation in the psychoanalytic language of demand and desire."[65] Yet, given that this psychoanalytic language was created without accounting for the experience of blackness—"neither Freud nor Adler nor even the cosmic Jung took the black man into consideration in the course of his research"—it cannot be used simply by Fanon. As Fanon argues, "A man who possesses a language possesses as an indirect consequence the world expressed and implied by this language."[66] Given that Fanon writes as a *black* man, his work demands that we ask what access the black man has to the "psychoanalytic language of demand and desire." Hortense Spillers's meditation on the use of psychoanalysis is helpful: "[L]ittle or nothing in the intellectual history of African-Americans within the social and political context of the United States would suggest the effectiveness of a psychoanalytic discourse, revised or classical, in illuminating the problematic of 'race' on an intersubjective field of play, nor do we yet know how to historicize the psychoanalytic object and objective, invade its hereditary premises and insulations, and open its insights, subsequently, to cultural and social forms that are disjunctive to its originary imperatives."[67] Building on Spillers, one way to read Fanon would be to demonstrate how he trans*forms psychoanalysis for the Antillean by invading its hereditary impulses and insulations and opening its insights to cultural and social forms that are disjunctive to its originary perspectives. The question, then, would not be how Fanon takes up insights from psychoanalysis, but how Fanon trans*forms psychoanalysis by accounting for the experience of blackness. Bhabha leaves unasked a crucial question: How does the experience of blackness inflect how the black man can take up psychoanalytic language? What position does the black man occupy in psychic life?

Because Bhabha does not account for the sexualized-biological role the black man occupies in psychic life, he describes Fanon's attention to embodiment as failure. He writes, "It is as if Fanon is fearful of his most radical insights: that the space of the body and its identification is a representational reality."[68] Unlike Bhabha, I think Fanon grapples with the role assigned to the black man in psychic life through the phylogeny, psychoanalysis-as-ontogeny, and sociogeny triad: as threatening sexual embodiment that exceeds its figurality. Bhabha dismisses Fanon's plea, "Why not the quite simple attempt to touch the other, to feel the other, to explain the other to myself?" as an "existential humanism" that denies "the question of desire."[69] How might Fanon's attention to—and desire for—touch refigure the psychic role assigned to the black man? How might it reckon with the embodied figuration—the biological—assigned to the black man in psychic life? Fanon's turn to touch is not a turn away from desire, but a way to refigure the black man's desire, a move away from the black man as sexual threat (excessive desire, sexual violence) to erotic invitation, a way to frame desire as part of the "leap of invention" Fanon theorizes that allows blackness to be imagined and lived outside of the frames provided by colonial modernity.

While Bhabha too readily dismisses Fanon's use of the body and touch as not psychoanalytic enough, Lewis Gordon desexualizes Fanon's desire. I quote a fairly long passage:

> The convergence of the "black problem" with desire ("want") already marks a distinction in Fanon's analysis. . . . By adding the dimension of what blacks want, Fanon raises and expands the question of the subjective life of blacks, of black consciousness, that parallels the Freudian question of women—What do women want? This question of want, of desire, is not as simple as it may at first seem, for the life of desire is prereflective and reflective. What one claims to want is not always what one actually wants. And what one actually wants could become discarded on reflection. . . . An individual's black desire may not comport with the structural notions of black desire.[70]

Here, Gordon points to the sociogenic effect, the metonym that transforms individual black desire into collective black desire, such that what one black individual desires is taken as what all black individuals desire. It is precisely this metonymic strategy that figures all black men as sexual threats. However, Gordon's move between individual and collective desire loses the gendered specificity that is foundational to Fanon's question: "What does the black *man* want?" ("Que veut *l'homme* noir?"). By *un*gendering Fanon's question—and this is strange given that Gordon uses a gendered analogy, Freud's "What do women want?"—Gordon loses the specific ways Fanon maps desire as embodied and sexualized, the specific ways black manhood is figured psychically and in representation as the biological. Moreover, Gordon's general, ungendered concept of desire ignores Fanon's own list about what the black man wants: sex with a white woman, recognition from a white man, touch, and freedom. If, as Bhabha and Gordon aver, desire can stage a political demand, a demand in the psyche for Bhabha and a collective demand for Gordon, that demand must engage embodiment, sex, and sexuality.

Desire as a political demand has been taken up most consistently in gay and lesbian writing. Figures including Guy Hocquenghem, Samuel Delany, and Audre Lorde have demonstrated how foregrounding desire produces different imaginations of the world, which, in turn, fuel political demands dedicated to building worlds in which queers can be possible. In a Fanonian vein attentive to sociogenesis, Hocquenghem recognizes that desire occupies the world made by colonial modernity: "Of all the political observations that can be made about desire, the most obvious is that there is nothing more racist than desire as it has been transmitted to us, and there is nothing more discriminatory than the absolute power of desire as it continues to tunnel along single-mindedly."[71] Hocquenghem takes on what has been described as the "autonomy of desire," a psychoanalytic (specifically Lacanian) and postpsychoanalytic (specifically Gilles Deleuze and Félix Guattari's) framing of desire as unconscious and polymorphously perverse, lacking any proper object and, as a result, able to attach to any object. In this scenario, queer offers not simply a range of affective and erotic possibilities, but also a variety of options for what constitutes a life beyond compulsory heterosexuality and, increasingly, compulsory homonormativity and couplehood in the era of gay marriage.[72] Yet, as Hocquenghem and Sharon Holland point out, this post-object, every-possible-object version of desire fails to consider the terms through which desire becomes possible. Holland asks, "How can one unmake the (queer) autonomy of desire—the thing that is shaped, like many other emotions, and circumscribed by the racist culture that we live in?"[73] To think about the politics of desire—to make desire political—demands reckoning with how it is produced and transmitted within the white supremacist order inaugurated by colonial modernity. To think about the politics of desire beyond the white supremacist order requires the Fanonian leap of invention, a speculative leap that imagines different configurations of desire and pleasure and livability.

If, as I have been arguing, Fanon's desire is embodied, sexed, and sexualized, how would it need to be reframed to imagine black queer life? I pose this question because even though the black man in *Black Skin, White Masks* is catachrestic ("the black is not a man," "the black man is not"), Fanon constructs a heterosexist world around this figure. Fanon provides some guidelines, but his work must be supplemented. Fanon writes, "I must constantly remind myself that the real *leap* consists of introducing invention into life."[74] And, "Why not simply try to touch the other, feel the other, discover each other?"[75] I juxtapose these two passages to ask how touch and feeling can be understood as leaps that introduce invention into life. What kind of invention might touch produce? What kind of *leap* might touch produce? I learn from black queer feminist thinking that the history of touch in colonial modernity is black and queer. Speculating about Middle Passage journeys, Omise'eke Tinsley writes, "During the Middle Passage, as colonial chronicles, oral tradition, and anthropological studies tell us, captive African women created erotic bonds with other women in the sex-segregated holds, and captive African men created bonds with other men. In so doing, they resisted the commodification of their bought and sold bodies by *feeling* and *feeling for* their co-occupants on these ships."[76] Tinsley offers an erotic economy that supplements, though it can never replace, the economies of enslavement and thingification. "The dream," writes Saidiya Hartman, "is to liberate [the enslaved] from the obscene descriptions that first introduced them to us."[77] In Tinsley's rendering, touch—affective and physical—generates relations of care and pleasure, ways of inventing and sustaining being together. Yet, as Holland writes, touch is not without risk: "touch can encompass empathy as well as violation, passivity as well as active aggression. It can be safely dangerous or dangerously safe. It also carries a message about the immediate present, the possible future, and the problematic past. Finally, touch crosses boundaries, in fact and imagination."[78] Touch risks invention, not simply affirming previous bonds and paradigms of filiation, as some thinkers of the Middle Passage have claimed, but generating new kinds of bonds.

Touch, leap, and invention meet in Audre Lorde's concept of the erotic. Lorde delivered "Uses of the Erotic: The Erotic as Power" at the Fourth Berkshire Conference on the History of Women in 1978. As Lyndon Gill notes, scholars and activists who engage Lorde's essay rarely discuss its historical context.[79] This absence means that while the essay has rightly been taken up as a theoretical intervention, the essay's specific intervention into the practice of women's history and history writ large is rarely discussed. I foreground the context of her work to ask how it intervenes in the work of history. I turn to Lorde for two additional reasons. First, *Sister Outsider*, her collected essays, opens with an article on Russia and closes with one on Grenada. It is not simply that her geohistories are expansive, but that her work moves so purposefully against the U.S.-focus of much U.S. scholarship, always critiquing U.S. nation and empire. Her prose, poetry, and activism move from Black Europe to Africa, modeling how to read across geohistories, across difference, toward freedom. Second, I engage with Lorde because she wrote and worked outside the legitimating framework of elite institutions and networks. As a non-institutional, independent scholar from Nairobi, also working outside of those elite institutions and frameworks, I am drawn to what Lorde's work makes possible, and to how her thinking and method might enable my own, and I wonder if the promiscuous generosity of her work was possible precisely because she wrote outside elite disciplinary frameworks, always knowing that her goal was freedom. For Lorde, the erotic was central to how freedom should be imagined and practiced, across geohistorical difference.

How might we read "Uses of the Erotic" as a response to Fanon's infamous remark about the black woman, "We know nothing about her"?[80] The conference was celebrating the fiftieth anniversary of the founding of the Berkshire group of women historians, a group formed to contest women's exclusion from formal institutions of history.[81] Reflecting on the conference, Alison Bernstein claimed it had "come of age." Not only had it attracted "over twelve hundred" attendees, but it had also "become an acceptable way for historians to make their reputations in the profession." And she notes that historians of women "are clearly heading toward new conceptualizations of the problem of writing women's history from a nonpatriarchal perspective."[82] Also offering reflections on the conference, Sue Benson and Barbara Melosh claimed the "atmosphere" of the conferenced provided "partial but powerful resistance to mainstream academic culture." Part of that resistance involved "a salutary concern with the historical study of women's relationship to other women and a diminishing interest in women's relationship to men." They summarize, "At the Berks, we share a place where women scholars and women's history is taken extremely seriously . . . and where the academic atmosphere is charged with the immediacy of feminist politics and surrounding social life."[83] At stake for the conference was not simply gaining recognition from mainstream historical institutions, including hiring committees and departments, but also challenging how history could be done.

Reading "Uses of the Erotic" as a way to think about how to do history, certain keywords stand out: "resource" (repeated at least twice); "information" (appearing at least twice); "knowledge" (appearing at least ten times); and "source" (appearing at least four times).[84] Lorde earned a master's degree in library science from Columbia University and, in conversation, referred to herself as a librarian. She writes, "I had been 'the librarian who wrote'" describing how she was viewed in the late 1960s.[85] In conversation with anthropologist Gloria Wekker in 1992, Lorde also described herself as a "simple librarian."[86] This biographical information helps to situate Lorde as someone trained in and aware of knowledge economies. The connections she makes between and among "resource," "source," "information," and "knowledge" emerge from this training. In a 1986 interview with the German scholar Marion Kraft, Lorde says, "If we are to create a new order, we must go back, back, back to what is primary, and those are our feelings; and take those feelings and bring them forward enough, so we can cobble a new way out of them."[87] Lorde emphasizes the importance of transformative knowledge economies when she argues later in the interview that women should "not require from each other the kinds of narrow and restricted interpretations of learning and the exchange that we suffered in the universities or what we suffered in the narrow academic structures."[88] Lorde's turn to the erotic as a "source" and "resource" asked historians to imagine and create history beyond the narrow confines of archival records, to draw on their own experiences of their lives and bodies to write usable histories. Lorde's call has been answered in a range of ways by Omise'eke Tinsley, who imagines erotic lives for enslaved women; Katherine McKittrick, who urges us to "believe the lie" of the enslaved woman who declares she was born free; and Treva B. Lindsey and Jessica Johnson, who urge us to consider that enslaved women, including Harriet Tubman, had erotic subjectivities.[89] Following Lorde, these scholars have taken seriously the charge to consider black women's feelings and erotic lives as grounds for how to do history and how to produce knowledge. They move beyond a history of blackness as a history of violation by taking the erotic as the grounds from which to theorize.

The erotic, writes Lorde, "is a resource within each of us that lies in a deeply female and spiritual plane, firmly rooted in the power of our unexpressed or unrecognized feeling. In order to perpetuate itself, every oppression must corrupt or distort those various sources of power within the culture of the oppressed that can provide energy for change."[90] Locating the "erotic" in a "deeply female and spiritual plane" extends Fanon's claim that "The black is not a man" by finding interiority *elsewhere*: if the black man is excluded from the domain of the human marked as white, then what counts as interiority—the psychic domain mapped by Freud, Lacan, their peers and their followers—needs to be remapped. A different geography of interiority is required to apprehend black life, and Lorde's "deeply female and spiritual plane" provides possible coordinates for that geography. In conversation with Adrienne Rich, Lorde seizes the universal, and claims that she believes the "Black mother" exists in "each of us, whether we are Black or not"; she "exists more in women; yet she is the name for a humanity that men are not without."[91] In a later conversation with Marion Frank, Lorde says, "I speak of the Black mother as that part of us which is chaotic, messy, deep, dark, ancient, old, and freeing."[92] It is a not a stretch to imagine Lorde's "Black mother" as a riposte to Freud: if a mythical Greek man—Oedipus—can be established as the grounds for universal family and social dynamics, then an equally mythical black mother can play a universal role, naming what is "chaotic," rather than disciplinary. Too, given the economy of black motherhood in colonial modernity, governed by *partus sequitur ventrem*—"that which is brought forth follows the womb"—an economy "which dictated that the children of a slave woman inherited the mother's non/status," the black mother Lorde imagines as grounding psychic alterity demands an altogether different genealogy of the human, of myth, of fantasy, of psychic life, and psychic possibility.[93] Unlike the violated and voiding and traumatic interiority bound to trauma and mourning and unfreedom generated by colonial modernity and, specifically, the phylogeny, psychoanalysis-as-ontogeny, and sociogenesis triad, Lorde posits that an alternative, "freeing" interiority is possible. Within that geography, in a space created by and as the erotic, Lorde meets the Fanon who desires "to discover and love man, wherever he is." In generating the black mother as interiority, Lorde takes the "real *leap*" of "introducing invention into existence."

Lorde considers the erotic—and the joy it provides—as an essential way of establishing and sustaining relations across difference. The erotic lubricates interactions, not by eradicating difference, but by creating a shared feeling and practice through which difference can be approached:

> The erotic functions for me in several ways, and the first is providing the power which comes from sharing deeply any pursuit with another person. The sharing of joy, whether physical, emotional, psychic, or intellectual, forms a bridge between the sharers which can be the basis for understanding much of what is not shared between them, and lessens the threat of difference.[94]

Beyond helping to lessen the threat of difference, the erotic creates grounds for staging political demands in which feeling is central. Joy and pleasure do not become incidental to political, social, economic, and cultural undertakings. Instead, they become central to imagining how such undertakings should proceed and how those proceedings should be evaluated. Have those undertakings intensified joy? Have they multiplied pleasure? Have they generated conditions of livability that make the social more pleasant? These questions take center stage when political work attends to the erotic. It becomes more possible to imagine a shareable world when that world is imagined as joyful.

An approach that prioritizes the erotic reimagines how collectivity should function. Lorde moves between the personal—"me" and "I"—and the collective—"we," "our," "us"—to demonstrate how the erotic can build worlds:

> Once we begin to feel deeply all the aspects of our lives, we begin to demand from ourselves and from our life-pursuits that they feel in accor-

dance with that joy which we know ourselves to be capable of. Our erotic knowledge empowers us, becomes a lens through which we scrutinize all aspects of our existence, forcing us to evaluate those aspects honestly in terms of their relative meaning within our lives. And this is a grave responsibility, projected from within each of us, not to settle for the convenient, the shoddy, the conventionally accepted, nor the merely safe.[95]

Notably, in this quotation Lorde's pronouns are "us" and "we," as she imagines how collectives that value the erotic can produce political and social critique while advancing a vision of collective life that foregrounds pleasure. Lorde's emphasis on the erotic as sharing and joy and pleasure textures Bhabha's claim that Fanon retreats into "an existential humanism that is as banal as it is beatific." In fact, Fanon's desire to "touch the other, feel the other, discover each other," a desire interested in curiosity and pleasure beyond the limits created by white supremacy, is precisely the kind of political demand produced by an attention to psychic life.

Where Fanon's *leap* of invention consists of taking desire as the starting point for rethinking black subjectivity, even knowing how that desire has been pathologized by white supremacy, Lorde's *leap* of invention consists of foregrounding the erotic, taking Fanon's tentative questions about touch and using them to map a freeing interiority, the black mother.

Love and Touch

Again, as though for the first time: What does the black man want? I'm listening to Rihanna's "Work" as I turn to this concluding section, and it reminds me of why I remain attached to Fanon: his attention to love, touch, and the body. Even though many of us write about Fanon's "lived experience," processing it through a range of thinkers, we remain detached from such writing, refusing to risk what Fanon risked. I worry that we lose the Fanon to whom we remain attached as we process him through disciplinary methods. In the first iteration of this writing in 2008, I read Fanon through Adler, Freud, Lacan, and Hegel, following the path that I thought he had prepared. At the time, as a graduate student, I lacked the courage to follow his antimethod, to risk the opening he provided in writing, "O my body, make of me always a man who questions."[96] That one quotation helped to ground my thinking. Luce Irigaray and M. NourbeSe Philip showed me how to think through the body as forming, demonstrating how language creaked and fractured faced with bodies it did not know how to form.[97] Audre Lorde and Essex Hemphill gave me erotics: "Now we think / as we fuck," Hemphill writes.[98] Patrick Califia and Samuel Delany showed me how to think with fucking, how fucking could lead to thinking, and how thinking could lead to fucking.[99] Tricking in Pittsburgh, Pennsylvania; Seattle, Washington; Portland, Oregon; Champaign, Illinois; and Chicago, Illinois with what Delany calls a "statistically significant" number of partners taught me the kind of questions a fucking body could ask.[100] As I traveled through these geographies—as a student on a visa and then as a worker on a visa—I carried *Black Skin, White Masks* with me, not because it explained what I experienced, but because it shared my ongoing disorientation. Fanon's questioning body and my fucking body met on the grounds of shared deracination. Perhaps it was easier for my twenty-four-year-old body to encounter the twenty-five-year-old author—I leave as a possibility that something as arbitrary as proximity in age makes a difference to how one reads Fanon.

We met and continue to meet on the grounds of Fanon's question: "Why not simply try to touch the other, feel the other, discover the other?" Fanon offers this possibility against the world organized in terms of "Superiority? Inferiority?" This possibility also reveals the limits of and extends beyond "what does the black man want?" gathering bodies and genders and sexes that Fanon could not have imagined: the woman of color, trans*, intersex, queer. If the disoriented Fanon provides one model, the Fanon who imagines tenderness provides another. Touch Fanon is a world-building Fanon, a world-reimagining Fanon, who tries to imagine the possibilities for pleasure and joy and risk. While I am drawn to the formally experimental Fanon, to the modernity-reimagining Fanon, to the angry Fanon, and to the anecdote-telling Fanon, I keep returning to the Fanon who insists there's a place for the body that questions, who believes that an attempt to touch might *do something*, who believes that intimate life matters.

In addition to asking what the black man wants, *Black Skin, White Masks* asks what happens to the possibility of love under conditions of oppression: "Today we believe in the possibility of love, and that is the reason we are endeavoring to trace its imperfections and perversions."[101] Elsewhere, I argue, "Fanon argues that love cannot flourish in racist societies where the socio-politically dominant are deemed more, or inherently, loving and lovable."[102] Within colonial modernity, authentic love is impossible: "true love, real love—i.e., wishing for others what one postulates for oneself when the postulate integrates the permanent values of human reality—requires the mobilisation of psychological agencies liberated from unconscious tensions."[103] This Fanonian view of love as sociogenic goes against the grain of thinking in black studies and black diaspora studies, both of which have often reinforced a distinction between the public and the private by insisting that the enslaved and the colonized loved deeply and honestly as a bulwark against unhumaning. Such love was a source of renewal and strength that enabled the enslaved and the colonized to face the depredations of colonial modernity. As Spillers argues, intimate life for the enslaved was always subject to the arbitrary invasion of property relations, and the possibility of such invasion shaped affective possibilities: love did not remain untouched.[104] Following Fanon, we might ask what happens to the possibility of love for those considered unloving and unlovable.

I am wary that I have moved from the questioning body to the fucking body to the loving body, wary because the fucking body is so easy to disregard and discard, so easy to dismiss as the preoccupation of queer studies rather than black studies and black diaspora studies. These fields have met on the grounds of shared vulnerability and, albeit in different ways, have pursued the roles of pleasure in surviving ongoing unhumaning and crafting freedom dreams. Fanon gestured toward but could not imagine the possibilities of the fucking body: he desired a fucking body for the black man free from "unconscious tensions," but could not desire the same kind of body for the woman of color or the homosexual. From him, we can learn that our abilities to experience pleasure and love are attenuated by oppressive structures, and we can learn to yearn for something more, for the world in which we can say, "Yes to life. Yes to love. Yes to generosity."[105]

2

Mourning the Erotic in René Maran's *Batouala*

How did colonial modernity shape how African and Afro-diasporic people interacted? How did colonial modernity impress itself on the inchoate experiences of desire and intimacy? This chapter explores these questions through an extended formal analysis of René Maran's *Batouala* (1921), the most significant black diasporic novel of the 1920s. *Batouala* influenced Harlem Renaissance authors, Negritude authors, and authors in Cuba, and is widely recognized as a foundational novel in shaping twentieth-century black diaspora aesthetics.[1] Subtitled *Véritable Roman Nègre*, *Batouala* provided an ambivalent message for its readers. In what sense could a novel (*roman*) be true (*véritable*)? Furthermore, given that the term *nègre* "had extremely negative connotations in the early 1920s," as Brent Edwards writes, in what sense could fiction tell a true story about negation?[2]

Set in colonial Africa, *Batouala* is an ethnographic novel, much like Thomas Mofolo's *Chaka*, Chinua Achebe's *Things Fall Apart*, and Flora Nwapa's *Efuru*. It uses the tools of ethnography, including extended descriptions of customs, rituals, and kinship, to depict an African community undergoing change. Simultaneously, it imagines forms of erotic freedom that invite Afro-diasporic and African readers to recognize how enslavement and colonialism damaged and attenuated erotic diversities, while exploring the possibility that the erotic can be a meeting ground for Africa and Afro-diaspora.

Even though *Batouala* is set in the early twentieth century, a period of colonial rupture, Maran switches between this framing and a backward glance that imagines a time before the ruptures of colonial modernity. When characters in the novel describe a time prior to the white man coming, they suture the periods of enslavement and colonialism. For instance, the novel muses: "Since the boundjous had come to settle in their lands, the poor good black had no other refuge but death. That alone released them from slavery. One could now find happiness only there in those distant and shadowy regions from which the whites were strictly excluded."[3] Settler colonialism, as present in Africa as in the United States, Canada, and Australia, requires "slavery": forced labor, cruelty, unhumaning, commodification, truncated black lives, and unfreedom. Maran is using "slavery" not simply as a metaphor for European colonialism. He is marking how the practices and logics of enslavement not only subtend the practices and logics of colonialism, but also extend them in new, dynamic ways. *Batouala* is, thus, a speculative experiment, in which Maran tries to imagine African life prior to enslavement through the lens of ongoing colonialism. This speculative experiment is ruptured, however, by Maran's colonizing, ethnopornographic gaze: he composed *Batouala* while a French colonial administrator in Central Africa. If Maran's imagining of the pre-enslavement past might be considered a freedom dream, how does this freedom dream function alongside the colonial present he represents? How might Africa and Afro-diaspora meet at this multitemporality where the imaginative pursuit of freedom grapples with the banality of colonial domination? What temporal fantasies of each other might Africa and Afro-diaspora need to invent shared ground?

In this chapter, I am interested in the frottage—the pleasures and irritations—between Afro-diaspora and Africa. In Maran's work, this frottage takes place between the aesthetic and the ethnographic, in the space where Afro-diaspora desires and dominates Africa. It is also a space where Afro-diaspora desires freedom for itself and Africa, and where the erotic permits difference to be less threatening.

The shared ground Maran invents takes erotic diversity as crucial to weaving together Africa and Afro-diaspora: embodied, erotic pleasure is central to the work of imagining freedom dreams. I use "erotic diversity" to suggest the limitations of using familiar identity categories—homosexual, heterosexual, bisexual—to apprehend imagined African pasts. While an increasing body of work by scholars and activists argues that precolonial Africa had a range of gendered and erotic practices, these claims are often staged in the language of identity-based rights—"there was homosexuality in precolonial Africa."[4] This approach effaces a broader range of erotic and gendered practices that do not fit within postsexological taxonomies (homosexual, heterosexual, bisexual, man, woman) and frames (perversion, pathology, deviance, transgression).

Moreover, Nigerian philosopher Nkiru Nzegwu speculates that Africa's erotic diversities, those that existed prior to the ruptures of colonial modernity, may be remembered more acutely by Afro-diaspora.[5] I am intrigued by the opening she creates to imagine Afro-diaspora as re-membering and performing erotic memory work for Africa, and by her broader claim that, counter to notions that Afro-diaspora's histories and memories and practices are to be found in, and authenticated by, Africa, the traffic in histories and memories and practices is multidirectional and dynamic. Africa has as much to learn about its past from Afro-diaspora as Afro-diaspora has from Africa. Maran's ethnographic novel fantasizes and remembers erotic diversity for Africa and Afro-diaspora. In *Batouala*, Africa and Afro-diaspora meet on the shared grounds of memory and fantasy, imagination and ethnography, enabled by the form of the ethnographic novel.

Batouala embeds a love triangle within colonial modernity in Ubangui-Shari, the present-day Central African Republic. The novel's eponymous protagonist is a village leader (*mokoundji*) who is wrestling psychically, ideologically, and materially with changes produced by co-lonial modernity. He laments that his people, the Banda, no longer have autonomy: they are burdened by taxes that compel them to work for the colonial government and even their moments of pleasure are attenuated. For instance, the community's most significant dance, which combines male and female ritual initiation with a sexual orgy, must be scheduled when the local area commandant is away. The Banda must steal time and space to participate in "the first of dances, that from which all the others derived" (87). In *Batouala*, the depredations of colonial moder-nity manifest themselves as a generational struggle in the realm of the intimate. Batouala's favorite wife, Yassigui'ndja, is sexually unsatisfied: "young and rich in unused passion," the "fire which devoured her could not be quenched by the one sexual experience her husband provided her each day" (45). She is infatuated with the younger Bissibi'ngui, who has already had affairs with Batouala's other eight wives. Jealous, Batouala plots to kill Bissibi'ngui. However, this plot goes awry and Batouala is fatally wounded. In the final scene of the novel, Batouala lies dying while Yassigui'ndja and Bissibi'ngui have sex within his line of vision; he rises, attempts to kill them, and dies in the process. Yassigui'ndja and Bissibi'ngui flee: "Alone in the world and masters of their destiny," convinced that "nothing could prevent them from belonging to each other now" (148).

I take Maran's novel as an occasion to explore what happens when Afro-diasporic authors figure their relationship to Africa through erotics. By focusing on the erotic as the meeting place for Africa and Afro-diaspora, I interrupt the scholarly tendency to frame this meeting place through tropes of hetero-kinship. I seek to enlarge vocabularies and frames of diasporic encounter to include lover, fuck buddy, and trick, the potential for a range of erotic desires and encounters. I ask what it means for Afro-diaspora to desire Africa, and track the compromised routes through which such desire travels in colonial modernity. I place the erotic at the heart of Afro-diasporic and African encounters as an object of desire and mourning. In "Mourning and Militancy," Douglas Crimp asks about the relationship between mourning and eroticism. He writes, "Freud tells us that mourning is the reaction not only to the death of a loved person, but also 'to the loss of some abstraction which has taken the place of one, such as fatherland, liberty, an ideal. . . .' Can we be allowed to include, in this 'civilized' list, the ideal of perverse sexual pleasure itself?"[6] To extend Crimp's question in a different direction, to what extent might black diasporic representations of African erotic practices be described as forms of mourning? I will argue that Africa and Afro-diaspora meet on the shared grounds of mourning the loss of erotic diversity because of the disruptions of colonial modernity. In *Batouala*, Maran mourns black erotic practices that were attenuated (though never erased) under slavery and colonial modernity. Ultimately, this mourning situates erotic pleasure and diversity as practices of freedom, complicating dominant visions of diasporic encounter as hetero-normative kinship.

Beyond Diaspora as Hetero-Kinship

In the body of literature stretching from Alex Haley's *Roots* (1976) to the present, which includes works as disparate as Barack Obama's *Dreams from My Father* (1995) and Saidiya Hartman's *Lose Your Mother* (2007), the encounter between Afro-diasporic populations and Africans is framed through hetero-kinship. When Haley reaches the Senegambian village of Juffure, for instance, from where his ancestor, Kunta Kinte, was taken, the villagers receive him as one of their own through a special ceremony:

> I don't remember hearing anyone giving an order, I only recall becoming aware that those seventy-odd people had formed a wide human ring around me, moving counterclockwise, chanting softly, loudly, softly; their bodies close together, they were lifting their knees high, stamping up reddish puffs of the dust. . . .
>
> The woman who broke from the moving circle was one of about a dozen whose infant children were within cloth slings across their backs. Her jet-black face deeply contorting, the woman came charging toward me, her bare feet slapping the earth, and snatching her baby free, she thrust it at me almost roughly, the gesture saying "Take it!" . . . and I did, clasping the baby to me. Then she snatched away her baby; and another woman was thrusting her baby, then another, and another . . . until I had embraced probably a dozen babies. I wouldn't learn until maybe a year later, from a Harvard University professor, Dr. Jerome Bruner, a scholar of such matters, "You didn't know you were participating in one of the oldest ceremonies of humankind, called 'The laying on of hands'! In their way, they were telling you 'Through this flesh, which is us, we are you, and you are us!'"[7]

Blood calls to blood, family calls to family, flesh touches flesh, and kinship is affirmed through "one of the oldest ceremonies of mankind." As the women offer their children and take them back, a cycle of life is affirmed. Simultaneously, the act of giving and snatching away repeats how Kunta Kinte was stolen away; unlike that earlier theft into the Middle Passage, this giving and taking away of bodies takes place within an enclosing circle, within the safety of hetero-kinship.

Where Haley depicts a ceremony designed to welcome him back to Africa, Hartman finds no such uncomplicated welcome. Traveling to Africa decades after Haley, Hartman emphasizes the economic and ideological difference between their respective journeys:

> There was nothing exceptional about my journey. Any tourist with the willingness and the cash could retrace as many slave routes as her heart desired. But there was something particular, perhaps even peculiar, about

it. My generation was the first that came here with the dungeon as our prime destination, unlike the scores of black tourists who, motivated by Alex Haley's *Roots*, had traveled to Ghana and other parts of West Africa to reclaim their African patrimony. For me, the rupture was the story. . . . The holding cell had supplanted the ancestral village.[8]

Unlike Haley who travels as a genealogist, to find history and kinship, Hartman enters the post-Haley world of "heritage tourism," a world of economic exchange dominated by the idea of the returnee-as-tourist as opposed to the returnee-as-kin. As anthropologist Jemima Pierre documents, contemporary Afro-diasporic travelers engaged in heritage tourism create their own rituals of mourning and remembrance, seeking connection with the past instead of with possible surviving African kin.[9] Yet, whether one seeks connection with present African kin, as Haley does, or with the past of lost kin, as Hartman does, hetero-kinship remains at the heart of Afro-diasporic and African imaginations and encounters.

This focus on hetero-kinship as an affective, ideological, and material method of connecting Afro-diasporic and African populations, as present in scholarly approaches as it is in autobiographies, obscures other modes of imagining connection. It is not that Afro-diasporic and African populations don't connect as friends and lovers and fuck buddies, but that these forms of encounters rarely take central stage as the grounds for theorizing Afro-diasporic and African relationships. What happens when the erotic is at the heart of how Afro-diasporic and African populations encounter each other? What happens when the erotic is at the heart of how they imagine each other? Maran's ethnopornographic gaze stages an encounter between Afro-diaspora and Africa on these grounds.

Upon its publication in 1921, *Batouala* won the Prix de Goncourt, the most prestigious literary prize in France. It was the first time this award had been granted to a black author, and Maran's win was celebrated within Afro-diasporic circles.[10] An exuberant reviewer for the *Cleveland Gazette* declared *Batouala* "the greatest novel that a Negro has ever written," emphasizing it was "a novel that no Afro-American should be without and leave unread, even if it is necessary to pawn the most necessary 'valuables' to buy."[11] Harlem Renaissance intellectuals

Alain Locke and Jessie Fauset praised *Batouala*. In a 1923 essay, Locke credits Maran with instantiating a "revolutionary change" in French colonial fiction by making the native human. Maran's work, Locke argues, moves "from sentimentality to realism, from caricature to portrait."[12] In so doing, Locke would argue in a later, 1925 essay, Maran provides a model for "young Negro writers," inspiring them to "dig deep into the racy peasant undersoil of the race life."[13] Beyond Locke's voyeuristic class condescension—the assumption that "racy peasant undersoil" should be available for his consumption—this description points to the erotic charge *Batouala* held for him, and the permission he thought it granted young writers to explore the erotic more explicitly.

The novel had an extended reception in *The Crisis*, the journal Fauset edited: the February 1922 issue of *The Crisis* promised a review of the novel; the March issue featured a review by Fauset; the May issue featured an image of Maran on the cover and a brief discussion of the novel's influence in France; the September issue featured another review by Fauset on the novel's translation into English; and the October issue featured a full-page advertisement that cited approving quotes from the *New York Times,* the *New York Herald*, the *Negro World,* and the *Living Age*.[14] Fauset's March review praised the novel's veracity while noting its revolutionary potential: "'Batouala' is really what its subtitle indicates, a story of actual Negro life (*véritable roman nègre*) and because it is it differs from any concept which we in this Western World have of life."[15] For Fauset, "actual Negro life" is distinct from what those in "this Western World" imagine and experience as life. From the attenuated life available in the "Western World," the "orgies of the native feasts and dances" in the novel are "shock[ing]," because "they are too raw, too unvarnished."[16] It would be presumptuous to claim that Fauset was untouched by the modernist primitivism that drove European and North American artists and writers to seek vitality and inspiration in non-Western cultures.[17] But to attribute Fauset's perspective on *Batouala* primarily to a modernist primitivist framework risks missing her broader criticism that the Afro-diasporic black person's entry into Western modernity severed a relationship to the erotic. *Batouala* offered a glimpse that life itself could be conceptualized and experienced differently.

Contrast Fauset's view with that of an unattributed 1922 review in the *Savannah Tribune*: "Avowedly the apostle of his own race, Maran's book is not the passionate representation of the cause of the denizens of the Dark Continent." It continues, "Maran does not flatter these dusky inhabitants of the African brush. On the contrary, he portrays in the crudest colors their hideous vices; the sordid existence of masses who think only of sleeping, eating and women."[18] Unlike Fauset, this reviewer evaluates *Batouala* through the limiting frames of Western civilization, frames that, as James Campbell has shown, inspired generations of African Americans to travel to Africa to convert the natives to Christianity.[19] Striking a balance between Fauset and the *Savannah Tribune* reviewer, Mary White Ovington, an author and chair of the NAACP's board of directors, celebrated the novel for winning the Prix Goncourt, but worried that it depicted "a grossly sensuous tribe held in subjection by a brutal government," and argued that the novel depicted the depredations of colonial modernity: "One who has read much of Africa knows . . . that the great festival that under French rule has become merely an orgy once had a deep religious significance."[20] Ovington's review implicitly endorses an erotic view of spirituality that has room for gendered and erotic diversity, even as she laments that French rule, including the French frames that dominate how such rituals are apprehended, subject African lives and rituals to an ethnopornographic gaze that even the sympathetic reader cannot escape.

More recent Africanist criticism has excoriated the novel for how it depicts Africans, especially Maran's focus on erotic scenarios. E. C. Nwezeh argues Maran "did not hide his aversion for black Africans" and singles out Maran's depiction of an erotic dance in the novel: "the hideous portrait of the blackman . . . attains its climax with the author's description of the dance of love."[21] Similarly, Naminata Diabate lambastes Maran for depicting Africans as "sexualized," claiming that the novel's explicit focus on sexual desires and acts "caters to a certain image of Africa that reinforced [racist and colonial] stereotypes."[22] It would be simple to dismiss these critiques as conservative and antisex, and, certainly, Africanist scholarship tends to be sexually conservative. However, such a dismissal overlooks the complicated question of how Africa and Afro-diaspora relate, a question that must consider the white supremacist frames through which such engagement takes place. As Fanon records, Martiniquans who underwent French colonial education were taught to regard black Africans as savages, and to strive to distinguish themselves from such savages.[23] Those who excelled in this education system, as Maran did, were taught and absorbed French colonial ideas of Africans as primitive and overly libidinal. Knowing these aspects of Martiniquan education, African critics are justified in their suspicion of Maran's novel. I do not dismiss this friction—frottage—between African and Afro-diasporic readings of the novel. Instead, I move away from critical irritation to the possibilities of mutual pleasure. I want to reframe Maran's novel as black diasporic rather than French colonial to posit that Maran is developing strategies to bridge Afro-diaspora and Africa while acknowledging the ravages of colonial modernity, especially the loss of erotic freedom.

Framing Maran's Ethnographic Novel

In the preface to *Batouala*, Maran insists on the novel's fidelity to ethnographic realism: "I have spent six years incorporating in [this novel] what I had heard in Africa, and describing in it what I had seen there." Maran repeats this claim for ethnographic fidelity several times: "I have extended my objectivity even to the point of suppressing thoughts which could have been attributed to me"; "So this novel is completely objective. It doesn't even try to explain: it states facts. It doesn't show indignation: it records"; "this [is a] novel of impersonal observation" (7–8, 13). These claims are, in part, pragmatic: Maran worked as a French colonial administrator and, no doubt, wanted to safeguard his job. Beyond the pragmatic aspect, these claims position his work in relation to European discourses on Africa. Christopher L. Miller observes, "Repetition, quotation, and plagiarism . . . are all parts of the African tradition in European writing."[24] By emphasizing that his novel is objective, Maran distances himself from this tradition. As Fauset and Ovington aver, Maran was trying to create a frame through which to apprehend African life beyond the frames created by European colonial fiction.

Given Maran's claims that *Batouala* is objective, it is not unreasonable to ask why he wrote a novel as opposed to an ethnography. What possibilities did he seek in the aesthetic? From at least the late nineteenth century, African and Afro-diasporic intellectuals pursued a double strategy of writing and publishing in specific disciplines while also creating aesthetic works. Pauline Hopkins wrote speculative philosophy (*A Primer* of *Facts Pertaining to the Early Greatness of the African Race and the Possibility of Restoration by Its Descendants*) and fiction (*Of One Blood*); W. E. B. Du Bois published foundational work in sociology (*The Philadelphia Negro*) and fiction (*Dark Princess*); Zora Neale Hurston published fiction (*Their Eyes Were Watching God*) and ethnography (*Tell My Horse: Voodoo and Life in Haiti and Jamaica*); Aimé Césaire published poetry (*Return of a Native to the Native Land*) and anticolonial critique (*Discourse on Colonialism*); C. L. R. James wrote fiction (*Minty Alley*) and political history (*The Black Jacobins*); and Léopold Sédar Senghor published poetry and political philosophy. In the latter part of the twentieth century, this strategy continued in work by Kamau Brathwaite (historian and poet), Édouard Glissant (novelist and philosopher), Sylvia Wynter (novelist and philosopher), and Micere Mugo (poet and literary critic). These writers understood that in pursuing freedom for African and Afro-diasporic people, they had to challenge not only the disciplinary conventions that wrote them out of history and pathologized them, but also the imaginative and affective elements that subtend disciplinary rules.

In his inaugural address as the president of Liberia College in 1881, Caribbean-born Liberian intellectual Edward Wilmot Blyden argued that African students should study work from the classical through the medieval period; everything after that, he argued, was tainted by white supremacy and would damage the students. He writes, "We have in our curriculum adopted some years ago a course of study corresponding to some extent to that pursued in European and American colleges. To this we shall adhere as nearly as possible; but experience has already suggested, and will no doubt from time to time suggest, such modifications as are required by our peculiar circumstances."[25] Liberia could not adopt education wholesale from Europe and the United States because of how that education interpellated black subjects:

> In all English-speaking countries the mind of the intelligent Negro child revolts against the descriptions given in elementary books—geographies, travels, histories—of the Negro; but, though he experience an instinctive revulsion from these caricatures and misrepresentations, he is obliged to continue, as he grows in years, to study such pernicious teachings. After leaving school he finds the same things in newspapers, in reviews, in

novels, in *quasi* scientific works; and after a while—*sæpe cadendo*—they begin to seem to him the proper things to say and to feel about his race, and he accepts what at first his fresh and unbiased feelings naturally and indignantly repelled. Such is the effect of repetition.[26]

Here, Blyden describes the affective, cognitive, psychic, and ideological damage created by knowledge systems grounded in and dedicated to advancing white supremacy. As he moves from "elementary books," early training in school, to "newspapers," "reviews," "novels," and "*quasi* scientific" works, he maps how what begins as *mis*representation soon transforms into what Sylvia Wynter describes as *over*representation, where the black person is constantly faced with the white man being represented as though he is the human itself.[27] For the black person within *over*representation, the problem is not simply feeling inferior: "A feeling of inferiority? No, a feeling of not existing."[28] It is a feeling that is reinforced by educational and cultural systems, by the scholarly and the aesthetic.

Blyden pays especial attention to the joint effect of intellectual work and aesthetic work produced during colonial modernity. He writes,

I know that during these periods some of the greatest works of human genius have been composed. I know that Shakespeare and Milton, Gibbon and Macaulay, Hallam and Lecky, Froude, Stubbs, and Green belong to these periods. It is not in my power, even if I had the will, to disparage the works of these masters; but what I wish to say is that these are not the works on which the mind of the youthful African should be trained. It was during [the Renaissance] that the transatlantic slave trade arose, and those theories—theological, social, and political—were invented for the degradation and proscription of the Negro.[29]

And Blyden concludes, "The special road which has led to the success and elevation of the Anglo-Saxon is not that which would lead to the success and election of the Negro."[30] Blyden's movement between leading aesthetic figures—Shakespeare and Milton—and influential historians and political thinkers—Gibbon, Froude, and Macaulay—indicates the intimate connection among the aesthetic, the intellectual, and the political. Within colonial modernity, these three dimensions buttress each other, with the intellectual finding ways to justify the political based on aesthetic elements, for instance. The aesthetic dimension often subtends intellectual projects, including how disciplines and fields are imagined and created. Black intellectuals who engaged these fields and disciplines needed to reckon with how the black was *figured* within them—with the aesthetic dimension—just as much as they needed to challenge faulty data and racist arguments. It was not enough to present better data or more complete archives or even more sophisticated arguments so long as the aesthetic dimension to post-Renaissance discourses remained unchallenged. The ethnographic novel has been central to these efforts.

The twentieth-century African and Afro-diasporic ethnographic novel reimagines the human by placing black people at its heart, not as objects to be studied by colonial ethnography or to be imagined by colonial fiction, but as richly imagined individuals embedded within complex communities. Let me offer three examples of this work. Claude McKay's *Banana Bottom* (1933), which I discuss at greater length in chapter 4, reimagines the Jamaican peasant away from the white supremacist frames provided by leading historians of Jamaica Edward Long and James Anthony Froude. Where these two depict Jamaican peasants as unruly and disorganized, lacking any coherent systems of being or patterns of behavior, McKay creates a portrait of a community navigating the ravages of post-emancipation life, while also inventing new ways to be together. Similarly, Zora Neale Hurston's *Their Eyes Were Watching God* (1938) embeds its protagonist, Janie Crawford, within richly imagined black communities, most notably, the town of Eatonville, which has an all-black population. Hurston enjoins her readers to imagine how black towns develop strategies for living together, for creating and sustaining thriving forms of community. And in Flora Nwapa's *Efuru* (1966), the eponymous protagonist wrestles with community expectations that an Igbo woman must bear children to fulfill her duties to the community. However, Nwapa imagines a belief system rich and flexible enough for Efuru to thrive based on her religious and ethical practices. In doing so, Nwapa's work resists colonial descriptions of African women as overly libidinal and as oppressed by traditional patriarchal frameworks. In each of these works, the aesthetic provides a way to imagine black women as creative and ethical agents, departing from the colonial ethnographies and colonial fictions that tend to fix black women in restricted, unimaginative roles, often awaiting white male saviors.

New Appetites

In the figure of Yassigui'ndja, Maran breaks out of the duty-over-desire paradigm advanced by Blyden, who had argued that African women are duty-bound to marry and reproduce, by depicting a woman who, in the new moment of colonial modernity, privileges desire over duty.[31] Batouala's first and favorite wife, Yassigui'ndja, does not believe that duty abolishes desire, nor does she compartmentalize the two. When she is unable to bear Batouala children, she supports and even encourages his marrying eight other women, understanding that the marriage contract involves bearing children. The novel extends beyond this hetero-reproductive injunction, however, and foregrounds the role of sexual pleasure in cementing intimate relations. Thus, Batouala has sex with his wife "each morning before getting up for good" (24). Even though the text describes this act as his fulfilling "his male desires" by enacting "daily liberties," it also complicates what could be taken as an act of male dominance (24). When the narrative shifts focus later in the day from Batouala to Yassigui'ndja, it emphasizes the mutuality of desire:

> [Yassigui'ndja] shivered suddenly and stretched, prey to a desire which bathed her with languor and softness. In spite of her age she still felt young and rich in unused passion. The fire which devoured her could not be quenched by the one sexual experience her husband provided her each day. Why was it surprising that her virtue became more and more un-stable each day? Batouala's stinginess was becoming quite insulting. (45)

What Batouala understands as ritual and right, Yassigui'ndja under-stands as a right and a service. It is Batouala's duty to satisfy her sexual needs.

Yassigui'ndja emphasizes that pleasure is a right that trumps the man-dates of duty. Conversing with her fellow wives, she claims, "bed, food, manioc bread, men, dancing and tobacco, that's all that really counts" (59). This emphasis on value, "all that really counts," alludes, if indirectly, to the colonial struggle over value—economic, moral, spiritual—that inflects the entire novel. Yassigui'ndja critiques the colonial imposition of an order that attempts to re-value quotidian pursuits, material goods, affective states, labor practices, and intimate experiences. This enumeration of "all that really counts" that privileges physical pleasure reflects the novel's argument that colonialism stole pleasure. As Batouala notes, "at first, not happy with trying to suppress our most cherished customs, they didn't cease until they had imposed theirs on us," concluding, "In the long run, they have succeeded only too well there. Result: the gloomiest sadness reigns, henceforth, through all the black country. Thus the whites have made the zest for living disappear in the places where they have taken up residence" (72). The final sentences of this complaint extend its geography from the novel's setting in Central Africa to the entire colonized world. It's a moment that breaks the novel's frame, explicitly connecting colonized Africa to the entirety of settler colonialism. Maran refigures settler colonialism's geohistory, rendering it as affectively saturated with "the gloomiest sadness." The loss of the "zest for living" is taken as seriously as the loss of land and freedom.

Yassigui'ndja's flexible system of value also enables her to imagine a range of intimate diversities extending beyond those offered by her immediate surroundings. At one moment, she speculates on the possibility of interracial sex:

An idea which made her laugh again came to her. It was frequently said of the whites, or "boundjous," that their male organ was ordinarily smaller than that of black-skinned men. It was added, in compensation, that they did surpass the latter in the art of knowing how to use the only tool whose sight always fills women with pleasure and plunges them into raptures.

She had wanted to be able to taste their embraces so that she could compare them to those of Batouala. In what way could the first differ from the second? Whether men are white or black, they have only one way of penetrating women in their short frenzy. Just the same, some say that certain whites act with women like two male dogs who mount each other. Such taste seemed so abnormal and so foul that it couldn't be true. Perhaps it was up to her, Yassigui'ndja, to gain insight on this point. Would the commandant of the Bamba rebuff her if she made advances to him? (48)

At the level of form and content, this passage exemplifies and challenges the tangled web of fact and fiction, what Fanon describes as "a thousand details, anecdotes, stories" that characterize black sex practices, and extends that frame to slyly include white sex practices.[32] The second and third sentences in the above passages lack active agents—"it was frequently said"; "It was added" (by whom?). As such, they mimic the paradigms of scientific observation and reporting that ostensibly absent the subjective observer, while also invoking the slyness of gossip. Crucially, the novel notices that white sex practices are as much an object of speculation and gossip as are black sex practices, subject to the same assessments based on notions of normality and pleasure—the idea of sex practiced like "two male dogs who mount each other" is "abnormal" and "foul." Yassigui'ndja objects not to same-sex acts—two male dogs with each other—but to the prospect of what sounds like sex in a position where partners cannot see each other's faces. Yassigui-ndja's sexual preferences, her tastes for what she likes and what she's willing to try, reveal a sophisticated erotics, an *ars erotica* that refuses racist depictions of African and black women as indiscriminate sex partners, too intent on satisfying appetite to care about how they are satisfied.

Yassigui'ndja's sexual fantasies also challenge racist rhetoric about black women's sexual appetite, because fantasy is an act of the imagination, an act of the mind. Whereas in racist thought black women are often depicted as mindless appetite, Maran foregrounds Yassigui'ndja's psychic life. Yassigui'ndja assumes the role of a sexual empiricist, intrigued by the possibility of comparing how differently raced men approach sex. She muses on the "abnormal" lovemaking strategies ascribed to whites, but, like a good scientist, she refuses to accept rumor as fact, and considers the possibility of finding "insight."

Yassigui'ndja's fantasy life also distinguishes her from Batouala because she is willing to contemplate new pleasures available through colonial modernity. As feminist scholars on Africa have noted, even though the sex-gender systems imposed by colonialism attenuated some of women's power, colonialism also granted women new opportunities to reimagine themselves.[33] Batouala, as with Chinua Achebe's Okonkwo, insists on ossifying tradition: "The old customs are always the best. For the most part, they are founded on the surest experience. So one would never be able to follow them too closely" (23). This emphasis on "customs" characterizes his relationship with Yassigui'ndja, as captured in a song he hums early in the novel:

> *Man is made for woman.*
> *And woman for man.*
> *And woman for man.*
> *Yabao!*
> *For man.* (24)

The repetition of "woman for man," twice explicitly and once implicitly in the final line, as opposed to the single "Man is made for woman" privileges men's needs, downplaying the possibility of women's fantasies and needs. It also suggests a conventionality that Yassigui'ndja shares only partly. She claims, "A woman should never refuse the desire of a man, especially when that man pleases her. That is a functional principle. The only law is instinct. Cheating on one's man is not so important, or rather it ought not to be" (36). Sexual pleasure is key to how women respond to men's desire. African philosopher Nkiru Nzegwu argues that across a range of African communities, from West to Central and East Africa, older women taught younger women to expect sexual pleasure and to facilitate it.[34] This expectation of pleasure provides Yassigui'ndja with a philosophical position: if pleasure is privileged, then fidelity within marriage "ought not to be" "so important."

Completely breaking with Blyden's paradigm of duty over desire, Yassigui'ndja exclaims to Bissibi'ngui, "living is sleeping with the man you desire, and also breathing the odor of his desire" (108). But this is not a desire disconnected from material realities; instead, it is enabled by colonial modernity. At this point in the novel, Yassigui'ndja has been accused of killing Batouala's father through witchcraft. She is undergoing various ritual trials to prove her innocence, including taking the "poisons of ordeal" (106). Her "tormentors," including Batouala's other jealous wives, seek to get rid of her. Consequently, she approaches Bissibi'ngui and suggests they run away together:

> My most secret flesh will be happy to serve as a sheath for your sword. In the meantime, let us flee. I will do your cooking, wash your laundry, sweep your house, clear and sow fields—all that, provided we leave.

Shall we be on our way? We'll get to Bangui. You can get a job there as a tourougou [militiaman in the colonial service]. Once a tourougou, would any M'bi dare complain about you? (107)

Maran twines the sexual with militarized colonialism as he moves from the metaphor of sex as weaponized, a "sword" entering a "sheath," to the possibilities opened up by colonial administration to young African men. Yassigui'ndja's "secret flesh" becomes part of the arsenal arrayed against colonized Africans. But I want to be careful not to read her sentiments according to an older political vocabulary of those who resisted and those who collaborated with colonialism: the starkness of this binary overlooks the numerous forms of interactions between colonizer and colonized that do not fit neatly within such narrow parameters.

Yassigui'ndja seeks to enter more fully into the ambivalent promises of colonial modernity. Before she married Batouala, Yassigui'ndja worked for a white commandant as a "boyesse," a house servant (46). While the novel does not elaborate on this brief comment, except to note that she did not sleep with the commandant, even though rumors said otherwise, it would not be a stretch to speculate that Yassigui'ndja observed the privileges of working for the colonial service from her intimate location within the house. She understands the structure of colonial governance. Ironically, the deal she attempts to strike with Bissibi'ngui replicates the relationship she had with the commandant: she will act as a "boyesse," except this time sex will be part of the deal. To save her life, she is willing to enter into a position of servitude. But this is not all.

Yassigui'ndja's proposal that Bissibi'ngui become a tourougou, a position that even a M'bi cannot contest, registers the evolving generational politics created by colonial modernity. Prior to colonialism, many African societies followed elaborate rituals that marked transition from one stage of life to another. Briefly, young men had few resources of their own and had to wait until they were older and were granted property by the older generation, their fathers, before they could contemplate settling down and marrying: the older generations controlled the younger ones economically. Colonial modernity ruptured these economic dependencies: young men could leave home, earn their own money, acquire property, and marry when they wanted. Through the status offered by colonial administrative structures, young men contested the dominance of older men. Younger men such as Bissibi'ngui embraced the opportunities offered by colonial modernity:

> Let the hunts finish. Right after that, I shall go to Bangui to join the tourougou service, to become a militiaman, as the whites say, with a rifle, cartridges, and a big knife hung on his left side by a leather belt. The militiaman is well-dressed. His feet are shod in sandals. He wears a red tarboosh. He is paid every month. And every Sunday, as soon as the 'tatalita's' of the horn have sounded 'break ranks' he goes to enjoy a little leave in the villages, where the women admire him.
>
> To these immediate advantages, other, more important ones are added. Thus, instead of paying taxes, it is we who help collect them. We do that by ransacking both the taxable villages and those who have paid their due. We have the rubber worked and recruit the men who are needed to carry the sandoukous. (108)

While Yassigui'ndja focuses on the power Bissibi'ngui will gain, over her and the local chief, Bissibi'ngui muses on the pleasures proffered by colonial modernity: new clothing, more efficient weapons, fawning attention from women, and authority over laborers and taxpayers. The pleasures are psychic and material, as he imaginatively refashions himself: subjected to colonialism and also newly empowered to act by colonialism.

Bissibi'ngui's soliloquy—it extends for another full page—notably diminishes Yassigui'ndja's presence in his life. While she seeks his protection and pledges to devote herself to him, he notes, briefly, in one paragraph, that he will protect her, and then muses, in ten succeeding paragraphs, on all the benefits to be gained by joining the militiamen. This imbalance suggests the uneven opportunities provided for women within colonial modernity. Although colonial modernity created new opportunities for women and men to reenvision their lives, such opportunities came at a high cost. Yassigui'ndja is giving up the privilege and respect accorded to her as Batouala's first wife. In the frame provided by the novel, the freedom from tradition she envisions places her within a position of domestic servitude to Bissibi'ngui. More precisely, she chooses domestic servitude to Bissibi'ngui as an alternative to a traditional mode of life that has become too threatening. However, given

Bissibi'ngui's narcissistic reaction to her proposal that he become a militiaman, the novel suggests that she exchanges one form of precarity for another.

And here the frame that started this section changes: while the novel suggests that it's possible to privilege desire over duty, to choose the precariousness of a love affair over the duties of marriage, it also insists that affairs of the heart are also affairs of the hearth, enabled by historically situated material circumstances. Colonial modernity enables new psychic and material possibilities, but it exacts a heavy toll. Yassigui'ndja abandons the attenuated freedoms of custom for the equally attenuated freedoms of modernity. Through the figure of Yassigui'ndja, Maran directs us to consider African women's strategic forms of action within colonial modernity.

"Desire was the only master"

Arguably, the most controversial chapter in *Batouala* focuses on the two-part ga'nza ceremony that combines an initiation rite, which transitions boys and girls into gendered and sexual adulthood, and a sexual orgy, where "all things are permitted, even perversions and sins against custom" (85). The ceremony also assembles the disparate Banda people, helping to forge and sustain social, political, and cultural bonds through shared embodied and erotic rituals. Toward the beginning of the novel, Batouala issues a drum message inviting "His men, their wives, their children, their friends, the friends of their friends, the chiefs whose blood he had drunk and who had drunk his" to the "Ga'nzas" (33). A chorus of drums responds to his invitation:

> "We have heard you, and heard you well."
> "We have heard you and understood."
> "You are the greatest of the M'bis, Batouala."
> "The greatest of the great chiefs, Batouala."
> "We will come. Surely, we will come."
> "And our friends will be there."
> "And the friends of our friends will be there."
> "Feasting! . . . Yabao! We're going to have a good time."
> "We'll drink like fish."

"That is to say, like whites."

"No, like true M'bis Bandas, because true M'bis drink more than . . ."

"We'll dance."

"We'll sing."

"Afterwards we'll show the women that we know how to use them."

"You can count on me."

"On me."

"On me." (34)

No simple RSVP, these responses range from flattery to description to affirmation to debate to boast. Batouala's call produces an aural collective—these intricately patterned drum responses create a public sonic space of vibrations and reverberations. Their transcription as text, the making literal of "drum voices," also registers a black diasporic longing for intimacy filtered through ethnographic epistemology.

Reading Maran's descriptions, it is difficult to remember that he's describing drumming, so intent is the desire to render legible native sound. This desire is not unique to Maran; it is a recurring feature of Afro-diasporic and African ethnographic novels that are filled with narrative breaks, where story is supplemented by ethnographic explanation. As one of the first Afro-diasporic ethnographic novelists, and as a colonial administrator, Maran attempts to imbue African practices of sounding with saturated meaning, a meaning that overflows in the two ellipses in the above passage. If this too-faithful rendering (transcription? translation? transliteration?) indexes a colonial will to know, it also registers a black diasporic longing for intimacy, a desire to bridge the sonic-disrupting histories of slavery.

While the visual arrangement on the page suggests a linear order to the responses, the ellipses offer a richer hint of the overlapping drum voices, a metonym for the expansive diversity of the Banda people, who are figured as "friends" and "friends of friends." Banda-ness emerges as a shared devotion to appetite and pleasure—an intent to feast, to drink to excess, to dance, to sing, and, for the climax, to perform virility for "the women." By emphasizing appetite and pleasure as the basis for collectivity, Maran reworks racial and colonial paradigms that depicted such pleasurable pursuits as the absence of society or community. Within a logic codified by Freud, one enters civilization and organized community by managing and repressing libidinal urges.[35] Freud is unable to envision how pleasurable pursuits can form the basis of collectivity. Against that frame, Maran suggests a genealogy for pleasure as collectivity-producing and collectivity-sustaining that will be pursued in queer art and scholarship by figures including Samuel Delany and Patrick Califia.[36]

Simultaneously, Maran creates an ideological and sensual space for Banda-ness that helps to redefine diasporic blackness. In *Black Skin, White Masks*, Fanon defines blackness as subjection to a white gaze, always threatened by dissolution. As the white gaze confers recognition to the black individual, the black person cannot simply turn away from the white gaze, but must solicit its approval. As Fanon puts it, "the former slave wants to *have himself recognized*," explaining in greater detail, "I appealed to the Other so that his liberating gaze, gliding over my body suddenly smoothed of rough edges, would give me back the lightness of being I thought I had lost, and taking me out of the world put me back in the world."[37] However, this reliance on the white gaze for recognition renders the black person vulnerable to psychic dissolution: "But just as I get to the other slope I stumble, and the Other fixes me with his gaze, his gestures and attitude, the same way you fix a preparation with a dye. I lose my temper . . . I explode."[38] To escape this mode of blackness as psychic precarity, back-to-Africa advocates including Blyden argued that one needed to leave sites of interracial subjectification to imagine a different way of being in the world. They imagined that it was possible to craft a mode of blackness that did not rely on white recognition or, less utopically, was not as vulnerable to the psychic dissolution created by proximity to whiteness. Maran's Banda-ness reclaims pleasure in and for black subjects across the diaspora.

Although the drum responses envision a Banda-ness distinct from colonial blackness, they also affirm a troubling masculinism, especially in the unusual syntax of the climactic moment: "we'll show the women that we know how to use them." "Show" invokes demonstration and performance, gesturing toward the public nature of the sex acts contemplated. But these are not simply brute ruttings; they are demonstrations of knowledge, of an *ars erotica* that proves masculinity to the women. Yet, this *ars erotica*, this knowledge, is modified by the word "use." Masculinity is predicated on the ability to "use" women. "Use" implies that the demonstrations of sexual prowess are as much for the women, a method to interpellate them as women, as they are for the men. During this public spectacle, men will be watching each other "use" women. To be a man is to "use" women, a performance that is central to the gender-making labor of the ga'nza, a ceremony in which young men and women are gendered through ritual initiation. And, while the still-tender initiates probably do not take part in the orgiastic rituals, those rituals affirm gendering.

And disrupt it.

In *Batouala*, the ga'nza is a sacred occasion featuring "the great dance of love, the one which is never allowed except on the evening of the ga'nza"; "during this glorious dance all things are permitted, even perversions and sins against custom" (85). What does it mean that collectivity is sustained, through a diversity of erotic acts and pleasures, "perversions and sins against custom"? What kind of labor might the erotic perform? More crucially, what is the relationship between the two parts of the festival: the first, which affirms normative gendering through ritual initiation, and the second, which creates an intimate space for disrupting hetero-gendered sex?

Regrettably, the paradigms of colonial modernity rupture the experience of guilt-free pleasure and modify the ga'nza, segmenting it through the colonial lexicon of ethnopsychology ("perversion"), religion ("sin"), and anthropology ("custom"). This disciplinary triad is rendered by the omniscient narrator and marks a moment of mourning: the narrator cannot abandon the epistemological frames imposed by colonial modernity. The remark following the comma, "even perversions and sins against custom," yanks the celebratory occasion into the time-space of a disciplinary colonial modernity; as it does so, the comma acts as a silent wail, a moment of deep mourning for the epistemological tax exacted by colonial modernity. This mourning is an undertow that inflects the ga'nza dance's ecstasies with a deep longing for a time before the disciplinary frameworks of colonial modernity.

Between the ritual initiation and the communal public orgy, a public performance of gender-confounding sex is staged, a reminder of the sex-gender possibilities and practices lost through the disciplinary ruptures of the black diaspora. The loss, as I have suggested, is both phenomenological and epistemological: although queer sex-gender practices survived the ruptures of the black diaspora, they took on new epistemological configurations, shifting from "glorious" to transgressive. Reading Maran in the twenty-first century, the terms that come to mind—transgressive, voyeuristic, masculinist—register the impress of black diasporic ruptures. I offer the following extended quotation from the book with a deep sense of grief that it cannot be read otherwise:

Two women made their appearance at just that moment. The more beautiful of the two was Yassigui'ndja, the wife of Batouala the mokoundji. The other had never known a man.

Both were naked and shaven. Glass necklaces adorned their necks, rings hung from their noses and from their ears, and bracelets jangled on their wrists and ankles. Their bodies were covered with a dark red glaze.

Yassigui'ndja wore, besides these jewels, an enormous painted wooden phallus.

It was held by strings to the belt encircling her waist, a male symbol which indicated the role she was going to play in the dance.

At first she danced only with her hips and her loins. Her feet did not really move, but the wooden phallus bounced with her every hip movement.

Then slowly, she glided toward her partner. The girl drew back in fear. The woman did not want to give in to the male's desire! Her gesture and her leaps expressed her fear.

Disappointed, Yassigui'ndja, as the male, stepped back and renewed her advance, stamping the ground violently.

Meanwhile, having overcome her irrational fear, the maiden now offered herself from afar. She offered little resistance. She threw off all restraint, and melted to the ardor of the phallus as a fog melts in the rising sun, covering with her hands sometimes her eyes, sometimes her sex parts.

She was like flushed-out game who had suddenly given up.

For a little longer, she stirred the desire of the male figure by delaying his satisfaction. But when the latter seized her in his arms and brutally showed that he could wait no longer, she ended her resistance.

When the rhythmic acceleration of the dance had finally peaked in a breathless convulsion of short shivering moments, the dancers became immobile, happy, enraptured.

A strange madness suddenly seized the confused human throng surrounding the dancers. The men tore off their pieces of fabric which
served as their loincloths; the women also removed the rest of their
clothes. (86–87)

The first three paragraphs of this description weld gender and sex
normativity to modernist primitivism, a welding that, simultaneously,
begins to unravel sex-gender normativity. The first paragraph uses con-
ventional sex-gender markers and temporalities: the dance is staged by
women: one is more beautiful and married; the other is a virgin. The
comments on beauty, matrimony, and virginity confirm that womanhood is predicated on a relationship to men.

While hetero-gender norms govern Banda womanhood, that womanhood is also produced as an artifact of modernist primitivism, as evidenced in the elaborate description of the women's body decorations.
Through the gaze of the modernist artist, the women are also their orna-
ments: glass necklaces, rings hanging from noses and ears, bangles on
wrists and ankles, bodies glazed much like an earthen pot. Whereas the
first paragraph elaborates a sex-gender project of subjectification, the
second shifts into an aesthetic mode of objectification by depicting the
women as art objects. As Maran shifts more deliberately into the aesthetic, he begins to unsettle the sex-gender norms suggested in the first
paragraph. As the "women" are transformed into fetish objects, their
womanhood is suspended, a process that invokes the commodification
of black diaspora histories and the aestheticization of modernist primitivist practices. The "*theft* of the *body*" in black diaspora histories undoes
"*gender* difference . . . the female body and the male body become a
territory of cultural and political maneuver, not at all gender-related,
gender specific."[39] This black diasporic transformation of "flesh" into
"body," to use Spillers's terms, continues in modernist primitivist uses of
the black body where an "originary" commodification is newly repack-
aged through aesthetics. By joining commodification to aestheticization,
Maran creates a material affective link between the black diaspora and
modernist primitivism. Simultaneously, he suggests the sex-gender possibilities in the (always incomplete) transition from subject to object: in
the space of oscillation between subject and object, sex-gender becomes
subject to resignification.

This space of oscillation becomes a distinctly queer space as subject and object come together in the third paragraph: "Yassigui'ndja wore, besides these jewels, an enormous painted wooden phallus."[40] Within black diasporic histories, Spillers argues, "captured sexualities provide a physical and biological expression of 'otherness,'" confirming one's "distance from a *subject* position."[41] Time and space make a difference: by embedding his narrative within Africa (even colonized Africa), Maran asks whether black erotic practices can offer alternative ways of envisioning subject positions. It is not that he suggests erotic practices are the place of a fully knowing subject; instead, the erotic is a subject-making and subject-unmaking space, where sex-gender are less affirmed as stable positions and understood as more contingent.

The sex-gender performance by Yassigui'ndja and the unnamed virgin supplements the sex-gender refrain sang by Batouala, "Man is made for woman / And woman for man" (24). The performance of maleness and femaleness by Yassigui'ndja and the young woman denaturalizes "man" and "woman" and highlights "made," the construction of complementarity. Yassigui'ndja's sex-gender performance marks "man" and "woman" as sex-gender performances. Her use of a wooden phallus marks masculinity as prosthetic and cultural, a "privilege," to use Spillers's term, rather than a given biological fact. But the novel insists on the contingent nature of its premises: it oscillates between denaturalizing and naturalizing sex-gender. For instance, following the dance, Yassigui'ndja's declares to Bissibi'ngui, "living is sleeping with the man you desire," a statement that reinstates sex-gender stability by privileging hetero-gendered desire (108). However, her statement also supplements Batouala's: where his invokes the heteronormative duty advocated by Blyden, hers inclines toward the antinomianism of unruly desire. Despite this tension between duty and desire, an ongoing one in black diaspora intimate histories, Batouala's and Yassigui'ndja's accounts remain hetero-centric: they articulate how sex (as physical act) buttresses and produces binary gender: men desire and have sex with women and vice versa. The sex-gender performance between Yassigui'ndja and the unnamed virgin alerts us, however, to the performative and aesthetic aspects of Batouala's earlier declaration, which is a song he composes. By foregrounding the performative elements of such declarations, the text alerts us to the sophisticated understanding of gender in *Batouala*. Man and woman are performative roles maintained through consensus. This dance between Yassigui'ndja and the unnamed virgin is perverse, to use the novel's language, not simply because it involves two women and a wooden phallus, but because it demonstrates sex-gender as a performative system, exposing masculinity and femininity as roles rather than ontological states.

In fact, the description of the dance oscillates between role and being, obscuring the distinction between sex-gender as performative and as biocultural. The unnamed virgin solicits the desire of the "male figure," but this male figure quickly becomes male through a flurry of pronouns: "she" delays "his satisfaction," but "he" can wait "no longer" and seizes her in "his arms." This transformation of Yassigui'ndja and the unnamed virgin into pronominal forms, a sex-gender binary of he/she, unsettles what Oyèrónké Oyěwùmí terms a "bio-logic" that understands sex-gender as primarily biological.[42] In a Butlerian vein, gender performativity unsettles essentialized sex-gender configurations. But the stakes of my argument extend beyond a by-now too familiar queer emphasis on performativity.

This moment of sex-gender performativity in the ga'nza should compel us to rethink the sex-gender normalization central to black diasporic theories and histories. While the commodification of black bodies and practices of labor and punishment attenuated (or destroyed) gender differentiation, as several scholars have argued, such claims risk retroactively imagining sex-gender as stable prior to the ruptures of diaspora. They retroactively normalize sex-gender systems, or, at the very least, desire such normalization. As a consequence, black diasporic histories and theories become invested in defining black subjectivity in normative sex-gender terms. Although Maran's novel does not dispense with sex-gender normativity altogether, it creates spaces to imagine African and Afro-diasporic histories as sex-gender diverse.

Simultaneously, Maran's novel engages the ongoing construction of diaspora by black scholars through the late nineteenth and early twentieth centuries as a sex-gender normative enterprise. As outlined in the introduction, for Blyden the aggregative project of diaspora depended upon a normative sex-gender framework. Maran's ethnographic novel, empirical and imaginative, draws from the same methods used by Blyden in his attempt to advance a normative sex-gender framework.

But where Blyden absents sexual fantasy and queer practices, Maran's work engages the potential of fantasy to expand and unsettle normative sex-gender frameworks. In having the ga'nza performed outside the white gaze, when the commandant is away, Maran creates a space for what M. Jacqui Alexander terms "erotic autonomy." For Alexander, erotic autonomy "pose[s] a challenge to the ideological anchor of an originary nuclear family, a source of legitimation for the state, which perpetuates the fiction that the family is the cornerstone of society."[43] Where Alexander focuses on the postcolonial state, Maran takes on the disciplinary and normalizing imperatives of colonial modernity and provides a strategy through which to challenge the foundational role of normative gender and sexuality within black diaspora histories and theories as, to cite Alexander, "an ideological anchor." Maran emphasizes the role of erotic autonomy within black diasporic histories and theories.

However, this erotic autonomy as seen in the dance between Yassigui'ndja and the unnamed virgin is offered as a truncated possibility—while their sex-gender performance reaches a climax that subsequently envelops the entire community in a communal orgy, the orgy is interrupted by the unexpected arrival of the white commandant. His arrival is anticipated by, and parallels, Batouala's jealous rage when he discovers Yassigui'ndja engaging in sex with Bissibi'ngui, interrupts them, and chases after them. Given the logic of the ga'nza, a time when all things are "permitted," Batouala's rage at Yassigui'ndja's infidelity strikes an odd note in the novel. While it may register the banal fact that even the most queer occasions of sexual license cannot escape feelings of ownership and jealousy, especially as these are inflected by age-based factors (the younger lover versus the older), it also registers a shift in how desire is calculated. As the host of the party, the "greatest of the great chiefs," Batouala is socially and culturally desirable; indeed, one might argue that he is the most desirable man at the party because of the power he wields to provide pleasure to others. Although the novel does not clarify whether Batouala knows his other wives have cheated on him with Bissibi'ngui, those transgressions appear less important because they take place in private, away from public sites of desire. Batouala is angry because Yassigui'ndja and Bissibi'ngui have "the impudence to desire each other in front of him" (88). In choosing Bissibi'ngui over Batouala within a public space of desire, a place where one's status as desirable is publicly affirmed, Yassigui'ndja shifts the register of colonial modernity's incursion directly into the realm of the intimate. Her actions indicate that traditional modes of desire and paradigms of being considered desirable have been eroded by colonial modernity's new(er) paradigms: Bissibi'ngui incarnates a newly desirable body despite his socioeconomic lack among the Banda.

In publicly desiring each other, Yassigui'ndja and Bissibi'ngui introduce a new "perversion" into the public space of Banda sex and desire, a "perversion" rooted in the intimate opportunities offered by colonial modernity. They disrupt the intimate affirmations of Banda-ness as friendship and affiliation, cemented by ritual initiation and orgiastic sex, by refusing the prescribed hierarchies of desire. Although a (prematurely?) queer reading might celebrate this disruption of hierarchies by framing transgression as always liberatory, I want to suspend a celebratory reading of this transgression. Yassigui'ndja and Bissibi'ngui celebrate a new kind of public pleasure because their authority to transgress is subtended by the violence of colonial modernity.

Death after Death

Africa and Afro-diaspora meet in one of the signature tropes of the ethnographic novel: the death of an ancestral figure. When they interrupt the ga'nza, the white commandant and his men discover Batouala's father has died, presumably from the excitement of an already irrevocably altered ga'nza, as signaled by the bottles of Pernod at his side (89). As with the death of Bita Plant's father in Claude McKay's *Banana Bottom* (1933), Janie's grandmother in Zora Neale Hurston's *Their Eyes Were Watching God* (1937), Okonkwo's father in Chinua Achebe's *Things Fall Apart* (1957), and Waiyaki's father in Ngugi wa Thiong'o's *The River Between* (1965), his death signals not the end of a pure era, a "before" unable to persist in an aggressive present, but, instead, the meeting place, the point of frottage, between what Raymond Williams terms the residual and the emergent.[44] The Banda residual is understood as an unapologetic celebration of pleasure, evidenced in the novel's free indirect discourse over Batouala's father's death: "To die while drinking . . . There is no death more beautiful" (91). As with the collective voice of the drums earlier in the novel, this reflection on death is offered collectively, shifting the notion of free indirect discourse from being a relationship between a narrator and a character, to being a relationship between a narrator and a collective voice, a community. This death is "beautiful" because it is embedded in pleasure, in a moment when the potential benefits of colonial modernity, figured through Pernod, enhance the experience of the ga'nza.

Death is also "beautiful" because Batouala's father has escaped the punishment of colonial modernity: "Work is abolished [in death]. No more tax to pay nor sandoukous to carry. No cruelty, taxes! No whip!" (91). The shared experiences of slavery and colonialism joining Afro-diaspora and Africa are invoked in three terms: "work," "cruelty," and "whip." The sequence of the terms also narrates a diachronic history of colonial modernity: work sustains life prior to colonial modernity; it becomes forced labor when taxes are introduced; and that forced labor becomes even more cruel and coercive when the "whip" is introduced, a moment that marks the transition from coerced worker to enslaved laborer. Colonial modernity—as work, as taxes, as cruelty, as the whip—alters the meaning of dying and death: "Since the boundjous had come to settle in their lands, the poor good black had no other refuge but death. That alone released them from slavery. One could now find happiness only there in those distant and shadowy regions from which the whites were strictly excluded" (91–92). Just as the ga'nza represents a site of residual pleasure, one changed under colonial modernity from a scene of untrammeled pleasure to one of pleasurable transgression, death has shifted from whatever cosmological system governed its logic prior to colonial modernity. In fact, the novel offers no hint of any prior cosmological system, so thoroughly has the cruelty of colonial modernity reshaped the meanings of labor, life, and death.

I dwell on this relationship between pleasure and punishment, life and death, because the critical tradition around the novel has argued that Maran does not denounce colonialism. In an otherwise sympathetic reading, for instance, Jennifer Yee charges that the "plot itself is almost entirely dissociated from the topic of colonialism, centering on a story of adultery ending with an accidental death."[45] Similarly, Chidi Ikonné wishes that Maran "had reduced the emphasis on indolence, sex, and idle merriment" and portrayed characters who "resisted colonization."[46] Indeed, critics have often distinguished between the novel's preface, where Maran explicitly denounces colonialism as a "continuous evil" (10) and the novel itself. Introducing the Heinemann 1987 edition, Donald E. Herdeck warns that the "modern reader is likely to be disappointed" because the novel "does not contain more protest," including "a vivid dissection of the horrors of French colonial rule."[47] Cumulatively, these critics claim that the novel withdraws into an apolitical sphere, and that the erotic cannot be a place from which to launch a political critique.

In refusing to register the novel's focus on the disruptions of intimate life—the shifts in feeling and desire and pleasure produced by colonial modernity—these critics do more than simply depoliticize the intimate; instead, they join a long, ongoing tradition in Afro-diasporic, Africanist, and postcolonial scholarship that insists the intimate—often rendered as the family—is what Malek Alloula terms the "kernel of resistance" to colonial modernity.[48] Slavery and colonialism may have wrenched individuals away from communal life, transformed free individuals into enslaved labor, and even deracinated many individuals by dispersing them across space and time—be it to the Americas, to global wars fought on other continents, or to urban locations far from rural homes—but family feeling remains the peculiar element that resists efforts at commodification and dehumanization. The space of the intimate—defined as the space of kinship feeling—resists colonial modernity. As enabling as this tradition of thinking has been for building and sustaining affective and political collectivities through invocations of fictive kinship, it has also truncated our understandings of the intimate implications of colonial modernity. Insisting on fictive kinship as a grounding principle not only disavows queer experimentation, but also refuses to accept that feelings have histories.

Batouala's insistence on the intimate life of colonial modernity unsettles the claim that kinship ties, whether real or fictive, provided an affective and ideological armor against colonial modernity's intrusions. In its depictions of complaint, submission, acquiescence, pleasure, desire, fear, ambition, and ambivalence, it registers the impress of colonial modernity as a new structure of feeling, a structure that cannot be accounted for by paradigms of resistance and collaboration. Indeed, the novel's climactic moment is strangely suspended: "The indescribable clamor and jostling was followed by a dreadful, unexpected stupor" (88). Climax is arrested—and reached—by this "stupor," a term that registers the sudden aftermath of sex, the "little death"; the passing away of Batouala's father; and the commandant's arrival. "Stupor" names the intimate invasion of colonial modernity within this novel. It registers a sense of disbelief that the intimate, the ga'nza, the most sacred of dances, is not immune to colonial modernity's interruptions, be that in the form of newly publicly desiring couples, the arrival of the intrusive white commandant, or the presence of imported Pernod.

As a state of suspended action, an attenuation of feeling, "stupor" marks the novel's final scene, in which Batouala lies dying from a wound as Yassigui'ndja and Bissibi'ngui have sex in front of him. The narrative voice taunts Batouala: "Batouala, it is quite useless for you to continue to persist in not wanting to die. Don't you see only they exist. They have already forgotten you. You don't count for them anymore" (148–49). If the interrupted ga'nza represents the attenuation of community because shared rituals can no longer be sustained and thus can no longer sustain Banda-ness as practice, and, instead, relegate it to the place of fantasy and nostalgia, this scene of Batouala's death moves into potentially more dangerous territory. Within black diaspora studies, the hope has been that community might be dispersed, but that tiny spaces of family feeling remain, refuges that can save and reenergize. But the private is no longer a refuge in this novel: the public humiliation Batouala experienced is plunged into the privacy of his hut. The moment of his death is also the moment of his killing, where he is completely devalued, and doesn't "count anymore."

The scene is absurd: a nearly dead Batouala rouses himself and stumbles toward the enraptured couple to reclaim his honor and kills himself through what the narrator terms his "imprudent effort" (149). Batouala is unable to accept that his way of life is past; like his father, he is to be buried and forgotten. Yet this absurdity should give us pause, for it registers the uneven, breathless temporality of colonial modernity. Why, after all, should a man in his prime, a man who has just been feted by his friends, and who has just mourned his father's death, be confronting his own death? How do his contracted life and violent end gesture, if obliquely, to the shared grounds of violence and mourning that comprise the black experience of colonial modernity? And why should this dying take place in proximity to the erotic?

Mária Török elaborates an element of mourning that Freud disavows: soon after the death of a loved one, libidinal impulses are charged, and mourners want sex.[49] This linear sequence is not available for black people under colonial modernity: the increased precarity of life unmakes notions of sequenced life, whether understood as ritually sanctioned or biologically linear. Rather than unfolding smoothly, black diasporic life creases and wrinkles, bunches and snags; time itself stretches and contracts and tears in unexpected, surprising ways. Batouala's wounded death so soon after his father's and Yassigui'ndja and Bissibi'ngui's sex act as he is dying allegorize the truncated life possibilities of black diasporic temporalities. Certainly, Yassigui'ndja and Bissibi'ngui's sex act might demonstrate their selfishness. Simultaneously, though, their actions can also be read within the creased temporalities of the black diaspora, where the time of now, the time of then, and the time of perhaps tomorrow provoke new urgencies, and social death is mourned in a fully libidinal way. And, here, the Freudian script might be renarrated: the killing and lustful son becomes literalized through the time-creasing project of colonial modernity.

The final "Sleep . . ." which closes the novel, the narrator's injunction, is as tender as it is harsh: a moment of mourning confounded by the commanding logic of black diasporic temporalities, where one's time is calibrated by the whip, the lash, the command. The ellipses here invoke similar ellipses used to convene the ga'nza and to map its excesses: but where those earlier ellipses conveyed communal response, the role of antiphony in producing collectivity, this final ellipsis occurs in a sounding void, gesturing not toward a being-together in pleasure, but a fracture, a wail, a cut. Instead of this final ellipsis representing a radical shift from previous ones, it allows us to refract previous ellipses, allowing us to hear their inexpressible wails, their unbearable screams, their prolonged, if silenced, mourning.

This refractive glance becomes all the more unbearable once we recognize that previous ellipses invoke collectivity, potential, pleasure, and its absolute destruction. Listen, for instance:

> In concert, bellowing frogs, tympanic toads, buffalo toads, and smith tree-frogs play their anvil noises, their clicking voices and their bellowings.

"Ka-ak . . . ka-ak . . . Ti-tilu . . . ti-tilu . . .
Kéé-ex . . . kéé-ex . . . Kidi-kidi . . . kidi-kidi . . .
Dja-ah . . . dja-ah . . ."

Cattle bell tinklings, pestle poundings, sword clankings, uncontrollable retchings—discreet or clear, shrill or hoarse, the croakings of all kinds of toads and of all kinds of frogs make "yangba."

At the end of the day it makes a deafening tom-tom. All of a sudden it dies out. Then just as suddenly it begins again . . . (62)

The incomprehensible sounds Maran tries to approximate will live on in black diasporic histories of sounding, as song, as sound, as scream, as prolonged mourning for a brutally truncated back then, as an attempt to inhabit the sound of back there. To listen for and through the ellipses and the worlds they conjure is to listen for an erotics of being, to mourn for losses unfathomable, but deeply felt. Writing in the Chicago-based *Broad Axe* newspaper, Mary White Ovington, co-founder of the NAACP, claimed, "This book is great literature, but it describes things sexual with a particularity that is untranslatable." She registered, if inadvertently, how colonial modernity rendered "things sexual" untranslatable, illegible, lost. And captured, if inadvertently, the mourning that indexes that loss.

3

Ethnicity as Frottage in Jomo Kenyatta's
Facing Mount Kenya

Jomo Kenyatta was Kenya's first president, from 1964 to 1978, and, before that, a crucial figure in interwar Afro-diasporic London, where he engaged with black radicals, including C. L. R. James, George Padmore, and Amy Garvey. Scholarship on Kenyatta has tended to bifurcate his Kenyan and Afro-diasporic lives. Whether framed as a "native informant" or as an "indigenous anthropologist," Kenyatta has been positioned, on the one hand, primarily as an African speaking from an authentic vantage.[1] On the other hand, Gaurav Desai and Simon Gikandi have highlighted Kenyatta's cosmopolitan outlook, urging us to see him and his work as historically dense composites produced by the multiple contradictions of colonial modernity.[2] This chapter tracks the relationship between an ethno-national and an ethno-diasporic Kenyatta. I argue that Kenyatta sutures these disparate selves through a genealogical imperative that privileges normative gender and sexuality, and I argue that this genealogical imperative is seen most vividly in Kenyatta's use of ethnicity as a strategy to manage gender and sexuality.

More broadly, this chapter stages an encounter between African studies and queer studies as they are focalized through Kenyatta's ethnography, *Facing Mount Kenya: The Tribal Life of the Agikuyu* (1938). *Facing Mount Kenya* is Kenyatta's most explicit engagement with a school of anthropology influenced by sexology: Kenyatta studied under Bronislaw Malinowski, whose *Sex and Repression in Savage Society* (1927) contested the universal applicability of Freud's theories by examining non-Western spaces. Malinowski's engagement with sexology haunts Kenyatta's work, especially in *Facing Mount Kenya*'s detailed treatment of gender, sex, and sexuality. Yet, as I also demonstrate, Kenyatta's *Facing Mount Kenya* continues an ongoing project to manage the gendered and sexual disruptions occasioned by colonial modernity and experienced by Kenyatta as he navigated the rural–urban spaces of colonized Kenya and the national–diasporic circuits of interwar Europe.

Whereas the chapter on Frantz Fanon focused on a black diasporic philosophy of modernity and the chapter on René Maran highlighted a black diasporic aesthetics of difference, in this chapter I map the frottage between home and abroad, and demonstrate how Kenyatta navigated colonial modernity in Kenya and London. I track the theories of gender and sex that Kenyatta developed as a young man in colonial Kenya and show how those theories extended into his travels and stay in London. Amid the many changes of colonial modernity, he tried to make sex and gender stable concepts and practices that would ground him. Yet, as I argue, doing so meant locating himself out of history, and especially negating how Kenyan women were navigating colonial modernity and changing the meanings and practices of sex and gender. Kenyatta, thus, generates ethnicity as the frottage between temporalities and genres: urban modernity and traditional myth. And he can imagine ethnicity only by negating women's modernity.

To explore the relationship between Kenyatta as ethno-national and as ethno-diasporic, I begin by examining the figure of the African in late nineteenth- and early twentieth-century sexology. I argue that this figure shifts during colonial modernity, a shift indexed in Malinowski's work, and engaged by Kenyatta in *Facing Mount Kenya*. From this broad overview, I return to Kenyatta's Kenyan context and early activism to demonstrate the roles of gender and sexuality in his thinking. Following this exposition, I turn to *Facing Mount Kenya* to detail how it addresses gender, sex, and sexuality. I argue that Kenyatta uses a genealogical imperative to manage the geohistorical and geopolitical dissonance of being ethno-national and ethno-diasporic.

Africa and Sexology

In *Facing Mount Kenya*, Kenyatta forges a relationship between Kikuyu identity and homosexuality.[3] The final sentences of a chapter titled "Sex Life among Young People" read, "Owing to these restrictions, the practice of homosexuality is unknown among the Gikuyu. The freedom of intercourse allowed between young people of opposite sex makes it unnecessary, and encourages them to acquire experience which will be useful in married life."[4] These sentences conclude a section titled "Sexual Taboos," which includes prohibitions against incest; heterosexual sex in any position other than "the natural form," the "normal way," facing the "regular" position; and masturbation by circumcised boys and masturbation by all girls, regardless of their status.[5] The use of "natural," "normal," and "regular" invokes Edward Blyden's argument, outlined in the introduction, that African sexual and gender practices are produced through regular training.[6] The categories of "normal" and "natural" are produced as *effects* of training. They are not left to chance or inclination.

The logic of the section positions "the practice of homosexuality" as the most un-Kikuyu act, the one that indicates absolute deracination. Kenyatta attempts to cover all bases by disavowing homosexuality as "practice" and "knowledge": not only is it not done, but it is also not known about. As the paragraph concludes the entire chapter, it might be taken as the point of the entire chapter: to be Kikuyu is to disavow homosexuality as practice and knowledge. It is also to manage other forms of sexual impropriety so that they do not lead to homosexuality. To be Kikuyu is to manage the risk of homosexuality.

If the practice of homosexuality is unknown among the Kikuyu, why does Kenyatta hinge his chapter on this element? Of the contemporaneous book-length works on the Kikuyu—William and Katherine Routledge's *With a Prehistoric People: The Akikuyu of British East Africa* (1910), Charles William Hobley's *Bantu Beliefs and Magic: With Particular Reference to the Kikuyu and Kamba Tribes of Kenya Colony* (1922), and C. Cagnolo's *The Akikuyu: Their Traditions, Customs, and Folklore* (1933)—none had claimed the Kikuyu practiced homosexuality. How, then, do we make sense of Kenyatta yoking Kikuyu identity to disavowing homosexuality? This textual moment embeds Kenyatta's work within a longer history of evolving sexological discourses on Africans. In turning to European sexology to explore Kenyatta's thinking on homosexuality, I expand the contexts within which his work is framed and contest the view that *Facing Mount Kenya* is unmediated by the time he spent in Europe. I read *Facing Mount Kenya* as an active engagement with scholarship on gender, sex, sexuality, and belonging as these had been framed within sexological paradigms.

By 1886, when Richard von Krafft-Ebing published his field-defining *Psychopathia Sexualis*, the inchoate field of sexology had reached an uneasy consensus about Africans: they were not subject to "the vice." Describing what he termed a "sotadic zone," a space where homosexual acts were rife, British explorer and spy Richard Burton writes, "Anomalies of the sexual functions are met with especially in civilized races." He concluded that "the vice" was absent from indigenous Africa.[7] Prominent sexologists attributed sexual deviance to the influence of international trade and urbanization, creating links between zones of commercial and sexual traffic.[8] Homosexuality was also understood as a sign that a civilization was degenerating: it had reached a certain height and was now regressing from that height.[9] Given this temporal logic, Africans, who were understood as savage, did not fall into this most civilized of vices. Joining these ideas, Krafft-Ebing argues, "Large cities are hotbeds in which neuroses and low morality are bred, as is evident in the history of Babylon, Nineveh, Rome and the mysteries of modern metropolitan life. It is a remarkable fact that among savages and half-civilized races sexual intemperance is not observed."[10] African women and lesbians were aligned through comparative anatomy, as Siobhan Somerville has demonstrated, but African women were not framed as lesbians.[11]

The myth of the vice-free, indigenous African became central to colonial governmentality. If contact with the wrong kinds of spaces and foreigners corrupted Africans, the argument went, then colonial powers had an obligation to safeguard Africans by policing their interactions and their movements. The homosexual African enters the colonial archive through this heightened surveillance, as the product of colonial, paternalistic intervention. Neville Hoad has illustrated this process in a rich argument about homosexuality among the Baganda of Uganda. In 1885, the young ruler of the Baganda, Kabaka Mwanga, sentenced young Catholic pages at his court to death, creating the first Catholic martyrs in East Africa. Records from the time claim that the young men were condemned because they refused to succumb to the Kabaka's advances.[12] Mwanga was accused of being a homosexual and rumor said that he had "learned" the "vice" from Arabs. As Hoad demonstrates, this well-known story of the "homosexual" Kabaka who martyred innocent Catholic pages is complicated by the various power struggles at the Kabaka's court; the competition between Christian and Islamic leaders for influence among the Baganda; and the absence of any factual information about Mwanga's desires and actions. More broadly, Hoad speculates that this case gave an excuse for the British government to intervene in Baganda affairs and to impose colonialism.[13]

Managing intimate life was central to colonialism. Across a range of colonial spaces, the colonial government tracked intimate encounters, whether by passing laws requiring sex workers who interacted with colonial soldiers undergo mandatory inspections for venereal disease in India, or by changing inheritance and citizenship laws to manage identities of biracial children in the Dutch East Indies, or by forcefully removing children from their parents among indigenous communities in Australia.[14] In Africa, as well, colonial efforts focused on managing intimate and domestic life.[15] Disregarding indigenous clothing practices, colonial powers introduced Western modes of dressing that accorded with colonial sensibilities of how dress should distinguish gender; girls and women were instructed in domestic work and their outdoor labor deemed inappropriate; and power relations were reconfigured along what Oyèrónké Oyěwùmí terms a "bio-logic," that took embodiment as the key to gendered relations, disregarding other modes of evaluating gendered status and arrangements of social power.[16] The management of African intimate life was crucial to produce the right kind of African worker: appropriately gendered so that men could be recruited to work in domestic and service roles; sufficiently deracinated so that colonial demands on time superseded other commitments; and appropriately disciplined to submit to colonial authority.

The deracinated African became a central figure in colonial management, intimate life was central to how deracination was figured, and the prostitute came to embody the perils of deracinating modernity. Urbanized women across Africa were designated prostitutes, whether or not they participated in sex work.[17] Their financial independence, ability to navigate markets, and skills at negotiating the travails of colonial governmentality marked these women as dangerous: they unsettled order. Worse, they risked disorganizing colonial systems of management, as they sold their products and provided care to a range of figures across racial, ethnic, and religious lines. They created dissonant spaces of possibility, zones of instability where hierarchies were unsettled within markets of desire. The figure of the prostitute in colonial Africa came to represent a destabilizing queerness, not rooted specifically in same-sex desires and practices, but rooted, more precisely, in a reorganization of intimate life and socioeconomic arrangements. In turn, the urban zones associated with prostitution came to represent spaces of deracination that fostered queerness. The proximity of deracination to queerness became key to understanding colonial modernity. To be deracinated was always to be potentially queer.

In the 1920s, Malinowski described the relationship between the deracination occasioned by colonial modernity and queerness. Writing on the Trobriands, he argues,

> Freud has shown that there is a deep connection between the course of infantile sexuality and the occurrence of perversion in later life. On the basis of his theory, an entirely lax community like that of the Trobrianders, who do not interfere with the free development of infantile sexuality, should show a minimum of perversions. This is fully confirmed in the Trobriands. Homosexuality was known to exist in other tribes and regarded as a filthy and ridiculous practice. It cropped up in the Trobriands only with the influence of white man, more especially of white man's morality. The boys and girls on a Mission Station penned in separate and strictly isolated houses, cooped up together, had to help themselves out as best as they could, since that which every Trobriander looks upon as his due and right was denied to them. According to the very careful inquiries made of non-missionary as well as missionary natives, homosexuality is the rule among those whom white man's morality has been forced in such an irrational and unscientific manner.[18]

The formal similarities between this passage and Kenyatta's disavowal of homosexuality among the Kikuyu exemplify Gikandi's claim that Kenyatta "borrowed" from Malinowski's "vocabulary" to frame his Kenyan world.[19] Kenyatta emphasizes that prior to colonialism the Kikuyu, like the Trobrianders, had ready access to sex. Consequently, following Malinowski's logic, homosexuality would have been unknown among the Kikuyu because Freudian repression was absent. But if Kenyatta has saved the Kikuyu from homosexuality, he faces another problem: Malinowski attributes homosexuality to deracination, and Kenyatta belonged to the first generation of missionary-educated, urbanized men in colonial Kenya.

Managing Deracination, Managing Gender

Born in the late nineteenth century, Kenyatta grew up amid the most significant social, political, and cultural changes among the Kikuyu. Prior to the onset of colonialism in the late nineteenth century, the term Kikuyu described people who shared cultural practices (including farming), shared geographical space, and spoke similar languages. The Kikuyu were a loose, porous assemblage rather than a tightly defined, restricted ethnic group or nation. The administrative and political changes occasioned by colonialism transformed loosely affiliated people into an identifiable ethnic collectivity.[20] Kikuyu identity was formulated through colonial travel narratives, ethnographic accounts, and systems of administration that joined identity to place by using the concept of "native reserves" and issuing identity cards that policed movement. Simultaneously, Kikuyu identity emerged with strategic coalitions that involved trading with Europeans, guiding explorers, converting to Christianity, and staging armed resistance to colonial incursions. Two sites became especially central to this production of ethnic identity: the school and the city. These were the most important sites for Kenyatta's early formation.

Kenya's early schools were established by missionaries who were intent on producing colonial subjects trained to work for a range of colonial institutions as clerks, domestic servants, petty traders, artisans, local administrators, and mediators between ethnic communities and settlers. Because European missionaries and colonial administrators understood educated Africans as potential missionaries to their fellow Africans and go-betweens between Europeans and Africans, educated Africans had to be trained carefully. They had to be trained well enough to reject the most "savage" elements of their customs, but not to forget their status as subordinate to white Europeans. During a 1925 meeting between the acting governor, Edward Brandish Denham, and the local Kikuyu elders, Denham exhorted, "You are near education, you all want schools, they are one of the first things you will ask for. What do you want in those schools—you do not want the boys to be taught that they know more than their fathers, such schools are bad schools. You want a school making every boy more useful and helpful, you do not want the boys changed."[21] The key term in this passage is "boy," which indicates a position of inferiority. Denham reveals the colonial government's interest in prolonging African boyhood, which would be subject to the dictates of European manhood and managed by local elders sanctioned by colonial administrators. The key would be to keep Africans native, but not too native.

Perhaps the most vivid example of this strategic deracination in Kenyatta's life comes from his circumcision ceremony. Among the Kikuyu, ritual circumcision ushered young boys into the warrior class. However, European settlers complained that when natives returned from circumcision ceremonies they were no longer as docile as they had previously been; circumcision produced a changed disposition as boys acquired new sociocultural rights and privileges, including the right to have sex with women. Circumcision was soon associated with regression to savagery. To manage this regression, missionaries developed alternative circumcision rites for boys, helping them to transition from boys to warriors, but controlling the meaning of that shift by keeping the missionary-circumcised men away from other traditional rites and pedagogies that changed dispositions. Kenyatta, who arrived at a missionary station while prepubescent in 1909, underwent this missionary-initiated ceremony, fulfilling the formal requirement to be legible among the Kikuyu, but removed from the communal privileges provided to and obligations imposed upon those embedded within Kikuyu communities.[22]

Biographical accounts of Kenyatta describe him as unremarkable as a young student, unruly when he moved to Nairobi as a young man following school, and radical as a political leader in the mid-to-late 1920s, when he joined the Kikuyu Central Association (KCA), and founded and edited its newsletter, *Muigwithania*. *Muigwithania* helped to establish new ethno-national and ethno-patriarchal practices, as it envisioned Kikuyu masculinities different from traditional gendering practices, and rooted them, instead, in new political alliances and urban-based practices of sociality. For instance, a 1928 article reported that teams from Kiambu and Nairobi competed in a football match—Kiambu scored three goals, relaxed because they thought they had won; Nairobi then scored three goals, and the match had to go into overtime; Kiambu won.[23] These details, reported breathlessly, did more than simply recount how different Kikuyu groups interacted. They positioned Nairobi, home to the colonial government, in relation to Kiambu, and figured this site of colonial administration as equivalent to a traditional Kikuyu area through the use of a new, popular sport, football. In addition, a 1928 letter from Petro N. Kingondu of Fort Hall (Muranga) urged readers of *Muigwithania* to consider establishing "*Ngwataniro kana* companies" of different kinds—he lists twenty-six—that include companies to trade in cows, trade in chickens, plant vegetables, sell milk, build shops, build houses, and deliver mail. Establishing such companies, he argues, would provide work and discipline and curb vices ("nigwo waganu na uremi wa mithemba miingi uthire").[24] Establishing such companies would grow the ethno-nation, as the title of the article has it, "Uria Tungikuria Bururi" (How to build the nation).

The newspaper's masthead outlined the relationships the journal was attempting to forge. A text-box on the left-hand column identifies the journal as the "voice" (*mugambo*) of the Kikuyu Central Association in their service (*wiraini*) to the Kikuyu country (*bururi wa Gikuyu*). The center title announces the journal as the reconciler (*muigwithania*) of the people (*andu*) and country (*bururi*) of the Kikuyu. And a text-box on the right-hand side invites readers to join (*tonyai*) the KCA so they can help (*muteithie*) their country (*bururi wanyu*). This repetition of *bururi* imagines an ethno-nation comprised of disparate Kikuyu residents, and not Kenya as a multiethnic formation. Simultaneously, this repetition attempts to interpellate readers by affirming that they already own this country (*bururi wanyu*) and that the KCA is serving their cause. Building on colonial administrative practices that had imagined the Kikuyu as a discrete group, *Muigwithania* extended this logic to imagine the Kikuyu as a "people," as defined in colonial discourse, and also, more politically, as a country. The term *bururi* used to describe the Kikuyu assumes more significance when juxtaposed against other uses of the term in *Muigwithania* articles. A brief report on Australian Aborigines serves as a cautionary tale: they were conquered by the English (*Angeretha*), *Muigwithania* states, because their numbers were decreasing due to reproductive inability ("makoriruo ni kunyiha manyihaga ni undu wa kwiremwo kwao"). "*Kwiremwo kwao*" invokes impotence and infertility, placing heteroreproductive vitality at the heart of imagining resistance to colonialism and nation building. Resistance needs heteroreproduction. Freedom needs heteroreproduction. Too, the article adds, the Aborigines did not use land productively—they did not develop it. Aboriginal life and work practices could not withstand the English incursion, *Muigwithania* warns. Implicitly, Australian Aborigines were unable to move from *andu* to *bururi*. In contrast, the "Maorris" of New Zealand successfully negotiated identity as *"andu"* and *"bururi,"* in part because they worked hard, demonstrated they could adapt to modernity, and, in fact, elected political representatives, and so they provide a model for the Kikuyu.[25] These other uses of the term *bururi* indicate that Kenyatta uses it to suggest a conjunction of place (country), identity (people), and politics (nationalism, and, in this case, ethno-nationalism). Regardless of the historical veracity of his claims, Kenyatta is using these comparative frames to work out how the Kikuyu can navigate colonial modernity.

However, for the Kikuyu *andu-bururi* to succeed, it needs to be orderly; the gendered disorder created by urban modernity, where women owned property, rented to men, and had more material capital than men had to be managed.[26] *Muigwithania's* authors engage the question of how to establish and maintain an orderly, patriarchal household:

> Athomi aria meguthoma karatathi gaka ka Muigwithania ni gwenda kwaria na inyui, undu wa kiugo giki, kia uiguano. Kiugo giki ni kiugo kia bata muno kuri andu othe, tondu uiguano nigwo utumaga mundu murume ka mundu muka maikaranie thiini wa nyumba imwe, na hindi iria mari nyumba imwe magaciara ciana ni undu wa uiguano wao.[27]

> [Readers of this newspaper, I would like to chat with you about understanding. Understanding is very important to everyone because it permits men and women to establish a household and to have children.]

The author of these sentiments, G. H. M. Kagika, addresses the root word of *Muigwithania*, *uiguano*, which translates as "mutual understanding." Kagika insists on Kikuyu oneness ("Turi muhiriga umwe"—we are one clan) based on the myth of a solitary patriarch, Gikuyu, who birthed the nine Kikuyu clans. Kagika insists that the Kikuyu remember Gikuyu is their father ("Gikuyu ni ithe witu").[28] Strikingly, Kagika erases Mumbi, the mythical mother of the Kikuyu, who, together with Gikuyu, founds the mythical nine clans. In assigning Gikuyu the sole power to birth and name and manage Kikuyu identity, Kagika emphasizes the patriarchal nature of Kikuyu identity and social organization.

The turn to, and insistence on, a myth that placed the male Gikuyu as the foundation of Kikuyu identity and the imagined *bururi* attempted to mask the material distinctions between urban- and rural-based Kikuyu, differences that, arguably, lay at the heart of Kikuyu gendered identity as material practice. Traditional Kikuyu gendering was a life-long process rooted in material practices and exchanges, marked on the body, signified by clothing and decoration, and closely policed. One moved from one stage to another through ritual ceremonies: for instance, one moved from young childhood to prepubescence through a second birthing ceremony, in which mother and child simulated childbirth using a piece of animal skin to represent the umbilical cord. Rituals such as piercing ears among girls conferred different levels of access to social and cultural privileges. And even after ritual initiation, which many scholars have argued shifted one from childhood to adulthood, one entered stages of adulthood that changed as one became a parent or an elder. Modes of gendering did not tie gendered age and access to biological development; instead, biology was always subject to, and interpreted through, ritual.[29]

Colonial modernity disrupted prior practices of gendering, substituting new biological and cultural foundations for ritual ones; it also created new opportunities for gendering practices. When Kikuyu-born women moved to urban centers as petty traders and sex workers, with some converting to Islam and others becoming property owners and remitting portions of their income to rural relatives, they reorganized gender hierarchies of who could own and disburse property; when Kikuyu girls attended schools and donned cotton dresses and, in some cases, refused to undergo traditional initiation rituals, from having ears pierced to forms of genital cutting, they were reorganizing the material practices of gendering and sociality. Similarly, the young, urbanized men who formed the core members of the KCA had embraced the opportunities of colonial modernity to remake themselves. They argued that education and urban-based wage-earning jobs merited just as much respect as the more traditional rites of passage that involved joining the warrior class, raiding cattle, and defending villages.

For their part, rural-based elders worried about the material effects of colonialism and urbanization on health, fertility, and community. They came to associate practices such as wearing clothing with concealment, women's travels to and from urban centers as acts of prostitution, and young men's urban lives as sources of physical and moral degeneration. In 1912, a delegation of Kikuyu elders met with colonial administrators to express their concerns.[30] Elders worried that young men from rural areas who traveled to and worked in urban centers were being corrupted by urbanization. During the meeting the elders claimed, "After returning from work in the towns and wearing clothes our young men are spoilt. 'They are different men.' Those who return from monthly work are yet unspoilt but they don't bring their money to their fathers as before, they disobey the orders of the elders and think only of themselves."[31] The key word in the passage is "spoilt," a term that connotes that one is overly privileged and also that one is overly ripe—we speak of a spoiled fruit, for instance. Urban modernity had transformed young men, making them less useful to the elders and, in turn, the community. Equally notable, the only portion of direct, quoted (and presumably translated speech) is, "They are different men." Young, urbanized men had become illegible: their material practices produced unrecognizable forms of masculinity that could only be described as "spoilt" and "different."

The turn to a patriarchal myth in *Muigwithania* tried to create shared ground between rural-based male elders, who had vast amounts of social, cultural, and material capital, and urban-based male political activists, who were educated, but did not have the same cultural and political authority as the elders: both would unite to police and control Kikuyu women. A December 1928 letter to the editor demonstrates this need for patriarchal control. The writer warns that young initiated girls (*airitu*) and married women (*atumia*) who participate in trade are on a slippery slope to engaging in prostitution (*UMARAYA*). Although these girls and women might not want to participate in prostitution, trading exposes them to the risk of becoming prostitutes. The article calls on *Muigwithania*'s readers to restrict women's trading practices and travel to minimize the risk of their becoming prostitutes.[32] This letter echoes comments made during a November 28 meeting of the Kiambu Local Native Council. The title of the recorded minute is, "Prohibition of Kikuyu Women going to Nairobi to sell product as it leads to prostitution and disease."[33] While it is likely that the letter writer had attended the meeting and was simply repeating its message in the pages of *Muigwithania*, this speculation is impossible to prove. By publishing the letter, the young, urban men represented by *Muigwithania* aligned themselves with the patriarchal elders who wanted to control women's movement and activities. Myth created shared grounds for cross-generational homosociality, sutured by controlling women. *Muigwithania* provided a newly emergent Kikuyu group with patriarchal myths and practices that managed urban deracination and gender disorganization by envisioning Kikuyu identity and ethno-nationalism as gender and sexual normative.

Given *Muigwithania's* ethno-patriarchal focus, the one letter to the editor written by a woman, Tabitha Wangui wa Thomas Kamau, titled "Mugambo wa Mutumia" (A woman's voice), stands out. Published in the June 1929 issue, the letter contributes to the ongoing debates about *irua*.[34] Following an opening that pleads with the editor to publish the letter, Wangui affirms that *irua* is Kikuyu tradition and questions those who oppose it ("maundu maya maroimaku makuga ati ni wega gutiga kurua" [where are these ideas coming from that claim it's good to abandon *irua*?]). Rejecting *irua* leads to a crisis of sociality. She notes, for instance, that those who do not undergo the process are illegible to their peers. Though a woman may have gotten married and given birth, without undergoing the ritual she does not have the right to address mothers who have undergone *irua*. Men of the Christian church may address her as a woman, but she has no such standing among ritually initiated women ("Na athuri a Kanitha mekumeta Atumia no matingihota kwaria hari Atumia aria angi, Makiri atumia atia?"). The final question—"Makiri atumia atia?" How are they women?—speaks to the crisis of legibility created by the beliefs of different institutions, in this case, the Church and Kikuyu ethnonationalism. In fact, Wangui continues, women who do not undergo *irua* are exiled: from womanhood, from rural homes to urban centers, and from morality. She issues a stern warning: "angikorwo ni mukwenda Maraya maingihe muno niwega mukiuge ati ni gutige gucoka kuruo" [if you want the numbers of prostitutes to increase you might as well stop ritual initiation]. The letter is conservative. In it, Wangui apologizes for speaking before men as women do not have permission to do so ("ni nguigwa kieha muno tondu ninjui ati hatiri rutha mutumia kwaria mbere ya Arume"). It affirms ethnonationalist practices of gendering and supports gendered hierarchies, not only between men and women, but also between the ritually uninitiated and the ritually initiated.

Given the conservative tone of the letter, the final paragraph comes as a surprise, as it lays a claim to the importance of women's roles in political history. She writes, "Ni Mutumia wambiririe wira wa Bururi kuma Mwaka 1922 ni guo ndambiriirie gutungatira bururi uyu witu" [A woman started this nationalist work in 1922, and that's when I started serving our nation]. In 1922, Harry Thuku, a labor organizer, had been arrested for urging women to resist forced conscription by the colonial government. Following his arrest, a crowd of 7,000–8,000 gathered outside the jail to protest. As recorded by an observer, "Mary Muthoni Nyanjiru (from Weithaga in Location 10 of Fort Hall District) leapt to her feet, pulled her dress right up over her shoulders and shouted to the men: 'You take my dress and give me your trousers. You men are cowards. What are you waiting for? Our leader is in there. Let's get him.'"[35] Proper gender—the status of *mutumia*—provides the ground from which one can be properly political. A legible woman—made legible by undergoing shared rituals—has the power to mobilize men in nationalist causes. Mary Muthoni Nyanjiru acted not only in the name of a Kikuyu ethnonation, but also in the service of a Kenyan ethnonation assembled through its resistance to exploitative labor practices. Since I have found only one such letter, I do not want to overstate my case. However, Wangui's forceful statement suggests that *Muigwithania's andu-* and *bururi*-making project was contested and contingent, a moment of world-making and world-imagining within the ravages of colonial modernity.

I have dwelled on the sex-gender project of *Muigwithania* to emphasize that Kenyatta did not simply adopt sex-gender patterns and methods of thinking from his sojourn abroad and his studies under Malinowski. His tenure at *Muigwithania* taught him how patriarchal alliances could be forged through policing women and, more broadly, enforcing gender and sexual normativity. He learned how to manage the incoherence of Kikuyu identity by turning to myth and mystification, obscuring and appropriating practices such as initiation and marriage to control concepts of womanhood.

Before turning to Kenyatta's diaspora years and *Facing Mount Kenya*, let me reflect on how he envisioned his labor on *Muigwithania*. *Muigwithania* used the term *muthondeki* to translate "editor." *Muthondeki* means "maker," while the standard Kikuyu word for editor is *mutabariri*, which means "arranger or organizer." The root word, *thondeka*, can mean make or repair, and gestures to the reparative work between men the journal undertakes. Simultaneously, *muthondeki* skirts the gendering of creation in the Kikuyu language. In Kikuyu the term for creator is *Mumbi* (sometimes written as *Muumbi*), the name for Gikuyu's wife, the name erased by *Muigwithania*'s writers in their patriarchal fantasies. Scholar and translator Wangui wa Goro argues that *Mumbi* troubled the men who translated the Bible from English to Kikuyu as it aligned the Christian creator with the mythical Kikuyu mother. Consequently, they metaphorized creator as *Mwenye Nyaga* ("owner of the ostriches"), a suitably gender-neutral, hence patriarchal, designation.[36] In assigning himself the role of *muthondeki*, Kenyatta imagines himself as a latter-day Gikuyu, helping to fabricate and repair the very idea of a people (*andu*) and a country (*bururi*). The word *muthondeki* also indicates how Kenyatta understood writing and editing work as creative labor, as active fabrication, in which carefully chosen articles and letters from readers and pieces culled from other media would help to forge and sustain the *andu-bururi* connection *Muigwithania* sought to nurture.

Becoming Ethno-Diasporic

The *andu* and *bururi* of *Muigwithania*, the Kikuyu envisioned as a people and a country, are a distinctly modern formation, produced at the intersections of colonial technologies of surveillance and administration, precolonial technologies of capital production and management, and discursive technologies of urban-centered literacy and myth-making. School-trained, literate Kikuyus simultaneously participated in Afro-diasporic practices of translation and dissemination. C. L. R. James writes,

> Jomo Kenyatta has related to this writer how in 1921 Kenya nationalists, unable to read, would gather round a reader of Garvey's newspaper, the *Negro World*, and listen to an article two or three times. Then they would run various ways through the forest, carefully to repeat the whole, which they had memorised, to Africans hungry for some doctrine which lifted them from the servile consciousness in which Africans lived.[37]

James's brief anecdote offers rich possibilities for envisioning Afro-diasporic labor. It is unlikely that Garvey's journal was translated into

Kiswahili and other Kenyan languages. Kenyatta was probably describing a process that involved translating from English, probably into multiple languages; memorization as a technology for oral recitation; and widespread distribution of "doctrine" through oral means. In pointing to this labor of oral translation and circulation, I build on Brent Edwards's argument that periodical circulation was an essential practice of diaspora, and extend that argument to account for techniques of oral translation, recitation, and memorization.[38] Kenyatta's account, recounted by James, multiplies how we can understand periodical circulation and Afro-diasporic transmission—the number of copies sold and distributed has no necessary relationship to audiences reached.

While *Muigwithania* was devoted to establishing a Kikuyu country, an *andu-bururi*, it also participated in Afro-diasporic modes of exchange. The July 1928 issue vividly illustrates such exchange. It features a translated letter sent from the London-based West African Student's Union to *Muigwithania* in response to a letter that *Muigwithania* had sent: "Marua maku mega nimarikitie gukinya" [Your letter has been received warmly].[39] The unnamed author from the West African Student's Union claims to have been invited to speak at an important gathering of white young people ("ni njititwo kuheana uhoro thiini wa Mucemanio munene na wa bata wa anake a athungu"), and promises to mention Kikuyu anticolonial efforts. This mention is part of the letter writer's broader claim on the KCA, which is to forge a political connection. As translated by Kenyatta, the letter writer insists that the time has come for black people ("andu airo") to seek self-determination ("mekinyire na maguru mao"). The phrase "andu airo" as opposed to, say, "Africans," indicates the role diasporic centers played in mediating connections through race. Blackness became a mode of interpellating the Kikuyu readers of *Muigwithania* into a broader diasporic world.

Whereas *Muigwithania* envisions an ethno-nation, an *andu-bururi*, Kenyatta's translation-transcription of this letter imagines an ethno-diaspora, where Kikuyu identity is joined to a shared, diasporic blackness. This vision of an ethno-diaspora animated his departure from Kenya, his travels and studies in Russia and England, and his political and academic writing. Kenyatta's tenure at *Muigwithania* had placed him within diasporic circuits of print publication and circulation before he left Kenya.

Kenyatta left Kenya for England on February 17, 1929. He was traveling as a representative of the KCA and hoped to present Kikuyu griev-
ances to colonial administrators in England. Unsurprisingly, he was
unable to get a hearing because KCA was not recognized as a legitimate
political body. However, this initial trip nurtured a nascent diasporic
and pan-Africanist sensibility. He met with radical West African students and also allied himself with the communist-dominated League
against Imperialism. Through the late 1920s and early 1930s, communist newspapers such as the *Sunday Worker* and the *Daily Worker* provided him with a forum, where he framed Kenyan struggles in terms of
labor.[40] It was also during this initial trip that he most likely met George
Padmore, whose own participation in communist, pan-African, and
diasporic circles would provide a template for Kenyatta's own activities.

Kenyatta's alliance with communist-allied groups continued through
the 1930s, although it probably came to a premature climax in the early
1930s, when he spent one year (1932–33) as a student at Moscow's Communist University of the Toilers of the East (KUTV).[41] Kenyatta was an
indifferent Marxist. For instance, when accused of being a "petit bourgeois" by a fellow student, Kenyatta objected to the term "petit," saying
he wanted to be a "big" bourgeois.[42] Nonetheless, his time at KUTV
allowed him to meet black activists from other regions of Africa, the
United States, and the West Indies.

Despite his disenchantment with Marxism, it provided a crucial theoretical framework evident in his first significant publication, a short
essay titled "Kenya," published in Nancy Cunard's 1934 *Negro: An Anthology*. Written under the name of Johnstone Kenyatta, the brief article
provides a description of the country and its strategic, if exaggerated,
importance ("Kenya is the most important British colony in East Africa"); an account of European-African social and political relationships;
and a Marxist-inflected view of black exploitation. The closing line offers insight into Kenyatta's method: "Therefore, let us unite and demand
our birthright." This striking closing combines Marxist ("workers of the
world unite") with Christian and traditional Kikuyu ideas ("birthright").
As in *Muigwithania*, Kenyatta is envisioning an *andu-bururi* connection,
even as the frame has shifted from the Kikuyu ethno-nation to Kenya.
However, the *andu-bururi* model continued to dominate his conceptual
frameworks.

Kenyatta's participation in KUTV and inclusion in *Negro* are just two of the ways he was embedded within a broader black diasporic community, and both provide a point of departure from which to elaborate on how *Facing Mount Kenya* participates in black diasporic culture. *Facing Mount Kenya* may have been written while Kenyatta was a student at the London School of Economics, attending seminars by Malinowski, but it was also composed when Kenyatta was part of a vibrant group of diasporic thinkers, writers, and activists, including George Padmore, C. L. R. James, and Paul Robeson. In fact, Kenyatta was a founding member of the International African Service Bureau (IASB) in 1937, along with James and Padmore, a group that grew to include T. Ras Makonnen from Guyana, Kwame Nkrumah of Ghana, Peter Abrahams from South Africa, and Amy Garvey from Jamaica.[43] The group was responsible for organizing the 1945 Pan-African conference in Manchester, and also published a number of important books and pamphlets that, taken collectively, articulated both a pan-African and diasporic sensibility.[44] If we take this group as one of Kenyatta's key audiences for *Facing Mount Kenya*, we can examine how he attempts to stimulate conversation about the use of African histories and traditions within modern contexts. *Facing Mount Kenya*, like Blyden's *African Life and Customs*, was to be read within a black diasporic context. Its descriptions of native life were to create a "deep reserve" that was available to all diasporic black people.[45] If black people across the diaspora could not share space or politics, they could draw on the resources of imagined and invented traditions. For Kenyatta, it was crucial to write into being a form of blackness that bridged national and diasporic communities.

Kenyatta's attempt to forge bonds with his black friends and colleagues suggests that his ethnography is more fruitfully read as a diasporic rather than pan-African work. Brent Edwards provides a useful analytic distinction between the two terms when he points out that diaspora "has not been a dominant term of political *organization*," unlike pan-African, which is associated with political action.[46] It is not, he continues, that "'diaspora' is apolitical but that it has none of the 'overtones' that make a term like 'pan-Africanism' already contested terrain."[47] Pan-Africanism, for instance, risks focusing on continental Africa at the expense of other sites of African dispersal and sociopolitical organization. In contrast, diasporic works, though local and particular, do not offer a singular vision of political organization. As Edwards argues, the term diaspora "account[s] for difference among African-derived populations."[48] Discourses of diaspora, as Edwards has argued, are also fundamentally about trying to bridge cultural and historical gaps.

Reading *Facing Mount Kenya* alongside similarly diasporic texts demonstrates the historical and conceptual conversations in which it participated. To take just one example, shortly after *Facing Mount Kenya* was published, James published *The Black Jacobins: Toussaint L'Ouverture and the San Domingo Revolution*, his history of the Haitian revolution. While James's work articulated a radical revolutionary impulse that would become central to anticolonial and antiracist struggles through the 1950s and 1960s, Kenyatta's provided a history and culture of values and practices.

Juxtaposing the two texts illustrates how *Facing Mount Kenya* provides a useful prehistory to *The Black Jacobins*. This prehistory is important because James's history opens on a scene of destruction and disintegration that implies black people's history begins with the slave trade. His first chapter, titled "The Property," illustrates how Africans were enslaved. With the incursion of the slave trade, "Tribal life was broken up and millions of detribalized Africans were let loose upon each other. The unceasing destruction of crops led to cannibalism; the captive women became concubines and degraded the status of wife. Tribes had to supply slaves or be sold as slaves themselves. Violence and ferocity became the necessities for survival, and violence and ferocity survived."[49] Africa, in this telling, exists only as a site of loss and destruction, indicated by James's phrasing, "violence and ferocity survived," which collapses those Africans who survived the Middle Passage and those who remained in Africa. For the Kenyatta who had edited *Muigwithania*, using myth and fabulation to create cross-generational ethno-national affiliations, this framing of "detribalized Africans" marked by "violence and ferocity" would have been difficult to accept. If Africa and Afro-diaspora, both living in the aftermath of colonial modernity and in the afterlife of slavery, were to converse, Kenyatta needed a more expansive idea of history and blackness.

Especially interesting here is how James figures the status of women, and intimate life more generally.[50] Faith Smith argues that in *The Black Jacobins* James treats women as "little more than afterthoughts."[51] And

Aaron Kamugisha writes that it is only after World War II that James attempted to theorize gender relations seriously.[52] Although women do not take center stage in *Black Jacobins*, unlike men including Mackandal, Touissant, and Dessalines, they are central to how James theorizes power and the role of the intimate in revolution. Take, for instance, James's claim that "captive women became concubines and degraded the status of wife." He elaborates, "A mistress would poison a rival to retain the valuable affections of her inconstant owner. A discarded mistress would poison master, wife, children and slaves. . . . If a planter conceived a passion for a young slave, her mother would poison his wife with the idea of placing her daughter at the head of the household."[53] Even though some of these acts may be read as strategies for resistance and survival, James implies that women act in their self-interest, not for the good of the many.

When James turns to the maroon leader Mackandal, he writes, "the handsomest women fought for the privilege of being admitted to his bed."[54] More broadly, in writing about maroon communities in Haiti, he writes, "Those whose boldness of spirit found slavery intolerable and refused to evade it by committing suicide, would fly to the woods and mountains and form bands of free men—maroons. They fortified their fastnesses and palisades and ditches. Women followed them. They re-produced themselves."[55] Women follow men, wrestle over sleeping with prestigious heroes, and perform the work of reproduction for the revolution. Far from being marginal, women serve the revolution by producing and sexually serving its armies. Absent from James's writing is any speculation about how women imagined and pursued freedom. We are not far from how Kenyatta's generation of young men and Kikuyu elders envisioned women's roles.

For James, the form of intimate life adopted and practiced is one index of a successful society. Discussing mulattos, he writes of the "vice of their origin," a phrase that conflates the condition of enslavement that produced them with the violent and coercive forms of sex and desire that mulattos embody.[56] He cannot seem to distinguish the violence of white patriarchy from enslaved women's survival strategies. The masculinist cast of James's work is evidenced by his praise for Touissant's hetero-patriarchal virility: despite having numerous affairs with other women, Toussaint and his wife "lived together in the greatest harmony

and friendship."[57] Elsewhere, James depicts Toussaint as a noble patriarch, who ensured the safety of his former master's wife and, once in
power, took care of women and children, including those related to his
enemies.[58] Implicitly, James suggests that a large measure of Toussaint's
greatness lies in his ability to embody and rehabilitate respectable, patriarchal intimate life.

Given James's belief that *The Black Jacobins* could be a blueprint for
contemporary African struggles, the notion of intimate life he privileges
had serious drawbacks for someone like Kenyatta.[59] James advances a hi-
erarchical, European model of intimacy, privileging stable monogamous
marriage over concubinage, polygyny, or polygamy. Black modernity,
for James, turns away from the prehistory of slavery and colonialism
and looks toward a future shaped by European education and norms. He
writes, for instance, "The leaders of a revolution are usually those who
have been able to profit by the cultural advantages of the system they
are attacking, and the San Domingo revolution was no exception to this
rule."[60] As Belinda Edmondson has argued, James sought to have others understand him as a gentleman within the terms provided by English culture.[61] In privileging specific forms of intimate life and gendered
performance as central to black revolution, *The Black Jacobins* makes
articulations and practices of intimacy central to black diasporic political and historical undertakings. Read alongside *Facing Mount Kenya*,
though, we note the absence of a preslavery history of intimacy as well
as a post-independence account. James's account of revolution lacks the
intimate foundations to sustain a future. *Facing Mount Kenya* attempts
to fill this void.

In the preface to *Facing Mount Kenya*, Kenyatta positions the work
as a suture between African and Afro-diasporic people. *Facing Mount
Kenya*, he claims, was written for "those Africans who had been detached
from their tribal life."[62] "Detached" is a hopeful term that promises rapprochement between black people across the diaspora. "Detached" implicitly offers the promise of reattaching, avoiding the contemporary
rhetoric of "acculturation" and "detribalization" used by anthropologists
and policy makers to describe the irreparable psychic and ideological
violence enacted on "native" Africans by colonialism.[63] For instance, in
the inaugural issue of the journal *Africa*, Frederick Lugard argued that
contemporary anthropology would investigate the damaging effects of

the European incursion on Africans.[64] Lugard's claim about the potentially damaging effects of colonialism was echoed by Kenyatta's mentor, Malinowski.[65] Detached rather than damaged, colonized, urbanized Africans and their Afro-diasporic peers could forge strategies to reconnect, grounded in shared aspirations and norms. Indeed, while a people may be physically detached, their sense of attachment persists—this is, in fact, one of the major claims of recent diasporic theory.[66] Kenyatta advances an ambitious argument; he writes the book for "Africans," not Kenyans and not the Kikuyu. By describing Africans as "detached" he reaches both toward and away from continental Africa, creating a temporal and conceptual bridge between multiple forms of detachment, those arising from enslavement and the more recent ones caused by colonialism.

Kenyatta's Afro-diasporic colleagues attempted to apprehend him as Kenyan and African, terms which meant, variously, nationalist, illiterate, and uncivilized, although imbued with a great deal of energy. Kenyatta was, James writes, "a simmering volcano of African nationalism."[67] Kenyatta played a crucial role for the London-based radicals: as a native-born African, his presence sutured the continent to the largely Afro-Caribbean contingent.[68] Yet, as James's comment suggests, this fragile coalition was fissured by a colonial logic of developmentalism that framed native-born Africans—and Africa itself—as primitive. Writing to Richard Wright, for instance, George Padmore proclaimed, "I hate primitiveness . . . I will fight for a free Africa and Asia, not live there."[69] James and others were frustrated by what they understood as Kenyatta's dedication to ethnicity.[70] Given this context, it is likely that Kenyatta turned to anthropology because it offered a space that Afro-diasporic radicalism did not. If *Muigwithania* had offered the possibility of being ethno-national, joining *andu* and *bururi*, Kenyatta's experiences with London-based radicals suggested that an ethno-diasporic position was difficult, if not impossible, to sustain for political work.

Ombani na Ngweko: Ethnicity as Frottage

Facing Mount Kenya has been understood primarily as an ethno-nationalist, anticolonial text. Kenyatta defends Kikuyu land ownership, supports *irua*, and protests land alienation, thus expressing the most compelling issues around which rural Kikuyu identities and politics were forged. Continuing what Lonsdale and Berman term "the labors of *Muigwithania*," *Facing Mount Kenya* sets out not simply to describe but to create a Kikuyu nation out of disparate regions and widely differing customs.[71]

From at least the late 1890s, the Kikuyu had been the subject of articles in anthropological journals including *Man* and *Journal of the Royal African Society*.[72] In 1910, William Scoresby Routledge and his wife Katherine Routledge published *With a Prehistoric People*, their account of the Kikuyu as living in what Johannes Fabian has termed "allochronic time," a distinct temporality used by anthropologists to differentiate themselves from their subjects.[73] In 1933, Father Cagnolo, a Catholic priest with the Consolata Mission, published *The Agikuyu: Their Customs Traditions and Folklore*, and Kenyatta's classmate at the London School of Economics, Louis Leakey, had begun a three-volume ethnography of the Kikuyu, while his other classmate, Elspeth Huxley, had started work on an ethnographic novel, *Red Strangers* (1939). *Facing Mount Kenya* was published into an increasingly crowded field.

Published to dispel colonial speculation that the Kikuyu lacked indigenous forms of social and political organization, the ethnography is divided into twelve main chapters. The first two outline the relationship between ethnic identity and land tenure, a relationship based on myth and history: the Kikuyu inherited their land from Gikuyu and Mumbi and purchased it from previous inhabitants. In a strategy that recurs through the volume, Kenyatta covers his bases. The following three, "Economic Life," "Industries," and "System of Education," offer an extended description of Kikuyu labor and trading practices. The following ones, "Initiation of Boys and Girls," "Sex Life among Young People," and "Marriage System," outline a theory of ethnicity as a series of intimate practices. And, the chapters in the last part of the book deal with questions of governance, ranging from politics to religion and medicine.

Facing Mount Kenya shuttles between multiple formal registers, including anecdote and myth, description and speculation. In so doing, it sutures Kenyatta's multiple incarnations, especially as the editor of *Muigwithania* and the London-based, diasporic cosmopolitan. Kenyatta not only shuttles between textual and ideological registers, but, more crucially, he puts them in friction with one another: ethnicity, in his text, emerges as a mode of textual and cultural frottage, produced at the intersection of cultural times and practices and by the rubbing between times and practices.

On a formal register, *Facing Mount Kenya* bases its authority on the connection between autobiography and ethnography. Kenyatta writes, "Like any other Gikuyu child . . . I acquired in my youth my country's equivalent of a liberal education," adding, "[I] speak from personal experience."[74] As part of his personal experience, he describes learning from his grandfather, a famous medicine man, undergoing community rites to become legibly gendered, acting as an interpreter in a prominent land case, founding and editing *Muigwithania* as the "General Secretary" of the "Gikuyu Central Association," and traveling to England to represent the Kikuyu before several commissions, including the Hilton Young Commission of 1928–29, the Joint Committee on the Closer Union of East Africa in 1931–32, and the Morris Carter Kenyan Land Commission.[75] Even though Kenyatta describes his various experiences as a translator, administrator, political activist, and political representative, familiar with legal and parliamentary processes, these forms of experience are rarely mentioned when he is discussed as a native informant or indigenous anthropologist. Personal experience is understood as his having undergone Kikuyu rituals and lived as an authentic Kikuyu, where authenticity is measured through a narrow lens of what tribal life should be. No doubt, Kenyatta understood how he was framed, so he notes that "personal experience" is not sufficient and credits his training in anthropology with giving him "the necessary technical knowledge for recording the information scientifically."[76] It is worth repeating here that as the master discipline devoted to studying non-Western people, anthropology provided Kenyatta with an authoritative tool to write about Kikuyu life and social formations. Within the Afro-diasporic circles he was part of, anthropology was one of the few discourses available that gave him the authority to write about Kikuyu life "scientifically," without his thinking being dismissed as nostalgic.

To personal experience and scientific training in anthropology, Kenyatta added fabulation. Tavia Nyong'o writes, "A fabulist is a teller of tales, but he or she also discloses the powers of the false to create new possibilities."[77] Fabulation, he continues, "is always seeking to cobble something together, to produce connections and relations however much the resultant seams show."[78] The seams showed in *Facing Mount Kenya*. In an early review, Arthur R. Barlow, one of Kenyatta's former instructors at Thogoto, complains that Kenyatta's attempts to account for Kikuyu beliefs are untenable, as "the Kikuyu themselves are singularly unable to give any coherent or reasoned account of the tribal beliefs and customs."[79] Indeed, continues Barlow, Kenyatta's descriptions apply "mainly to the Kiambu section of Southern Kikuyu," and fail to consider other widely differing areas.[80] Many of Kenyatta's assertions, declares Barlow, are too "idyllic" and "the seamy side is glossed over."[81] Certainly, this review could be dismissed as white supremacy defending itself. After all, Barlow writes, "Unfortunately, almost every chapter contains some unsupported allegation direction against either the Administration or Missions in Kenya Colony."[82] Barlow defends the colonial mission and his right to know the Kikuyu better than Kenyatta.[83] Recent scholarship, however, has tended to agree with Barlow. Berman writes, "Kenyatta invented a homogeneous Kikuyu society that spoke with one voice."[84] Gikandi has argued that *Facing Mount Kenya* is "one of the founding texts of the literary tradition of the Kenyan 'national romance'" and Desai argues that it presents "an alternative picture" not "of how things really were but how things could have been."[85] If, following Desai, *Facing Mount Kenya* can be described as subjunctive, what work does that enable?

In part, the subjunctive nature of the text helps to clarify its genealogical, normalizing project, which projects an idealized past by stabilizing gender roles and sexual desires. "Tradition" and "identity" are secured by appeals to gendered and sexual stability. Kenyatta indicates as such when he claims that *irua* "is the most important custom among the Kikuyu. It is looked upon as a deciding factor in giving a boy or girl the status of manhood or womanhood in the Gikuyu community."[86] Without clearly defined gendered roles, the Kikuyu community would fall apart—and here, we hear echoes of *Muigwithania*'s critique of urbanized women whose independence unsettled gender roles. If *irua* provides access to gendered normativity, then frottage stabilizes sexual identity and creates a model for ethnicity as an intimate practice.

In *Facing Mount Kenya*, Kenyatta most fully develops his theory of ethnicity as a form of intimate practice. His most compelling metaphor for, and example of, ethnic intimacy comes in the chapter "Sex

Life among Young People," in his discussion of sexual practices between young men and women following ritual initiation:

> In order not to suppress entirely the normal sex instinct, the boys and girls are told that in order to keep good health they must acquire the technique of practising a certain restricted form of intercourse, called *ombani na ngweko* (platonic love or fondling). This form of intimate contact between young people is considered right and proper and *the very foundation stone upon which to build a race morally, physically, and mentally sound.* For it safeguards the youth from nervous and psychic maladjustments.[87]

The most jarring term in this description is "a race." Kenyatta rarely uses the word "race" in *Facing Mount Kenya*, preferring to use "Kikuyu" or "tribe." By using the indefinite article *a*, he creates an implicitly comparative frame. Those "races" that lack a ritualized method for introducing their young people to sexuality, and intimacy more broadly, are plagued by moral, physical, and mental problems. Undoubtedly, Kenyatta is engaging in a form of counterdiscourse: he builds on European anxieties about the effects of modernity on gender and sexuality, anxieties expressed most forcefully in sexology. He indicts Europe's degeneration, all the while praising unassailable black sexual propriety. Unlike repressed and, for that reason, neurotic and hysterical Europeans, Africans have cultural mechanisms for producing healthy sexual citizens. In using "race," Kenyatta also draws his diasporic colleagues into a broader conversation about African and Afro-diasporic sexual traditions. Kenyatta indicates that African sex practices are not a past that modern black subjects need be ashamed of, but can actually be used as a paradigm for modern conventions of black sexuality.

Ombani na ngweko is both a foundation and metaphor for ethnicity itself. *Ombani na ngweko*, Kenyatta explains, is an engine for socialization. Initiated girls (*airitu*) visit the young male initiates in a special hut (*thingira*, a young man's hut specially built for him to occupy after initiation), bringing with them food and drink. Typically, adds Kenyatta, such visits take place in groups; visits from individual girlfriends to their boyfriends are frowned upon and considered antisocial. During these group meetings the less popular ("ugly") boys benefit from the popularity of the more attractive ones. Following the meal, the girls are urged to select partners for *ngweko*. Kenyatta points out, "it is not necessary for the girls to select their own intimate friends, as this would be considered selfish and unsociable."[88] Indeed, *ngweko* is intended to build group feeling and solidarity through intimate exchanges with multiple partners.

Ngweko itself is highly choreographed. Older initiated girls taught younger ones how to prepare for the ritual. Initiation was supposed to take place once a girl had started puberty but before her first menses; typically, girls were between ten and twelve years old and, in rare cases, thirteen to fourteen. This point might explain the restricted nature of *ngweko*, as boy initiates ranged from fourteen to eighteen. According to Kenyatta's contemporary (and rival), Louis Leakey, senior girls taught younger ones how to tie their skirts so that full penetration could not take place; they also simulated the act of *ngweko* with the younger ones to provide them with practice. Leakey insists that this commerce between the two women was not "regarded as a form of lesbianism, but simply as instruction, and no shame attached to the teacher or pupil."[89] Leakey's insistence on the meaning of such "instruction" suggests the porous and unstable ways *ngweko* functioned; its threat to disrupt the terms and forms of ethnic intimacy required elaborate forms of justification.

As for the actual practice, Leakey provides an extended description that I cite in full:

> To start with, the girl had to lie on her left side with her left leg stretched out flat on the sleeping mat and her right leg bent and raised with the knee in the air. The left arm was also kept flat on the sleeping mat, the right arm being kept free for encircling the man's neck. When the man lay down he had to do so in such a way that his right leg rested on the girl's left leg. Then she brought her right leg over and enfolded both his legs under her right knee. She then rolled her trunk so that her breasts faced upwards; the man brought his chest down on to her breasts, and she encircled his neck with her right arm, thus helping to keep him in position. The man's penis was pressed against the girl's soft pubic apron. When the couple got too stiff in this position, they turned over and lay down on the other side in a corresponding position, with the girl on her right side and the man on his left.[90]

According to Leakey, junior girls were taught by senior girls that it was "good" to have several couples practice *ngweko* in the same sleeping area, simultaneously.[91] Notably, in his description of the ritual, Kenyatta omits this group aspect, most probably to discourage racist discussions of primitive group sex.

Kenyatta and Leakey privilege the couple form in their description of *ngweko*, Kenyatta by insisting that it takes place between one young man and one girl and Leakey by claiming that it is practiced by several couples in the same area. This privileging obscures the possible range of intimacies and pleasures and relationships *ngweko* created beyond the heterosexual couple form. We get hints of these possible intimacies from two accounts of *ngweko* narrated by Wanoi and Wamutira and documented by Jean Davison. Wanoi recounts,

> There was always one handsome man we called *kiumbi*. He was the one who was clean, good to talk to, and a good dancer. We girls would go to his place and all of us spend the night there. He had a very big bed. It would hold twenty girls with him alone. So we'd spend the night with him embracing each girl in turn. He would do nothing to us, as our skirts were tied to keep him from having intercourse with us.[92]

In her interview with Wanoi, Davison did not ask what kind of intimacies happened between the girls. At the very least, the actions of the single man as he moved from partner to partner were overshadowed by the frottage taking place between the girls—it's difficult to imagine a bed so wide that twenty girls could fit comfortably without touching each other. Wamutira offers a similar account to Wanoi, and elaborates it briefly:

> In those times, the man who was very attractive—who was *kiumbi*—had his own unmarried man's house, which was just one room. Girls, during dances, used to go there every night. We washed ourselves, beautified ourselves, and went to this man's house and spent the night and would not return home until morning. Our oldest mother taught us how to dress ourselves when going there to prevent anything from going wrong. . . .
>
> . . .
>
> We would spend the night there in his big bed being turned over and over by him all night. So in the morning we would go tell others of our agemates who had not come with us and then they would go that evening to be turned over.[93]

I offer these two voices, mediated though they are through Davison, because women's voices are rarely present in discussions of Kikuyu intimate practices. It is clear from Wamutira's account that the young women enjoyed themselves, since they attempted to recruit their friends. It also seems clear that the erotics at work here are not easily framed within postsexological terms and frames, nor am I interested in embedding them within those terms and frames. Instead, I am interested in how *ombani na ngweko* produces Kikuyu-ness as a relation of shared pleasure.

Kenyatta's emphasis on "technique" and "practicing" indicates that *ngweko* is a discipline designed to produce heteronormative, ethnic citizens. *Ngweko* serves as an apt metaphor for ethnicity as a practice of intimacy. It is, in part, because *ngweko* is so regimented and difficult to master that it can be "the very foundation stone upon which to build a race morally, physically, and mentally sound." In the interrupted temporalities of *ngweko*, Kenyatta finds a way to reframe the spatial and temporal disruptions caused by colonization and urbanization. *Ngweko*, after all, is a relation of continual return, an embodied reaffirmation of belonging: in a group setting, the male partner moves from one partner to the next, and, as he does so, the female partners also move, rubbing against different partners with each shift. Too, the focus on touch and rubbing rather than climax creates a sense of erotic sociality that extends beyond the *ngweko* session. Extended beyond the range of the newly initiated, it provides a model for men and women who worked in urban centers and returned to visit their families periodically, confirming their intimate sense of belonging: to return was to reencounter the erotic sociality one had enjoyed, to be surrounded by memories of flesh rubbing against flesh. Crucially, Kenyatta explains *ngweko* as a desire for and practice of proximity, one that is not reducible to sex. *Ngweko* is about desiring ethnicity. However, the line between desiring ethnicity and desiring (hetero)sex is not absolute in Kenyatta; in fact, though *ngweko*'s status as an interrupted form of intercourse may have queer implications, Kenyatta clearly focuses on it as a heterosexual practice. Unlike Leakey, for instance, Kenyatta does not mention that *ngweko* might take place between girls.

Following his discussion of *ngweko*, Kenyatta discusses taboos. In addition to incest, he claims that sexual positions are regulated: "any form of sexual intercourse other than the natural form, between men and women acting in a normal way, is out of the question."[94] Here, the terms "natural" and "normal" are notable for their complete lack of specificity. Given the intricate acrobatics involved in *ngweko*, we can only presume that the mandated sexual positions are relatively uniform. His discussion of masturbation is especially notable because of the way he genders the practice. Masturbation is forbidden among initiated girls but not among uninitiated boys. His description of it among boys is worth citing in full:

> Before initiation it is considered right and proper for boys to practice masturbation as a preparation for their future sexual activities. Sometimes two or more boys compete in this, to see which can show himself more active than the rest. This practice takes place outside the homestead, under a tree or bush, where the boys are not visible to their elders. It is considered an indecency to be seen doing it, except by boys of the same age-grade. The practice is given up after the initiation ceremony, and anyone seen doing it after that would be looked upon as clinging to a babyish habit, and be laughed at, because owing to the free sex-play which is permitted among young people, there is now no need to indulge in it.[95]

Kenyatta champions masturbation among boys because it establishes group dominance and prepares them for adult sex. For these boys, masturbation has nothing to do with sexual pleasure and, more to the point, has no homosexual implications. Kenyatta uses the terms "right and proper" to give respectability to what is, in reality, a messy group jerk-off. By highlighting the ritually imposed distinction between boyhood and manhood, he removes group masturbation from a homosexual economy. Although considered "right and proper," masturbation must take place "outside the homestead," away from the governing and, potentially, desiring eyes of "elders." As he continues, the gulf between childhood and adulthood expands, and by the last sentence, "boys" has turned into "bab[ies]," a regression through time, while those who have stopped masturbating are now described as "people." This final image of the masturbating adult combines ideas of desire, regression, underdevelopment, and antisociality, tropes familiar from sexology. Unlike the beneficial *ngweko*, adult masturbation serves no function. Although

Kenyatta does not explain the prohibition against girls masturbating, we might speculate that it, too, creates private individuals who value their own pleasure over the community's needs.

Kenyatta's chapter ends on an unexpected note, with a discussion of homosexuality. Its position at the end of the chapter suggests it might have been added for the sake of completion, so that Kenyatta might claim he had covered all his bases. On the other hand, its syntax hints that it may be the point of the chapter. He writes, "Owing to these restrictions, the practice of homosexuality is unknown among the Gikuyu. The freedom of intercourse allowed between young people of opposite sex makes it unnecessary, and encourages them to acquire experience which will be useful in married life."[96] Despite the brevity of the paragraph, Kenyatta manages to engage several dominant theories of sexuality. He opens with the slippery-slope theory, especially popular in the late nineteenth century, but still prevalent in the 1930s: homosexual urges were the result of abuse (via incest) or a natural consequence of self-abuse (masturbation). Because the Kikuyu forbade incest and allowed a limited and social form of masturbation, they were protected. Next, he takes on a theory popularized by Havelock Ellis that homosexual leanings were especially prominent among groups who had been sexually isolated in, say, boarding schools or military barracks.[97] Such leanings, as Ellis explains, are caused by privation and do not necessarily express "congenital" desire. According to this account, Kenyatta's generation of *athomi* would have been the first homosexuals because they had lacked access to *ombani na ngweko*. Kenyatta's knowledge of, and implicit claim that he participated in, *ombani na ngweko* safeguards him from accusations of perversion. Fictionalized autobiography and scientific objectivity become strategic partners in normalizing Kenyatta and his generation of *athomi*.

As a practice bound inextricably to heteronormativity and hetero-futurity, *ombani na ngweko* solders intimate performance to ethnic continuity. More crucially, as a heteronormative practice that is not immediately hetero-reproductive, *ombani na ngweko* binds the very concept of futurity to the promise of reproduction, and in so doing produces ethnicity as a hetero-promise. One becomes and retains full ethnicity in fulfilling this hetero-promise to reproduce. Translated into Afro-diasporic terms, *ombani na ngweko* envisions proper blackness, diasporic blackness, as a hetero-promise that is attained in fulfilling the implicit promise to "return" by reproducing.

Given that *Facing Mount Kenya* focuses exclusively on the Kikuyu and, to a lesser extent, on Kenya, it is possible to argue that it marks Kenyatta's turn away from the ruptures of diaspora toward a fictional ethno-national space that he had already explored in *Muigwithania*. Yet, as I have argued, *Muigwithania* navigated between an ethno-national (*andu-bururi*) and an ethno-diasporic stance, and *Facing Mount Kenya* attempts a similarly difficult balancing using tools available through anthropology. Might *ombani na ngweko* be taken not simply as a method for describing how Kikuyu-ness is produced in place, but, more generally, how ethno-nationalism and ethno-diaspora, both figured in Kenyatta, engage? Alongside that, might it be taken to describe how Afro-diaspora and Africa relate through various encounters of friction and irritation, of pleasure and anticipation, of recruitment (recall, the girls who recruit their friends) and coercion, of the fleshly ways relation is pursued? All my training tells me no. It tells me that it is absurd to suggest such a thing, especially when there are more concrete ways to figure such relation, including congresses and international meetings.

Yet. Queers need fabulation. We need to imagine and theorize and practice strategies that make our beings possible. Against our training. For something else. As described by Kenyatta and Leakey, *ombani na ngweko* opens the possibility that fleshly interaction, the pleasurable movement of bodies against each other, might provide a method for thinking about encounters between and among ethno-nation and ethno-diaspora, ethno-nation and Afro-diaspora, and ethno-diaspora and Afro-diaspora. Rather than presuming that a shared genealogical imperative grounded in real and fictive kinship creates the shared ground for interaction, we might pay attention to how difference is produced and negotiated as these various practices of collectivity engage. For queers, the space provided by an attention to friction and pleasure expands the ways we can claim and practice belonging across our varied positions as ethno-national, ethno-diasporic, and Afro-diasporic.

4

Antinomian Intimacy in Claude McKay's Jamaica

Claude McKay's *Banana Bottom* (1933) has frequently been read as a nostalgic text that retreats from his more explicit political concerns. Michael Stoff, for instance, claims that McKay depicts the Jamaican setting as "the metaphorical equivalent of Eden," suggesting that in turning to Jamaica in his final published novel, McKay hoped to recapture a sense of innocence untainted by his sojourns abroad.[1] Barbara Griffin argues that *Banana Bottom* is a "fictional precursor" for McKay's nostalgic, posthumously published memoir, *My Green Hills of Jamaica*, which views Jamaica through the eyes of childhood innocence.[2] If the lush Jamaican setting mimics the Garden of Eden, the novel's heterosexual pairings appear to reinforce the connection between nature and heterosexuality. In the concluding chapters, Bita Plant, the female protagonist, marries Jubban, her father's drayman, while her friend, Yoni Legge, marries the reformed playboy Hopping Dick. Adopting the model of the classic bildungsroman, in which marriage ostensibly resolves the tension between the individual and the society and, in this particular novel, the ostensible opposition between the peasants and the middle class, *Banana Bottom* is often considered McKay's most domestic and sexually normative novel.

This normative status has been reinforced by queer and diasporic scholarship on McKay that effaces *Banana Bottom*, and focuses on *Home to Harlem* (1928), *Banjo* (1929), and the unpublished *Romance in Marseilles*.[3] Queer interpretations of McKay's work have discussed the homosocial and homosexual relationships depicted in his novels and his male characters' resistance to heterosexual attachment.[4] As the eponymous protagonist of *Banjo* puts it, "a woman is a conjunction," suggesting that women join men to space and time in uncomfortable, pleasure-depriving ways.[5] Banjo implies that women domesticate men whereas diaspora, understood as constant, restless, dispersal, queers them.

Yet McKay also resists this opposition between a normative home and a queer diaspora. Take this scene from *A Long Way from Home*:

> I was often in the company of a dancer who was making a study of African masks for choreographic purposes. One evening, while he, my friend, Gladys Wilson, and I were together in my diggings in Fourteenth Street, a woman walked in to whom I had been married seven years before. A little publicity, even for a poor poet, might be an embarrassing thing. The dancer exclaimed in a shocked tone, "Why, I never knew that you were *married!*" As if that should have made any difference to *him*. I said that nobody knew, excepting the witnesses, and that there were many more things about me that he and others didn't know.
>
> All my planning was upset. I had married when I thought that a domestic partnership was possible to my existence. But I had wandered far and away until I had grown into a truant by nature and undomesticated in the blood. There were consequences of the moment that I could not face. I desired to be footloose, and felt impelled to start going again.[6]

As both "wife" and "dancer" remain unnamed, they function as structural analogues that represent the ostensible distinction between home and diaspora. McKay married his Jamaican sweetheart, Eulalie Imelda Lewars, in 1914, shortly after he dropped out of Kansas State College in Manhattan, Kansas, and moved to New York. The marriage was unsuccessful and she left for Jamaica after six months. In this passage, she symbolizes the conjunction of heterosexuality and place of origin.[7] In contrast, the male dancer represents the deracinated and queer potential of diaspora: his camp manner indicates he inhabits hegemonic masculinity improperly, and his profession embodies the disorienting, restless energy of diaspora. Implicitly, this scene represents the opposition between a normative home and a queer diaspora.

If wife and dancer represent respectively home and diaspora, then we might consider the pressure each one exerts on the black subject. Following the incident involving his wife and the dancer, McKay leaves Harlem: "Go and see was the command. Escape from the pit of sex and poverty, from domestic death, from the cul-de-sac of self-pity, from the hot syncopated fascination of Harlem, from the suffocating ghetto of color consciousness. Go, better than stand still, keep going."[8] In turning away from his wife, McKay rejects the domesticating imperatives of national identity, what he terms "domestic death"; simultaneously, he leaves the dancer, who represents the "hot syncopated fascination of Harlem," the pulsating excitement of diaspora. McKay does not oppose home and diaspora, seeing one as bondage and the other as freedom. Instead, he proffers that the two produce in him similar psychic and material effects.

Taking home and diaspora as co-constitutive rather than oppositional, and framing Jamaica as a space that conflates both, in this chapter I argue that McKay mines Jamaica's peasant histories to illuminate the central role of the black diaspora in creating unique histories and practices of intimacy that are foundational to what Paul Gilroy terms a counterculture of modernity.[9] I use the terms "intimate life" and "intimacy" to describe a wide range of bodily proximities and affective intensities that gain their meanings in the time-space of the black diaspora. In using the term "intimacy," I question whether sexuality necessarily assumes the shape of homosexuality, heterosexuality, or bisexuality within black diasporic histories. Given the ruptures of the black diaspora, the subject-making terms associated with sexuality too easily efface the histories of unhumaning that are foundational to the black diaspora. I use intimacy to name proximity and contact, pleasure and irritation, the many ways black diasporic individuals encounter and engage each other. An expansive notion of intimacy attuned to the particularities of the black diaspora has the potential to reorient not simply our objects but also our methods of study.

In the first section of this chapter, I trace a genealogy for McKay's work as rooted in Jamaican histories of labor and punishment. I explore how labor and punishment in Jamaica's slave and emancipation histories are especially rich sites for producing and circulating concepts and practices of gender and sexuality. From this historical foundation, I review McKay's *Constab Ballads* (1912), an underexamined volume of poetry based on his brief time in the Jamaican constabulary, and published before he left Jamaica for the United States. I argue that this volume demonstrates McKay's early and ongoing interest in the relationships among gender, sexuality, labor, and colonial governmentality, concerns that critics have often attributed to his post-Jamaican publications. By illustrating these concerns in his early work, I foreground the formative role of Jamaican practices of gender and sexuality to McKay's ethics, politics, and aesthetics. The final section of the chapter returns to *Banana Bottom*.

Set in "the Jamaican period of the early nineteen hundreds," *Banana Bottom*'s narrative takes place in "a time of inquietude." As McKay notes: "Queen Victoria had died with the nineteenth century. And the times were full of ideas. Socialist and Feminist and Freethought."[10] Strikingly, the novel interweaves the radical thought experiments from imperial Britain with the equally radical thought and life experiments in rural Jamaica. Rural Jamaica, exemplified in the village of Banana Bottom, is not McKay's escape from modernity, but his attempt to grapple with a distinct Afro-modernity. This experiment is embodied in the novel's main protagonist, Tabitha ("Bita") Plant. Raped as a pre-pubescent girl in her rural home of Banana Bottom, Bita is adopted by an English missionary couple, Reverend Malcolm and Priscilla Craig, who send her to England to be educated. They intend for her to be "an exhibit" to other rural Jamaicans when she returns.[11] However, instead of being transformed from "a brown wilding into a decorous cultivated young lady," Bita's "native pride" and imperial "education" combine to foster in her an "independence of spirit" that is manifested through her intimate attachments and choices.[12] Throughout *Banana Bottom*, intimate life provides the main terrain on which characters negotiate gender, class, and community. Taking Jamaican histories as the point of departure from which to examine McKay's queer aesthetic and practices decenters Europe and the United States and enables us to develop alternative languages for and strategies through which to understand McKay's queer labor.

Queer Genealogies

Although Wayne Cooper, McKay's biographer, claims that McKay owes his greatest intellectual debt to Walter Jekyll, a gay Englishman, Winston James credits McKay's elder brother, Uriah Theodore (U. Theo), with his intellectual development.[13] This debate pits an English colonial education against a Jamaican colonial education. One way to distinguish between the two is to note that U. Theo was a political activist who called for Jamaican self-government in 1922, anticipating later political movements in the late 1930s and early 1940s.[14] While Jekyll encouraged McKay's literary experiments, he also sought to limit them to broadly primitivist paradigms, trying to retain McKay's "native" intelligence and authenticity. As Gary Holcomb argues, the debate over McKay's education is also an argument over his sexual development. In privileging U. Theo's influence, James seeks to minimize Jekyll's impact on the impressionable McKay.[15]

Strikingly, most U.S.-based critics have followed Cooper's lead by implicitly endorsing the view that McKay learned about homosexuality from Jekyll. Michael Maiwald hypothesizes that McKay derived some of his ideas from reading Edward Carpenter, an important homosexual figure he encountered through Jekyll.[16] In these readings, indigenous Jamaica remains heterosexual and normative while McKay learns to be queer through his access to Jekyll. Less explored is how McKay functioned as an alembic, combining ideas about sexuality from his Jamaican heritage with the new Euro-American ideas of sexuality he learned from Jekyll. Although Jekyll undoubtedly influenced McKay, Jamaican histories of non-normative social arrangements also provided an important context. If we are to understand McKay's later fictional explorations of queer practices, we cannot discount his Jamaican background.

Fifty years into British rule, Jamaica had developed into what Orlando Patterson describes as "a monstrous distortion of human society": "This was a society . . . in which the institution of marriage was officially condemned among both slaves and masters; in which the family was unthinkable to the vast majority of the populations and promiscuity the norm."[17] Patterson represents one side in ongoing debates on the genealogy and implications of Jamaican, and more broadly, Caribbean intimate practices. Within the rich body of social science literature, scholars have debated whether Caribbean intimate practices derive from African survivals or whether they developed under slavery.[18] To this question of genealogy is added another of moral value. Whereas Patterson views nonmonogamous, nonmarriage-based practices as "monstrous distortion[s]," feminist scholars including Rhoda Reddock, Rhonda Cobham, and Barbara Bush have argued that Caribbean intimacies offered women autonomy and independence.[19] Building on this feminist scholarship, I mine Jamaica's intimate histories to argue that black diaspora histories help us to reenvision histories and theories of sexuality that, to date, have been dominated by white Euro-American experiences.

Jamaica became an experimental zone of intimate practices where a variety of nonmonogamous practices flourished, ranging from interracial concubinage to African-based practices of polygyny and polyandry. Sounding an alarmist call in his 1774 *History of Jamaica*, Edward Long warns that the indiscriminate nature of interracial intimacies indicated that white Jamaican residents had failed to fulfill the duties and obligations of hetero-citizenship and hetero-imperialism, both of which depended on maintaining racial distinctions. He declaims,

> Let any man turn his eyes to the Spanish American dominions, and behold what a vicious, brutal and degenerate breed of mongrels has been there produced, between Spaniards, Blacks, Indians, and their mixed progeny; and he must be of opinion, that it might be much . . . better for Britain, and Jamaica too, if the white men in that colony would abate of their infatuated attachments to black women, and, instead, of being "grac'd with a *yellow offspring not their own*" perform the duty incumbent on every good citizen by raising in honourable wedlock a race of unadulterated beings.[20]

Long weds race, marriage, citizenship, and colonial competition, and forges an important connection between intimate life and political identity. White citizens are duty-bound to marry and reproduce "unadulterated" children. For Long, citizenship is always hetero-citizenship: heterosexual, reproductive, and racially exclusive. Proper hetero-citizenship is essential for imperial ventures, for in foreign locations men risk producing bastards who might claim the rights of citizens. Building on the stereotype of black women as overly promiscuous, Long warns that the "*yellow offspring*" could belong to anyone. While their racial mixture may be apparent, their sire's identity may not be, and thus the gentry risked corrupting their class status by raising children who may have belonged to lower-class white men.

Intimate practices by white Jamaicans were antinomian because they refused to fulfill the duties of hetero-citizenship. As Trevor Burnard points out, white Jamaican men "held marriage" in "low esteem," and often preferred enslaved women.²¹ Not only did white masters prefer enslaved women, they often manumitted the resulting progeny, a practice that disrupted racial and social categories. Granting rights to illegitimate offspring weakened the racial distinctions on which imperial and colonial ventures depended. Even when white Jamaican men turned to white women, legal marriage was not guaranteed. Rates of marriage between white Jamaicans were relatively low and illegitimate unions were common.²²

These antinomian practices extended to enslaved and free black people, who eschewed monogamous practices in favor of a range of innovative intimate arrangements. Certainly, heterosexual monogamy and marriage were neither privileged nor hegemonic on the island. Long complains, for instance, "The [Creole blacks] are all married (*in their way*) to a husband or wife, *pro tempore* . . . so that one of them, perhaps, has six or more husbands, or wives, in several different places."²³ Both men and women participated in these antinomian arrangements: women chose their partners as freely as men. Black Jamaicans, Long summarizes, "laugh at the idea of a marriage, which ties two persons together indissolubly. Their notions of love are, that it is free and transitory."²⁴ Although Long's comments are meant to provide evidence of black Jamaicans' excessive sexuality and disregard for the norms of hetero-civilization, they provide us with an invaluable way to theorize enslaved black people's forms of intimacy.

By taking Long's claims seriously rather than dismissing them as racist fabrications, I build on Kamala Kempadoo's argument that "hypersexuality" is a "lived reality that pulses through the Caribbean body."²⁵ Kempadoo asks an important, ground-clearing question: "To what extent . . . can we read the 'excesses' or 'vulgarity' of Caribbean sexuality not simply as European inventions . . . that negate or demean the history and agency of the Other, but also as sedimented, corporeally inculcated dispositions that are lived and practiced every day?"²⁶ By drawing our attention to the everydayness of sexual practice, Kempadoo urges us to consider the Caribbean as a site for rich and robust intimate practices and theorizing about such intimate practices. She also directs us to consider the history of such practices. Created and maintained under extremely difficult conditions, black forms of intimacy had to be innovative and creative, running the gamut from short-lived, pleasurable attachments to more sustained, carefully choreographed forms of partnership and companionship.

In "Mama's Baby, Papa's Maybe: An American Grammar Book," Hortense Spillers argues that conditions under slavery disrupted gender formation, creating gender *un*differentiation. Under slavery, she contends, "we lose at least *gender* difference . . . and the female body and the male body become a territory of cultural and political maneuver, not at all gender-related, gender-specific."[27] Spillers describes how punishment produced gender. We imagine, she contends, that torture takes place only between men: it is "the peculiar province of *male* brutality and torture inflicted [on males] by other males."[28] To subject women to the same rituals unsettles gender differentiation. Scholars on Jamaica have demonstrated that men and women performed similar labor and received similar punishments. Implicitly, this similarity in labor and punishment produced men and women as equally ungendered subjects under the law and in social life.

Slave and colonial authorities were aware of undifferentiated gender under slavery, and in the period leading up to emancipation, they proposed a series of measures designed to properly re-gender black men and women. During the period of the Amelioration Acts (1823–34) and apprenticeship (1834–38), the colonial government abolished flogging for women and encouraged enslaved people to get married. The colonial secretary, Earl Bathurst, explained that bans on flogging were meant "to restore to the female slaves that sense of shame which is at once the ornament and the protection of their sex." Glossing Bathurst, Diana Paton notes that such measures were designed "to strengthen slaves' sense of gender difference," noting that the "specifically feminine 'sense of shame' was a common theme in both abolitionist and official discussions of women."[29] This sense that "shame" could be restored and proper femininity established for black women emerged in discourses that depicted domestic life in the post-emancipation period. Painting such a picture, one commentator rhapsodizes,

> Your wives, hitherto accustomed to be partakers in your daily toils running to the fields with you in the morning, and returning with you downspirited and dejected at sun set day by day, bringing no alleviations, will be enabled to remain at home, to look after your clothes, and your chil-

dren's clothes—your household affairs—your stock, your comfortable dinner, so that whilst you are at work at the field, as the day advances, instead of lagging in your work, you are more cheerful, more industrious, because moving in the certainty of finding every thing comfortable when you get home.[30]

In the post-emancipation period, women would be domesticated; their gendered status confirmed by the labors they performed in managing "household affairs" in the private space of the domestic.

Colonial officials encouraged newly emancipated black Jamaicans to get married, believing that marriage would create economically responsible individuals. Official statements from the period explicitly sutured three types of freedom: freedom from slavery, freedom to marry, and freedom to work. By joining marriage to economic responsibility, and depicting both as fruits of emancipation, colonial officials hoped to manage the labor habits of the formerly enslaved, whom they feared might "relapse 'into barbarous indolence.'"[31] Colonial officials tried to suture marriage's affective demands to economic need to ensure a steady, uninterrupted labor supply. Colonial officials insisted that good marriages were based on being good providers, and responsible husbands, wives, and parents were obliged to provide for their dependents. In providing for dependents, the formerly enslaved proved they loved their dependents and that they understood freedom as economic responsibility.[32]

For women, the freedom to marry came with the relative unfreedom of gender differentiation: by becoming dependent on men, they ceded the paradoxical gains of gender undifferentiation. The colonial officials who advocated marriage depicted it as a hetero-patriarchal structure; men would work outside the home while women would retreat into the space of the domestic to be supported by their husbands. It is instructive, for instance, that positions in colonial law enforcement were reserved for men.[33] Men would govern and women would be governed. Attempts to differentiate gender extended beyond the home/work dyad. Modes of punishment from the amelioration period through post-emancipation were tied to gender. Flogging was abolished for women and prisons were newly segregated by gender.[34] Moreover, prison authorities tried to distinguish between forms of hard labor: while men constructed roads and farms, women washed clothes.[35] Across a range of spaces and institutions, the colonial government tried to enforce gendered distinctions that, it hoped, would force newly freed men and women to continue working in a plantation-based labor market. As Holt points out, "[T]he problem of abolition was, at its root, a labor problem: how safely to transform a dependent laborer into a self-motivated free worker."[36]

As the colonial government promoted gender differentiation, it also intensified surveillance on intimate practices. By 1845, flogging was no longer allowed in Jamaica; it was reintroduced beginning in 1850 as punishment reserved for black men and meted out for sex-based acts including "rape, assault with intent to commit rape, sodomy, assault with intent to commit sodomy, bestiality, attempt to commit bestiality, carnally knowing children 'of tender years' or attempt to commit that crime."[37] While categories like "rape" and "assault with intent to commit rape" seem clear—even though filtered through racist ideas about black men—other categories are less so. For instance, "sodomy" and "assault with intent to commit sodomy" conflate desire and consent with sexual violence. Sodomy can never be a choice. Nonheteronormative desire must be disciplined. The overall effect of conflating these categories by punishing offenders was to gender all black men as sexual threats.

Jamaican women resisted attempts by the colonial government to turn them into economic dependents. In her study of Afro-Jamaican women from the nineteenth through the mid-twentieth century, Erna Brodber writes, "The absence of the man from the woman's day to day life and from observable interaction with her had been a social fact," adding, "Older women expect to, and in fact, urge younger women to separate their economic activities from those of their mates."[38] Like Brodber, Cobham argues that while peasant Jamaican women may have been emotionally and physically intimate with men, they remained economically independent.[39] Women's economic independence, often tied to their reluctance to get married, can be considered a strategy for resisting the hetero-colonial imperative that women should be married, economic dependents. Instead, women created a range of innovative intimate arrangements, in which they acted as surrogate mothers to needy children, who were both related and unrelated, and had a variety of intimate relationships with men, which ranged from short-term uncommitted affairs to long-term marriage-like arrangements.

Patterns of antinomian intimacy established during slavery continued well past emancipation and linger into the present. These forms of intimacy refuse to model themselves on hetero-colonial standards. In disregarding monogamous, heterosexual marriage as *the* standard, they refuse to concede the hegemony of hetero-citizenship as promulgated by former slave and colonial masters.

In his poetry, fiction, and nonfiction, McKay mines these histories of antinomian intimacy to critique heterosexual norms imposed by religion and class. For instance, in his posthumously published *My Green Hills of Jamaica,* McKay writes, "[N]atives of Jamaica do love excessively to indulge in that thing which caused Adam and Eve to be driven out of the Garden of Eden," noting, "When I was a boy in Jamaica it was established that there were about sixty percent bastard births," further commenting that childbirth out of wedlock and bastardy did not lead to widespread opprobrium. In a telling moment, McKay claims, "In our village we were poor enough but very proud peasants."[40] Although McKay's father started life poor, he had risen in class status by the time Claude was born. By identifying with the "poor . . . but very proud peasants," McKay embraces peasant values over bourgeois norms.

His class sympathies became more fully developed when he moved to Kingston for a short-lived stint as a constable in 1911. In the preface to his *Constab Ballads* (1912), he writes, "We blacks are all somewhat impatient of discipline, and to the natural impatience of my race there was added, in my particular case, a peculiar sensitiveness which made certain forms of discipline irksome, and a fierce hatred of injustice."[41] In this preface, then twenty-two-year-old McKay articulates a sense of antinomian blackness. While critics have focused on McKay's "fierce hatred of injustice" to explain his political commitments, his impatience with discipline is equally important. McKay's understanding of blackness as a form of "natural impatience" with discipline repudiates the discipline of the constabulary and critiques the various forms of religious, sexual, and political forms of intolerance he would oppose throughout his career.

By the time McKay met Walter Jekyll in 1907, he already had a framework for mounting a queer critique of sexual normativity, one rooted in specific histories of slavery and emancipation. By no means do I deny Jekyll's important influence. After all, shortly after meeting Jekyll, and especially after his mother's death in 1909, McKay moved to Kingston to be closer to Jekyll. However, focusing predominantly on a white Euro-American genealogy for McKay's queer aesthetics and politics forecloses a more complex engagement with Jamaican racial histories. In addition, discussions that understand queerness as primarily homosocial or homosexual marginalize McKay's radical critique of colonial sexuality.

Constab Ballads

Using *Banana Bottom* to examine McKay's queer Jamaican heritage is a chancy strategy because it was published more than twenty years after he left Jamaica. Given that temporal distance, it could be argued that *Banana Bottom* is a black Atlantic text, capable of being written only because of McKay's exile from Jamaica. To forestall the claim that Jamaica's queer histories only become visible to McKay following his departure from the island, I put into evidence McKay's Jamaican poetry from *Constab Ballads*. This early volume anticipates formal, ideological, and political concerns McKay pursued in his later work, even as these concerns were transformed by the rich experiences that inflected his politics and aesthetics—World War I, his life in Harlem and Marseilles, his travels to Moscow and Morocco, his encounters with Marxism, for instance. In turning to *Constab Ballads*, I emphasize how Jamaican modernity contributed to McKay's queer aesthetics.

Published in 1912, the same year as *Songs of Jamaica*, *Constab Ballads* contains twenty-eight poems written primarily, though not exclusively, in Jamaican vernacular. As these poems combine Jamaican vernacular with Standard English, they invoke and exemplify McKay's formal and informal registers, those learned in and out of the schoolroom. As he explains in the 1922 foreword to *Harlem Shadows*,

> The speech of my childhood and early youth was the Jamaican Negro dialect, the native variant of English, which still preserves a few words of African origin, and which is more difficult of understanding than the American Negro dialect. But the language we wrote and read in school

was England's English. Our text books then, before the advent of the American and Jamaican readers and our teachers, too, were all English made.[42]

Going beyond simply registering McKay's colonial upbringing and the hybrid subject it produced, the shifts in language in the poems index class affiliations and divisions. McKay's "Jamaican Negro dialect" acts as "vernacular glue," joining together Jamaican peasants, the urban working class, and antinomian constables, including the speaker in most of the poems.[43]

Vernacular Poetics

In the preface to *Constab Ballads,* McKay writes, "Let me confess it at once. I had not in me the stuff that goes to the making of a good constable; for I am so constituted that imagination outruns discretion, and it is my misfortune to have a most improper sympathy with wrongdoers."[44] This confession of waywardness speaks as much to McKay's formal strategies as it does to his actions. Poems slip in and out of formal, Standard English, as in the opening lines to "To Inspector W. E. Clark": "We welcome you, dear Sir, again; / But oh! de comin' brings us pain."[45] While in the first line, the black constables perform their subordination in Standard English, "We welcome you, dear Sir, again," they also inflect this subordination with familiarity by using "dear." Economic relations run through all of McKay's Jamaican poetry—they are especially prominent in *Constab Ballads*, as I explain in greater detail later in this chapter—and the single word "dear" points to the economies of the constabulary: subordination to a white officer is psychically and ideologically "dear" (expensive). Class and geohistorical difference are evidenced in the second line of the poem as it shifts from Standard English to Jamaican ("de comin'" as opposed to "the coming"). The "de" in the second line visually relates to "dear" in the first line, and while the pronunciation is different, the truncation (from "the" to "de" and, visually, from "dear" to "de") resituates "dear": "dear" shifts to "de," taking away the affective subordination expected of constables.

This multivoiced strategy continues throughout the poem: it ostensibly mourns that the commanding officer who has returned will one day leave again, but this explanation is undercut by the poem. Take the opening stanza,

> We welcome, you, dear Sir, again;
> But oh! de comin' brings us pain,
> For though we greet you glad to-day,
> Once more you're bound to go away:
> We grieve now deeper than before
> To know you'll be wid us no more.[46]

The welcome in the first line is immediately taken away in the second, where "de comin' brings us pain." While the third and fourth lines attempt to take away the sting of the second line—your presence is distasteful—that effort fails in the final lines of the stanza, which seem to "grieve" for the officer's eventual departure to another station, but are rendered so ambiguously that they also gesture to his death: "We grieve now deeper than before / To know you'll be wid us no more." In the second and sixth lines, the "us" is preceded by Jamaican vernacular, "de" and "wid" respectively, indicating that the "us" is made up of those who speak Jamaican vernacular. This sense of a language community intensifies in the third and last stanza of the poem in which the just returned officer is dispatched:

> Farewell, dear Sir, farewell again!—
> A farewell fraught wi' deepest pain:
> De very ringin' o' de bell
> Sounds like a wailin' of farewell;
> We feel it deeply, to de core,
> To know you'll be wid us no more.[47]

The insistent "farewell," which is repeated four times, has the force of a performative, even though in the second and fourth lines it is a noun rather than a verb. Not only are the constables bidding their superior officer farewell, but also the "ringin' o' de bell" joins and amplifies the "farewell." The reference to "deepest pain" intensifies the sense that the constables are not merely bidding a "dear" officer goodbye, but that they are cursing him: the feeling is more akin to "we wish you were dead" than it is to "we miss you when you are gone." As the superior officer is dispatched, the use of vernacular increases: it is used twice in the first stanza—"de" and "wid"—and used seven times in this final stanza—"wi," "ringin'," "o," "de," "wailin'," "de," "wid." In the final line of the poem, "wid us" takes shape and form because the commanding officer is gone. Although it is possible to argue that this poem demonstrates McKay's attachment to colonial order, as evidenced by the poem's regular tetrameter, rhyming couplets, and fondness for the commanding officer, closer attention to elements such as enjambment and Jamaican vernacular complicate that argument: the poem resists the discipline its form imposes.

Taking seriously the ballad as a narrative form, the collection follows a constable's life as he joins the constabulary and trains (poems 1–7), to when he assumes his duties and takes on the active life of a police constable (poems 8–19), through a growing disillusionment with the classist, racist, and colonial form of the constabulary (poems 20–24), to resignation from the constabulary and life imagined after it in a rural pastoral (poems 25–28). In its trajectory from urban modernity to rural pastoral, *Constab Ballads* anticipates similar trajectories in McKay's later fiction, from the urban and diasporic cosmopolitanisms of *Home to Harlem* and *Banjo* to the rural world of *Banana Bottom*. Yet, in *Constab Ballads*, this eventual retreat from urban modernity is not an uncritical celebration of a romanticized rurality, but a deliberate attempt to circumvent the affiliation-breaking depredations imposed by the constabulary as an instrument of colonial governmentality.[48] As McKay writes, "'Tis grievous to think dat / while toilin' on here, / My people won't love me again, / My people, my people, my owna black skin."[49] The use of the term "grievous" is a pointed reference to mourning, even as it carries hints of grievance. This grieving can be read in biographical terms—McKay joined the constabulary and subsequently left to pursue an aesthetic education under Walter Jekyll, both of which potentially alienated him from his fellow laboring Jamaicans subject to the colonial institutions of discipline he had ostensibly escaped. If McKay mourns this loss of intimacy, he also appears to resent the histories that have created this situation. These lines might articulate McKay's anxiety that his poetic "toil" under the mentorship of the white Jekyll might compromise his standing among his "owna black skin" or even that that forms of his poems—his use of the ballad form—might be taken as an aesthetic betrayal. Either option suggests a self-consciousness about his poetic "toil" that helps shift our understanding of his early poetry from what one early critic, William Hansell, dismissed as "sentimental."[50]

McKay's use of vernacular modifies the ballad meter he employs in most of the poems. Take, for instance, the opening stanzas in the first poem of the collection, "De Route March":

> In de fus' squad an' de front rank,
> 'Side me dear Will on de right flank.
> From de drill-groun' at the old camp
> We went marchin' on a long tramp.

> In de forefront was de gay band,
> An' de music it was ring grand;
> O how jolly were we boys, oh,
> As we marched 'long t'rough St. Jago!

> As we tramped on out de dull town,
> Keepin' time so to de drum's soun',
> All de folkses as dey ran out,
> Started dancin' with a glad shout.[51]

Written in iambic tetrameter, these lines invoke the discipline of the constabulary, with each rhyming couplet simulating the beat of the constables as they march alongside their partners. This formal twinning finds its corollary in the linguistic pairing of British colloquialisms such as "jolly . . . boys" and Jamaican-accented terms, ranging from the articles and conjunctions "de" and "an'," to the rounded, truncated words "groun'" and "marchin'." Combined these formal, syntactic, and semantic twinnings mark the sonic as an uneasy space of tension and conflict, where meaning and feeling rub against each other.

This conflict is suggested by the implicit juxtaposition and contrast between "fus'" and "front," both spatio-temporal markers that emerge from distinct histories. In using "fus'," as opposed to "firs'," to represent "first," McKay inflects the poem with a Jamaican accent, emphasizing the multiple sonic registers of his poem. Its written form captures, inexactly, multiple sonic traditions—those of the military with its "camp," and "fus[sy]" "drill-groun'" and "marchin'"; those of the Afro-Jamaicans whose bodies transform "marchin'" and "tramp-trampin'" into "swingin'" and "windin'," their bodily rhythms inspiring the "folkses" to join in "dancin'"; and the sonic traditions of the form it inherits and transforms, the rhyming couplets in iambic tetrameter and the narrative sequence of the ballad. McKay engages these traditions on a sonic "front": "fus'" and "front" represent sites of sonic engagement and conflict. The blend of English and Jamaican voices finds its corollary in the dull violence of military exercises encountering joyous dance, both of which demonstrate McKay marking the emergence of a new aesthetic attentive to the ambivalent fractures of colonial modernity.

If the sonic form of the poem captures the multiple voices of colonial modernity, Jamaican and English, the content of the poem registers themes that resonate in McKay's later work. The references to "dear Will" straddle the homosocial-homoerotic cleavage critics have traced in *Home to Harlem* and *Banjo*; the reference to "dancin'" anticipates the many club scenes depicting dance in poems such as "Harlem Dancer" and in impressionistic sequences in *Banjo*; and the pleasure within a situation of discipline captures McKay's reparative project, at once perverse and transformative, in which he depicts the social and affective possibilities available in undesirable sociohistorical situations.

The discipline expected by the constabulary fails to control unruly bodies whose infectious rhythms invite the "folkses" to appropriate a "route march" as an occasion for "dancin'"; this unruliness defines the aesthetic and affect of the poem. While McKay's truncated words look familiar, "marchin'," "dancin'," "trampin'," replicating strategies designed to fit meter—consider terms such as "o'er" or the Shakespearean "mak'st" and "deserv'd"—they skirt this metrical sonic requirement, registering not the discipline of meter, but the unruliness of *accent* as a geohistorical formation, where the iamb (iam'?) becomes reinflected by location. Just as those in "de fus' squad an' de front rank" transform "marchin'" into "swingin'," the poem's accents shift its geographical registers, exemplifying what Peter Hitchcock terms "Anglophone expression," a geohistorical modification to syllabic-accentual forms that creates a geo-accentual intervention into English poetry.[52]

This intervention becomes clearer once we focus on the relation between geography and affect in the poem. The "Route March" takes the colonial constabulary through the "ruins" of St. Jago—the "folkses" come out to dance as the constables tramp "on out de dull town." St. Jago was the capital of Jamaica when it was under Spanish rule. In an act of historical revisionism, McKay sutures its ruins to the presence of the black constabulary, implying that they march out of it and into the waiting "folkses" as nationalist heroes, having conquered the Spanish, a metonym for colonial power. Just as the "folkses" appropriate "marchin'" as an invitation to "dancin'," they similarly refashion the discipline of constabulary "trampin'" as an occasion to celebrate freedom from colonial domination. The "folkses" appropriation of an improper historical object, their misreading of a similarity in *form*, offers one useful paradigm for theorizing McKay's early poetics.

In an influential assessment of McKay's early poetry, Kamau Brathwaite argues that McKay wrote in "*dialect*," not "*nation*," because he "allowed himself to be imprisoned in pentameter."[53] Dialect arises from "the plantation where people's dignity is distorted through their language"; it is the language of "caricature." In contrast, nation language demonstrates the "African aspect of experience in the Caribbean," and is "like a howl, or a shout or a machine-gun or the wind or a wave . . . like the blues."[54] For Brathwaite, these sonic elements of colonial modernity fracture metered language. Throughout his discussion of nation language, pentameter indicates that a poet (or poem) is not yet attuned to the possibilities of resistant Afro-sonic modernities. Such resistance, at the formal level, would consist in trying to replicate the ineffable, reaching for the effect of the "wind," or a "howl," or a "shout." Rendered formally, the ineffable would fracture pentameter. However, if we begin from McKay's implicit poetic challenge that in a colonial situation form can be appropriated to different ends—"trampin'" read as "dancin'" and a daily exercise march taken as a moment of anticolonial triumph—we can certainly complicate Brathwaite's desire for form (as sound) to aspire to ineffability, and for ineffability to be the mark of a genuine Caribbean poetics.

Brathwaite's reading can be further complicated by attending to the bodily movements in "De Route March" not merely as the contents of the poem, but as formal elements. Fred Moten's description of black performance is apt here: "black performance has always been the ongoing, improvisation of a kind of lyricism of the surplus—invagination, rupture, collision, augmentation."[55] The transformation of "marchin'" into "dancin'" inserts a moment of improvisation into the colonial structures of discipline and surveillance signaled by the constabulary. The constables' movements are supplemented, ruptured, and augmented by the "folkses." After the "folkses" start "dancin'," the constables in training start "swingin'." The traffic is not one-way, between a passive folk and an active constabulary, but represents an important moment of cultural exchange across ostensibly divided lines: the constables in the service of the colonial government and the "folkses" the constables are supposed to govern.

Sound itself has been transformed, and this transformation is registered in the final stanza of the poem:

> To de music wid a good will
> We went tramp-trampin' up de hill,
> An' back to camp strode marchin' t'rough
> De sad ruins of St. Jago.[56]

Two cuts appear in this final stanza: the first, the hyphen that hiccups into "tramp-trampin'," marking a stumble, a visual and aural interruption into the movement of the line. Read aloud, the "p" in the first "tramp" is swallowed by the hyphen, rendered silent, anticipating the truncated "trampin'." In a moment of geo-accentual modification, McKay signals the distinction between the appearance of words and their sound(ing). The second cut is the affective change in the poem: gone are the "gay," "jolly," "happy," "boys" who march with "glad hearts." Instead, the poem ends on "sad ruins," because the fantasy that allowed the "folkses" to start "dancin'," the fantasy that the constabulary represents an anticolonial force, has been replaced by the reality of training in in the "camp," a place where implacable instructors promise, "Me wi' drill you ti' you mad."[57] It is not that the utopian promise articulated earlier in the poem is entirely dissipated, but its conditions of possibility are attenuated by its colonial setting.

Queer Will

The colonial histories that inflect McKay's poetry manifest themselves as moments of ambivalence and conflict exemplified by McKay's use of the term "Will/will" in *Constab Ballads*. "Will/will" is also, importantly, a site for queer orientation, and tracing its queer inflections is key to understanding McKay's queer labor. "Will/will" appears three times in "De Route March": "'Side me dear Will on de right flank" (line 2); "Me so happy by my dear Will" (line 14); "To de music wid a good will" (line 21). Short for William, and invoking McKay's colonial education, with its oblique references to William Shakespeare and William Blake—one hears faint echoes of W. E. B. Du Bois's famous claim, "I sit with Shakespeare and he winces not"—"Will" queers proximity to poetic history. Queers not only in the sense of declaring same-sex affection for "Will," but also in the syntactical form of the declaration. The first appearance of "Will" invokes the discipline of the constabulary through the syntax of "de right flank." This "Will" is "'Side" the persona, distanced, presumably, by the rules of form—the pattern of stresses in the ballad and the rules of the constabulary. Simultaneously, McKay rebels within the form in using the vernacular possessive "me" in this first instance, claiming "Will" as part of a Jamaican vernacular heritage, anticipating later appropriations of Shakespeare by Aimé Césaire, Julius Nyerere, and other Afro-diasporic and African writers.[58]

Read as an instance of black diaspora queerness, "me dear Will" embeds same-sex attraction within the nexus of capital and desire. The stress on the poetic line falls on "dear," invoking value and affection, that is, black diaspora histories of what Christina Sharpe has termed "monstrous intimacies": desires and erotics created, produced, and reproduced under conditions of de-subjectification.[59] That long history casts its shadow over this poem as the speaker's "dear Will" enables him to be "happy" within the constraints of constabulary routine and discipline. Indeed, "dear Will" attenuates the rigidity of the constabulary spatially and affectively: while line 2 has "dear Will" "on de right flank," positioned by constabulary protocol, line 14 has "dear Will" "by." This reframing of constabulary orientation from "de right flank" to "by" powerfully suggests the power of queer proximity to reformulate space and time and value.

Significantly, the shift from "on de right flank" to "by" takes place, in the time of the poem, after the troop encounter the "folkses" who appropriate "marchin'" for "dancin.'" Queer proximity becomes more possible through embedding in the "folkses." In this black queer diaspora rendering, queer proximity emerges at the intersection of the urban deracination of the constabulary and the rural hospitality of the "folkses."

What is queer about "dear Will" is not only the same-sex attraction to which it alludes, but also, more capaciously, the black diasporic histories of economic and erotic valuation that blend and jostle to produce black Jamaican bodies. These histories of constraint and possibility routed through the embodied "Will" continue to inflect all subsequent appearances of "will" and "Will" in *Constab Ballads*. Thus, when McKay writes of a "good will," or a "stubborn will," or an "aimless will," or a "cheery will," each of these suggest both the attenuated agency of the black diasporic subject and the erotic intensity borne by that subject.[60] These suggestions are amplified when McKay returns to "Will," but this time to suggest the hand of fate. In "Consolation," McKay discusses "man" as the "toy of a Will" and in "To W.G.G.," man is "De helpless playt'ing of a Will."[61] And while "toy" and "playt'ing" suggest an absence of choice, they are inflected by the erotic intensities of the earlier "dear Will." In queering "Will/will," McKay inhabits the ambivalence of black diasporic intimacies, never fully liberating, never entirely constrained.

In "De Route March," McKay uses the queer proximity of male bodies, the closeness to "dear Will," to delve into the making of postslavery subjects under conditions of colonial governmentality. The erotics of the poem, however, extend beyond the dyad of speaker and "dear Will" to create affiliations between the constabularies in training and the "folkses" they are training to monitor. McKay's antinomianism, his rebellion with and against forms, draws from and gestures toward modes of world making embedded in Afro-Jamaican socialities.

Gender Dissonance

While poems other than "De Route March" similarly focus on the queer proximity of male bodies, notably "Bennie's Departure," "Consolation," and "To W.G.G.," prioritizing same-sex male intimacies as the primary sites of McKay's queer labor sidelines his ongoing engagement with

Jamaican modernities as innovative sites of gender-making. Because Jamaican women are so central to these innovations, I examine the poem "Disillusioned" in *Constab Ballads*, which features a woman speaker. In doing so, I build on and depart from Winston James's argument concerning the significance of women speakers and characters in McKay's poetry.

Writing on McKay's two early volumes of poetry, *Songs of Jamaica* and *Constab Ballads*, James emphasizes "the extraordinary degree to which the experience of Jamaican women is woven into the overall tapestry of [McKay's] work."[62] "In fact," continues James, "not an insubstantial number of his poems were written in the female voice, and even more had women as subject matter," concluding that these early poems amply demonstrate McKay's "feminist sympathies."[63] As James rightly notes, McKay features many women and many women's voices in his work; however, this representation need not necessarily suggests a "feminist" stance on McKay's part. The aesthetic labor of representation is not necessarily equivalent to the political work invoked by the term "feminist."[64] In foregrounding how McKay represents women in his early work, especially peasant and working-class women, James enables us to reassess evaluations of how McKay depicts women in his later work and to consider the intertwined transnational dimensions of McKay's representations of women. We can consider, for instance, how a poem like "Harlem Dancer" might appear placed within the context of McKay's long-term, ongoing interest in women as laborers. Framed through labor, words in the poem like "sway" and "sang" and "danced" become (haunted) performances of bondage and freedom within a labor economy populated by postslavery subjects. Such a reading further textures the poem, without mitigating the problem of the male gaze and voice.

Strikingly, none of McKay's post-Jamaica poetry is written explicitly in the voice of a woman. As Gilroy notes, black diasporic modes of affiliation and practices of legibility are often predicated on affirming normative ideals of gender, and it's tempting to speculate that leaving Jamaica impeded McKay's ability to write in a woman's voice, because he was compelled to voice masculine protest.[65] It is worth noting, for instance, that McKay's most famous poem in the years soon after he left Jamaica was "If We Must Die," a poem of defiance and resistance in the tradition of black male protest. And while McKay's well-documented queer explorations unsettle notions of heteronormative black male sexuality, they often do so by advancing masculinist, homosocial ideals. The forms of gender play in his Jamaican poetry are simply not available in his post-Jamaica poetry.

What if McKay's representations of women demonstrate his feminist sympathies *and* express forms of queer gender play? This "*and*" does not represent a progressive utopia, but the location of frottage, where feminist sympathies rub up against queer gender play, producing a range of effects and affects: queer gender play in the hands of a male author can displace women and reconsolidate gendered binaries, even as it has the potential to destabilize gender and sexuality. This ambivalence suffuses the poem "Disillusioned."

"Disillusioned" features the lament of a rural-born woman, Fan, who followed her lover, Dan, as he traveled to the city to become a "Constab."[66] In the poem, a now-pregnant Fan mourns that her lover has left her for "a to'n-bred miss":

> Can you leave me, leave me so,
> Full me heart wid grief an' woe,
> Leave me to a bitter fate,
> When I'm in dis awful state?[67]

Although the poem's "feminist sympathies" may lie in its depiction of women like Fan, rural victims of a capricious and cruel urban modernity, it is, for the most part, a difficult poem to claim as feminist. One may feel sympathy for the abandoned Fan, "undefile'" until her relationship with Dan, but she is an unlikely feminist heroine, certainly nowhere near as bold and aggressive as the speaker in "The Apple-Woman's Complaint," who lambastes the "pólice" for "oppressin' we."[68]

Sexually pure until she met Dan, Fan subordinated herself to him during the relationship. After leaving her "mudder's home" against parental advice, she supported his career as a constable, emotionally and financially. She indicates as much when she asks about the "to'n-bred miss,"

Will she warm you where you're chill?
Will you get of lub you' fill?
Will she starve herse'f fe you,
As I always use fe' do?

Will a to'n gal go bare-feet,
Jes' fe try mek two ends meet?
Will she car' water an' wash,
Jes' fe help you' lee cash?[69]

Less feminist icon or even descendant of the fiercely independent Jamaican women who, at the turn of the twentieth century, challenged gender-normative arrangements, Fan inhabits two seemingly incommensurable economies: a financial one, where her labor keeps her independent, and an affective one, where her attachment to the constable compromises her independence. Acknowledging her problematic nature, might a reading through the figure of the speaker offer other interpretive possibilities?

The thirteenth poem in *Constab Ballads*, roughly halfway through the twenty-eight-poem sequence, "Disillusioned" interrupts the constab's voice that has been narrating his training and its travails. It is the first instance of a distinct woman's voice in the collection, and it textures the homosocial-homoerotic world of the constables by emphasizing the economic and affective structures that subtend their urban existence—women feed the men, provide them with "lee cash," and act as emotional anchors, allowing the constables, ironically, to pursue other economic and affective attachments. Once we begin to frame the poem through Fan's labor, a more complex picture emerges: this is no helpless village naïf, an object of condescending sympathy. Indeed, it's possible to see how the abandoned Fan might evolve into the speaker in "The Apple-Woman's Complaint," who warns her "bastard" "son-son," "Jes' try to ha' you' mudder's min' / An' Police Force you'll neber jine."[70]

An important split takes place between the affect of the poem, which seems to gender Fan relentlessly as a dependent woman, and the description of Fan's labor, which undermines the presumed normative gendering between employed male constable and unemployed female lover. The poem's dissonant economies, one rooted in affect the other in labor, both make visible and unstable a third economy, that of gender. It's worth recalling that, as Paton points out, in the post-emancipation period Afro-Jamaican men were recruited into the military service, a strategy designed, in part, to create and enforce gendered distinctions between working, masculinized men and the stay-at-home feminized women they would support. In this poem, the constab's masculinity is depicted as a form of affective and economic theft:

> Dem wi' ondly try fe rob
> All de good you mighta hab;
> An' 'fo' you can count de cost,
> You wi' find you'se'f lost, lost.[71]

Combined, the terms "rob," "good," and "cost" emphasize and multiply the poem's many economies. For instance, "good" points to a moral economy, suggesting that the constab has stolen a morality attached to an idealized rural femininity. Yet, this reading of moral femininity is complicated by the suggestion that the "good" robbed from the speaker is gender itself: the gender that emerges from labor practices is imagined as a "good" that the constab "rob[s]," leaving the speaker "lost, lost." In this queer reading, what is "lost, lost" is not only moral character and material goods, but also the gender-making, subjectivity-producing work these two subtend. Constab masculinity is predicated on a theft from Fan.

It is only by stealing from Fan that the "heartless Dan" can pursue the "risky to'n woman." What is at stake for Dan in the poem is the gender stability promised by his association with the urban woman. The poem takes great care to highlight the femininity of the urban woman: she is described as a "to'n-bred miss," suggesting an emphasis on cultivation and manners, a protected, class-inflected femininity. Although obliquely, the poem also suggests that this "to'n gal" will not work to support Dan: her function is to stabilize his sense of masculinity by simultaneously performing a helpless femininity and exploiting his need for an economically rooted and affectively performative masculinity. This performative masculinity is evident in how Dan treats Fan:

> Now, sake ob a to'n-bred miss,
> You mus' treat me laka dis!
> Tramplin' me under you' feet,
> Tu'nin' me out in de street.[72]

The physical and material violence meted out to Fan is part of the act of theft the poem indicts; these are not simply assertions of masculinity, certainly not the dissonant, affectively complex masculinity featured in the prior twelve poems. Instead, they are attempts to stabilize constab masculinity by ejecting the rural, laboring woman's body that is its economic foundation.

While framing the poem through multiple economies—labor, affect, morality—helps to unsettle the normative gender assumptions that an initial reading of "Disillusioned" would support—that it is a poem about rural female disempowerment at the hands of an urban male—it would be irresponsible to claim that the poem enacts a kind of gender utopia beyond the strictures of normative gender. Even a cursory reading of the final stanza disabuses us of this notion:

> Will you leave me, heartless Dan,
> For a risky to'n woman?
> When I'm burdened do'n wid woe,
> Will you leave me, leave me so?[73]

The pathetic Fran who opened the poem returns here in full force: "burdened do'n wid woe," lonely and desperate. Despite Dan's cruel treatment, she wants him back. Despite her critiques of him, even in this stanza, she wants him back. And while it might be possible to argue that she wants to retrieve what he stole from her, such an argument is far too convenient. Instead, McKay depicts gender as an incomplete, in formation, contested project, one riven by the historical modes of its production and circulation as these are mediated by labor and location.

Long neglected by critics, the poems in *Constab Ballads* do more than recount McKay's life as a constable; neither rehearsals for the formally experimental work he undertakes in *Home to Harlem* and *Banjo* nor the queer aesthetics in these works and the unpublished "Romance in Marseilles," these poems contend with the gender- and sexuality-making projects of Afro-Jamaican modernities. And while the shape, texture, and sound of McKay's queer project changed over the course of his travels around the world, his early poetry theorizes his investment in Afro-Jamaican gender and sexual dissonance.

Banana Bottom

As the omniscient narrator explains, the community of Banana Bottom has a queer origin. The founding patriarch, a "strange Scotchman," bought a vast estate in the 1820s, liberated all the black slaves, "married one of the blackest of them," and sold off small portions of his estate to those blacks who wanted to buy them.[74] Although Scots in Jamaica may have been opposed to slavery, they did not tend to interfere with the system, and so this Scotchman's actions disrupt a historical trend.[75] In marrying a woman who was formerly enslaved, he also goes against the hetero-colonial mandate that depends on maintaining racial difference. Moreover, he disrupts standard interracial relationships in Jamaica. As Catherine Hall succinctly puts it, "England was for families, Jamaica was for sex."[76] Even when sexual relations extended into decades—for instance, Thomas Thistlewood, an eighteenth-century Jamaican planter, kept an enslaved woman for sex for over thirty years—this distinction between marriage and sex remained.[77] By contrast, this Scotchman refuses to follow the script in which black women are acceptable only as concubines.

Through the figure of the Scotchman, McKay queers the very notion of genealogical descent by unsettling its literal and metaphorical grounding in nature: the family tree is rooted in perverse ground and produces strange fruit. McKay suggests that blood has the potential to queer place. The idea of the natural does not exist untouched by history, but gains meaning precisely as it comes into intimate contact with history as embodied in the Scotchman and his descendants. In Banana Bottom, the Scotchman becomes one with the land. His blood "has flowed down into a dark-brown stream deep sunk into the soil" (3). "His Negress bore him plenty of children. And his children begat a lot of children," and through them the Scotchman's "strange" blood inseminates and fertilizes the land, producing a place full of "natural aberrations" and "curious little aberrations" (3, 177). Founded on miscegenation driven by fetishistic desire (the "blackest" of women), Banana Bottom is despised by whites from other towns who describe the village and the descendants of the Scotchman as "a picture of decadence and degeneracy" (4). While this founding narrative seems laudatory—enslaved people were freed, marriage offered rather than rape, economic opportunities provided—it is still rife with ideological problems. For instance, how are we to read "the blackest of them" and "His Negress," descriptions that suggest, despite emancipation and marriage, that the Scotchman's black wife remains a fetish object? While McKay traces the forms of cultural and biological hybridity that subtend Banana Bottom, he does not gloss over the troubling racialized histories that persist and create hierarchies. Indeed, these histories trouble intimacy and desire, refusing to read either as resolutions to the complications of history. For McKay, hybrid formulations are queer: odd, anomalous, troubling, and unsettling. And their queerness resonates across generations. The desire and marriage between a formerly enslaved woman and a wealthy former enslaver within a predominantly slave-owning community inaugurates a perverse genealogy—"his children begat a lot of children."

Queering genealogy also unsettles the longstanding metaphorical bond between women and land that takes women's bodies as metonyms for the nation. McKay illustrates the ideological and material labor that conflates body with place. The Scotchman's "blood" inseminates the land of Banana Bottom. Jordan Plant, Bita's father, returns to Banana Bottom, his mother's ancestral home, and "plants" himself there, forging a material bond with the land through cultivation; Aunt Nommy, Bita's stepmother and aunt, roots herself in Banana Bottom by planting luxurious flowers in her compound; Crazy Bow stakes his claim on the land by walking all around Banana Bottom; and Bita establishes her connection to the land by immersing herself in the life and rhythm and geographies of the land. In *Banana Bottom*, the connection to land is neither natural nor inevitable; it emerges through a series of ongoing negotiations and practices, and is not restricted to any one gender.

"Curious Little Aberrations"

Midway through *Banana Bottom*, Bita's fiancé, Herald Newton Day, who is handpicked by her patrons, Reverend and Priscilla Craig, is found in a compromising position with a nanny goat. Importantly, the text does not portray the actual event: "The rumor ran through the region that Herald Newton had suddenly turned crazy and defiled himself with a nanny goat" (175). Subsequently, his family sends him to Panama to escape the scandal. As with Bita, whose rape leads to her leaving, Herald Day's sexual misconduct leads to his exile. It is unclear what sanctions, if any, Herald Day would have faced if he stayed. Banana Bottom is, after all, a town founded by a "tradition-breaking European," an "unpuritan liberator," and incorporates, as one of its values, tolerance for the "good sinner" (9, 39). Indeed, the villagers' nonchalance regarding all matters sexual suggests he might have become the butt of jokes, but little else.

Herald Day's actions set the stage for an important epistemological debate between Squire Gensir, the local eccentric Englishman interested in peasant culture, and Teacher Fearon, the local schoolmaster, a debate that implicitly invokes the figures of Walter Jekyll, McKay's English mentor, and U. Theo, his schoolmaster elder brother. Squire Gensir cannot reconcile Herald Day's behavior with his vision of black peasantry. Following late nineteenth-century sexology and theories of cultural contact, he believes that aberrant sexuality happens to "a different kind of peasantry—a kind that had been stunted and worn out by civilization," not the "primitive," "strangely unfathomable" peasants of Banana Bottom (176). Squire Gensir offers a quasi-Foucauldian account that binds perverse behavior—even the designation "perverse"—to modernity and especially to modern spaces. It should not exist in the hetero-Eden of Banana Bottom. For Squire Gensir, perverse behavior is linked to "culture," not "nature."

Countering this view, Teacher Fearon explains,

> It's all in nature. If I should tell you about my experience with the kids. The curious little aberrations that crop out among them with all kinds of things. Playing with themselves just like toys in their hands. . . . When they grow up they will throw away the toys quite naturally. . . . The only thing strange about this is that one of Herald Day's toys may have remained with him and he growing up with it without being aware. (177–78)

Well aware that peasants are Squire Gensir's hobby, and that he collects indigenous forms of expression, especially songs and stories, Teacher

Fearon avoids providing any specific information, offering, instead, a series of elliptical and euphemistic renderings. "If I should tell you," seems to offer the promise of narrative, one which seems to be somewhat fulfilled by "The curious little aberrations" and "playing with themselves like toys in their hands," but the narratives don't quite add up—they satisfy neither an anthropological demand for detail nor a scientific demand for classification. At most, Teacher Fearon suggests that young children might masturbate. In Glissant's terms, Teacher Fearon asserts his "right to obscurity."[78]

By framing Herald Day's actions within a history of natural childhood play, Teacher Fearon avoids implicating Herald's actions, and by inference the Banana Bottom community, within a Euro-American theory of sexual perversity. His interpretation of Herald Day's actions offers a gentle, even humorous, reminder that intimate practices live within multiple epistemological frames that are historically and geographically specific. Furthermore, Teacher Fearon critiques the assumption that Banana Bottom exists outside of history, while suggesting that the area's history demands we rethink, and mark the limits of, Euro-American sexological categories, which do not account for Afro-diasporic histories and experiences of sexuality. Describing Herald Day's actions through a notion of childhood play, Teacher Fearon refuses to participate in creating normative/non-normative, primitive/civilized binaries that are central to sexology.

If, as I have suggested, Teacher Fearon, and by implication McKay, refuses the normative, disciplinary imperative of Euro-American sexological categories, how do we account for the resonances between Teacher Fearon's developmental explanation and psychoanalytic models of sexual development? Teacher Fearon's explanation about childhood play is remarkably similar to Freud's description of children as polymorphously perverse. Is McKay, as Paul Jay claims, "infected" by dominant discourses?[79] Although the idea of play shares an affinity with psychoanalytic categories, it refuses the foundational category of the perverse. Freud's notion of the polymorphously perverse hinges on the term "perverse," a relation to an implied normative that Teacher Fearon's account does not acknowledge. For instance, Teacher Fearon claims that Herald Day grew up with his toy, eschewing the psychoanalytic (and colonial) language of arrested development. For McKay, the twin notions of play and development are not circumscribed by a notion of normativity. These competing etiological theories dramatize McKay's attempt to queer genealogies of diaspora. He contests normative and normalizing concepts of gender and desire—in hetero-Eden, men desire goats—and foregrounds moments of improper gender and perverse desire.

Perhaps no single character embodies Banana Bottom better than Crazy Bow Adair. A third-generation descendant of the Scotchman and his black wife, Crazy Bow is a brilliant student who is sent by his family to a private institute for boys at Jubilee, the nearest town. During his second year there, Crazy Bow discovers music and "shot right off the straight line and nothing could bring him back" (5). He teaches himself how to play piano and can no longer function within normative conceptions of domesticity and labor. On his return to Banana Bottom, he spends his days wandering about, popping into houses when he hears a new, exciting piece of music, but otherwise itinerant.

Crazy Bow's characterization reveals McKay's syncretic method in *Banana Bottom*. He represents a queer blend of the stereotypes of Creole blacks and figures from McKay's Jamaican childhood. Edward Long, a crucial figure McKay rewrites, claims, "Creole Blacks . . . without being able to read a single note, are known to play twenty or thirty tunes, country dances, minuets, airs, and even sonatas, on the violin; and catch with an astonishing readiness, whatever they hear played or sung, especially if it is lively and striking."[80] A living archive who knows "village tunes, hymns and anthems, jubilee songs and snatches of high music," Crazy Bow is the unofficial pagan priest of Banana Bottom. Each time he plays, he bewitches, seduces, and lulls the residents (6).

His unofficial but crucial priestly rank is confirmed during a religious revival in Banana Bottom. Following an extended three-year drought, during which the villagers sicken from "drinking bad water" and village children come down with "rickets and yaws," a "Briton" named Evan Vaughan begins a "Big Revival" (232). Vaughan attempts to establish himself as the new patriarch of Banana Bottom, recruits all the local young women to be "Sisters in Christ," and, in the process, disrupts social practices such as dances and tea-meetings, which depend on these young women (243, 255). At the height of the revival, Crazy Bow appears at Teacher Fearon's schoolroom, where Bita is playing a selection from Handel's *Judas Maccabaeus*. Taking over from her, he plays the entire oratorio, a string of spirituals that make the "people weep, recreating again the spirit of the ancient martyrdom that still haunted the crumbled stones and rusted iron of many a West Indian plantation," and then turns to dance and tea-meeting tunes that inspire his audience to dance (258). As he plays, news of his performance spreads and the community gathers around to hear him. In retelling the history of the community through music, Crazy Bow reconstitutes its various components. He reconstitutes a history of mixing and blending, marrying the oratorio to the spirituals, invoking the strange marriage of opposites that founded and sustains Banana Bottom. Crazy Bow breaks the "spell" of the revival.

Before moving to the rape, it is equally important to contextualize Bita Plant. The Plant family is anomalous within Banana Bottom. Bita's grandfather, Jaban Plant, is a native of Jubilee, where he worked as a "local agent and purchaser" of coffee beans, and also where he developed a close friendship with the Reverend Angus Craig, Reverend Malcolm's grandfather (18). Following Jaban's death, his son, Jordan, returns with his mother to her native village of Banana Bottom, where she owns a plot of land. Through hard work, he adds to the land he owns and becomes the most prosperous peasant in the village: "Rooted in the soil, Jordan then was obviously the one thriving Plant" (27). Jordan claims a place in Banana Bottom through his unnamed mother, a woman who springs from a perverse land, and is himself planted into the perverse soil of Banana Bottom.

Tabitha, Bita, is Jordan's only child. Born at seven months, she "killed her mother," a description villagers use to describe a child whose mother dies in childbirth. Although a "fragile" baby, she soon becomes "remarkably strong and self reliant." "As a child," McKay writes, "Bita had been given lots of rope to roam around and had developed tomboyish traits" (7). While her abbreviated history is less colorful than Crazy Bow's (she is, after all, only twelve), it is still strange. Born premature, her birth "killed" her mother, suggesting there might be something unnatural about her. Certainly, the villagers have marked her difference. As a child she displays remarkable, and gender-bending, independence, developing "tomboyish traits." She has been given lots of "rope" to roam around. This roaming aligns her with Crazy Bow's vagabond impulse.

Crazy Bow and Bita embody the perverse legacy of the queer land: both practice gender in antinomian ways, both challenge notions of discipline and desire, and both incarnate the queer potential of their genealogical histories. These three factors shape how we interpret Crazy Bow's rape of Bita. As the novel opens, we are told, "Bita was a girl with a past. Between the years of twelve and thirteen she had been raped. She had been raped by Crazy Bow Adair" (2). Despite this forthright statement, critics have debated whether the novel depicts a rape. Kenneth Ramchand, for instance, consistently terms it an "incident," and claims that it "establishes Bita's natural connection with the Banana Bottom world."[81] Echoing, while historicizing Ramchand, Geta LeSeur claims that due to the "setting and era" of the story, "the idea of rape is not developed." As a result, "what its treatment indicates about the culture and about the place of women in that culture is bothersome for contemporary readers."[82] Extending LeSeur through an important feminist intervention, Barbara Griffin argues that by opening the novel with Bita's rape, McKay foregrounds women's "subjugation" as central to the sociocultural world of Banana Bottom.[83] Read together, LeSeur and Griffin bring into focus the conceptual difficulty created by the afterlife of slavery's ungendering: how does one write about sexual violence directed against black girls? Is it possible to write about sexual violence against black girls without subsuming it into the category of violence against black women? Can there be a specificity attached to sexual violence against black girls when the historical category of girlhood is denied to black girls? McKay himself is unambiguous that Bita was raped, and in stating this point emphatically, he demands that we reckon with how to discuss a category of sexual violence that was not recognized as such during (and because of) colonial modernity.

Bita and Crazy Bow are neighbors and playmates, even though he is twenty-five and she is twelve. Although all the other village children are afraid of him, Bita enjoys "romping" with him. The rape takes place as they are romping:

> As they romped, Bita got upon Crazy Bow's breast and began rubbing her head against his face. Crazy Bow suddenly drew himself up and rather roughly he pushed Bita away and she rolled off a little down the slope.

Crazy Bow took up his fiddle, and sitting under a low and shady guava tree he began to play. He played a sweet tea-meeting love song. And as he played Bita went creeping upon her hands and feet up the slope to him and listened in the attitude of a bewitched being.

And when he had finished she clambered upon him again and began kissing his face. Crazy Bow tried to push her off. But Bita hugged and clung to him passionately. Crazy Bow was blinded by temptation and lost control of himself and the deed was done. (9–10)

This passage draws on a tradition of writing that identifies black girls in the tropics as sexually precocious; during slavery and its afterlife, this tradition denied black girls the protective status of girlhood. Even though Crazy Bow Adair has a central place in Banana Bottom, he is still a descendant of the founding family, and this rape invokes the histories of white supremacy and patriarchy that made Banana Bottom possible, the violence that subtends a pastoral ideal.

Characters in the novel struggle to assign meaning to Bita's rape: it occasions glee from those who envy Jordan Plant's middle-class status and, subsequently, envy from those who want Bita's "advantages," including being adopted by the Craigs. Aunt Nommie views it as a premature sexual affair, Sister Phillby evidence of Bita's precociousness, and Priscilla Craig abuse. We have no evidence of how Bita views the event as it transpires, although, later, when she runs into Crazy Bow, she describes it as "that trouble of his adolescence," echoing Teacher Fearon's assessment of Herald Day, and placing full responsibility for the sexual violence on Crazy Bow (257). As the novel nears its conclusion, she terms what happened rape, following a meditation on how memories are shaped: "For a child's actual experiences and those that are related by older relatives are so inextricably mixed in the dawning consciousness of childhood's memories that it is difficult to separate one from the other" (287). Here, she registers the conflicting frames provided by her aunt (it was a "premature sexual affair"), by Sister Phillby (Bita was precocious), and by Priscilla Craig (it was rape), all frameworks she absorbed and attempted to navigate as a girl.

In offering conflicting perspectives on what happened, while retaining the word rape, McKay directs us to consider how kinship (Aunt

Nommie), medicine (Sister Phillby), race and religion (Priscilla Craig) produce different kinds of sexual epistemologies. As in the debate between Squire Gensir and Teacher Fearon that pits a "traditional" versus an "organic" intellectual, these differing perspectives by women interpellate Bita into different frameworks. Like Teacher Fearon, Aunt Nommie embeds Bita's rape into a narrative of sexual experimentation, an interpretation that circumvents pathology and sin, even as it draws on an idea of black girls as sexually precocious. Sister Phillby's report similarly embeds Bita within peasant mores, a blend of malicious gossip and medical concern, although shaped by racist discourse about black girls' sexual precociousness. Her goal is to challenge the implicit relationship between class status and sexual morality then prevalent in Jamaican discourse in which the middle classes measured their distance from peasants by embracing sexual restraint.[84] Bita's "fall" demonstrates middle-class hypocrisy. Where Sister Nommie and Sister Phillby attempt to credit Bita with agency, Priscilla Craig insists that Bita is a "child" and must "have been abused" (16). Of the three women, Priscilla Craig grants the status of black girlhood credibility; simultaneously, in an imperialist vein, she proffers white women as black girls' saviors. For critics, the problem is both formal and ideological. On a formal note, it inhabits the same neighborhood as McKay's use of the ballad, tetrameter, and, in his later works, the sonnet, even for his most radical poems, such as "If We Must Die." We cannot simply ignore the racial histories of these forms and, with Brathwaite, we can ask what using these forms makes impossible. Similarly, McKay borrows and steals from available frameworks to render the complexity of Afro-diasporic life across multiple spheres: some readers may not like that Priscilla Craig names the problem of child abuse, but she helps to create a space to consider black girls *as* girls.

Bita's rape plays a foundational role in *Banana Bottom*: it is the event that drives and haunts the narrative. It plays a genealogical role that enables the very possibility of narrative. This aspect is crucial given that Crazy Bow does not literally impregnate Bita. Instead, the rape engenders rumors, songs, and a novel. By placing Bita's rape as the start of Afro-diasporic narrative, McKay reminds us that even our pursuits of queer diasporas must reckon with the foundational (sexual) violence through which black people enter colonial modernity.

The Marriage Problem

Bita's marriage to Jubban toward the end of the novel appears to mark the limits of McKay's queer labor and suggests a turn toward conservatism, a narrative that accords with one conception of McKay's biography.[85] Within histories of Jamaica and the novel, marriage represents the point of rapprochement, when unruly individuals reconcile their desires with those of society and assume their positions as social subjects. And, certainly, within black diaspora histories more broadly, nothing confers respectability quite like marriage. Combined, these various perspectives seem to support the argument that *Banana Bottom*, much like McKay, moves beyond queer play into heteronormativity. Remarking on the ostensible conservatism of McKay's poetic form in his later career, when he adopted more standard forms like the sonnet, William J. Maxwell argues that McKay "struggle[s] to produce a faithful lyric poetry of modern cataclysm."[86] Extending Maxwell's comments to *Banana Bottom*, we might consider how the form of the novel registers the complex histories of Afro-modernity.

The claim that *Banana Bottom* moves from queer to heteronormative succeeds only if we ignore McKay's genealogical labor and efface the multiple epistemological debates that he stages around the problem of intimacy. From the Scotchman's troubling, fetish-driven marriage to a freed slave, to Herald Day's experiments in bestiality, to Bita's rape, McKay queries how we assign value and meaning to intimate relations. Indeed, as Leah Rosenberg argues, Bita's relationship with Jubban and their first sexual encounter are "troubled" by their "close associations with incest and necromancy": Jubban is Bita's adopted brother and they first consummate their passion in a cart bearing Bita's dead father.[87] Arguably, they follow the path of antinomian intimacies that created and sustain Banana Bottom. Their marriage may have the same formal structure as those privileged in Jamaican colonial histories and in histories of the novel, but its embedding within Banana Bottom's histories requires that we attend to its queer genealogies.

Toward the end of *Banana Bottom*, in one of its more overtly polemical formulations, Bita muses on the meaning of love. Reflecting on her life with Jubban, she distinguishes her present conception of love from her "early romantic" idea that "thought of love as a kind of mystical force, incomprehensible and uncontrollable" (313). She rejects this formulation as "a borrowed thing, an exotic imposition," privileging instead the "real intrinsic thing that had flowered out of the mind of her race" (313). This turn toward a genealogical, even organic notion of indigenous love should be read within the context of the perverse land Bita inhabits. It is not simply a racialized turn divorced from history, but a turn toward the forms of love that "flower" from a community grounded in a perverse land. Bita's striking formulation binds an organic metaphor, "flowering," to the act of imagination, "the mind of her race," a conjunction that foregrounds Afro-diasporic modes of intimacy as innovative rather than genealogically normative.

In the conclusion to *The West Indian Novel and Its Background,* Ramchand argues, "After all his journeyings and all his explorations of roots and affinities, and because of these, Claude McKay was able to return to his island spiritually and imagine in *Banana Bottom* a community to which it is possible to belong."[88] Ramchand's rich phrase, "to which it is possible to belong," captures the essence of McKay's expansive imagination. In *Banana Bottom* McKay depicts flexible modes of belonging rooted in a wide range of intimate practices. Against the exclusionary practices privileged by hetero-colonialism and, later on, hetero-nationalism, McKay suggests that queer genealogies of intimacy provide powerful paradigms for creating dense, rewarding networks of association and affiliation, spaces and practices where queer diasporic radicals can belong.

beginnings, in seven movements

1.

Frottage starts in a matatu, with a makanga yelling "kaa square," changing a fourteen-seater van into a multi-configuration of mothers handing their children to strangers to hold, luggage being squeezed into multidimensional crevices, capacity being stretched beyond meaning, and then beyond that. Bodies move against each other, learning new choreography with each twist and turn, each bump and pothole, each alighting and gathering. Our silences mingle with our conversation, our fantasies with our quotidian, and, for the length of a journey, we are rubbing along.

2.

Frottage begins with your fingers flipping through pages, feeling the texture of paper or screen, shifting position on your chair, perhaps adjusting a cushion or tucking a blanket, holding a pet or moving it to the side, pausing to touch your hair, scratch an itch, grab a pen to take notes, or slide your finger along a screen to underline something. Scratching your head in frustration, moving with the liquid of the words, resisting their lure, demanding friction, a more textured argument, a more rigorous engagement with this or that, a scene that grapples with the unbearable. A stop. There is syncopation. Geographies start and stop. A beat continues.

3.

What's touching you now? Who do you want to touch you? Where do you want to be touched? How do you want to be touched?

4.

Frottage pauses at the motion of trends and waves, the still-dominant, too-dominant Hegelian *aufhebeng* that is supposed to guide critical thinking. First this, then that, then a this-and-that which becomes a this. Permit this vulgar rendering. I experience this as unconvincing. Raymond Williams gets closer to it—what it? truth? experience? knowledge?—when he discusses the dominant, the residual, and the emergent. One experienced as present, the other as the past-that-is-not-past, and the other as the inchoate future-in-the-present.

From the position of arrest that is blackness—from the afterlife of slavery—I continue to ask why the coordinates feel so familiar. Why the cartographies of the world's waterways—the Indian Ocean, the Atlantic, the Mediterranean—continue to be saturated with black people's suffering. Why residence time continues to be extended:

> The amount of time it takes for a substance to enter the ocean and then leave the ocean is called residence time. Human blood is salty, and sodium . . . has a residence time of 260 million years. . . . We, Black people, exist in the residence time of the wake.[1]

And against this deep untimely time, the interruption: the noose the bullet the lynching the poisoning the bombing the camps the mass graves the killing that makes futures difficult

but not impossible

never impossible.

5.

Frottage is the frantic rubbing of a tongue against the mouth's soft palate, the scratch-red eyes that announce pollen season, fertilizing season, harvest season. The cautions not to rub your eyes as you try to grab that thing inside that will not cease, that prickle, that scratch, that irritation.

6.

Frottage is wool-scratch fabrics that promised to be soft, detergent-washed towels that promised to be soft, plush sofa seats that promised to be soft, eco-conscious cushions that promised to be soft, sand-grit beaches that promised relaxation. The endless ways skin is reminded it is present, and feels.

7.

Frottage is this: my words in your hands, my words on your eyes, my words in your mind, rubbing along and against, perhaps working your last nerve, perhaps extending something, perhaps sitting, pressure that builds into rubbing, perhaps pleasurable, perhaps not.

We rub along and against.

Frottage.

ACKNOWLEDGMENTS

Many people have dared me to risk thinking. They have provided space, with love and patience, for eccentric prose, stylized ideas, the play of fashion(ing) and substance. They have indulged flights of fancy and the extended life of intuition that too often functions as my thinking. And they have taught me how to imagine together, across difference, across geohistories, toward freedom.

In Kiswahili the word *Mwalimu* conveys immense respect and gratitude. It translates as teacher. I invoke it here as an inadequate way to acknowledge the many teachers who have shaped my life. My immeasurable thanks to Linda Kinnahan, who first valued my thinking; to Dan Watkins, who first let me know that black queer studies mattered; and to Beth Rich, who valued my obsession with Harlem Renaissance poetry.

At the University of Illinois at Urbana–Champaign, I encountered a community of thinkers, who taught me it was possible to join the words "community" and "thinkers" without irony. I am grateful to my teachers: Ania Loomba, Tim Dean, Martin Manalansan, Jean Allman, Antoinette Burton, and Matti Bunzl. Bill Maxwell trusted that I could think about Claude McKay, and I hope I have justified that trust.

At the University of Maryland, College Park, I was privileged to have colleagues who valued my thinking. I'm grateful to Bob Levine, Zita Nunes, Kandice Chuh, Mary Helen Washington, and Carla Peterson. Sangeeta Ray made my life immeasurably richer.

Over a meal in Nairobi, Tavia Nyong'o convinced me that this manuscript should leave my hard drive. I am grateful to him and the other series editors of Sexual Cultures—Ann Pellegrini and Joshua Chambers-Letson—for giving *Frottage* a home. At NYU Press, I'm grateful to Eric Zinner for walking me through the publication process, even with the seven-hour time difference. I thank Dolma Ombadykow for her meticulous work and care. And I'm grateful to the production team—copyeditors, designers—for their wonderful work.

For intellectual community and friendship, I thank Elizabeth Angell, Adia Benton, Darius Bost, Sarah Jane Cervenak, Petero Kalulé, Dina Ligaga, Grace Musila, Chris Taylor, and Rinaldo Walcott.

For imagining freedom and working toward it, I am grateful to Mariame Kaba.

This work would not have been possible without Praseeda Gopinath, Melissa Free, Christina Walter, Christina Hanhardt, and Dana Carluccio.

Other friends made my life possible in too many ways to enumerate. My thanks to Martha Nell Smith, Marilee Lindemann, Christina Sharpe, Kweli Jaoko, Sofia Samatar, and Aaron Bady. Christina, Sofia, and Aaron have been ideal readers, full of generosity and care.

For their capacious, freedom-making imaginations, I thank Mukami Kuria, Nanjala Nyabola, Wairimu Muriithi, Ngwatilo Mawiyoo, Lutivini Majanja, Neo Musangi, Aleya Kassam, and Bethuel Muthee.

This book exists because of Siobhan Somerville and Jed Esty. Thank you.

Melissa Girard has lived with my thinking and my passions and my idiosyncrasies and my obsessions for far longer than I would have imagined possible, and with grace and love. Because of her, I did not have to read Foucault to understand that friendship is a way of living.

NOTES

INTRODUCTION: FROTTAGE

1 Haley, *Roots*, 150.
2 See Sharpe, *Monstrous Intimacies*.
3 Haley, *Roots*, 179.
4 For recent examples, see Foster, *Love and Marriage* and Hunter, *Bound in Wedlock*.
5 Robinson, *Black Marxism*, 113.
6 Spillers, "Mama's Baby, Papa's Maybe," 69.
7 McKittrick, "Mathematics Black Life," 16–17.
8 See Weheliye, *Habeas Viscus*.
9 Hartman, *Lose Your Mother*, 6.
10 I take this language of "writing back" and my critique of it from postcolonial studies. I am especially grateful to James Hodapp, whose dissertation critiquing the "writing back" paradigm in African studies helped to shape my thinking.
11 Morrison, *Playing in the Dark*.
12 Sedgwick, *Touching Feeling*, 150–51.
13 On speculation as a critical method, see Kazanjian, "Scenes of Speculation."
14 Lewis, "To Turn as on a Pivot."
15 Ngai, *Ugly Feelings*, 6, 7.
16 See Herskovitz, "The Negro in the New World" and Frazier, "The Negro Slave Family."
17 Berlant and Warner, "Sex in Public," 548.
18 See Delany, *Times Square Red, Times Square Blue*; Hanhardt, *Safe Space*; Luibhéid, *Entry Denied*; and Reddy, *Freedom with Violence*.
19 Crummell, "The Race-Problem in America," 167, emphasis in original.
20 Mintz and Price, *Birth of African-American Culture*, 65.
21 Mintz and Price, *Birth of African-American Culture*, 66.
22 Mintz and Price, *Birth of African-American Culture*, 66, emphasis in original.
23 Berlant and Warner, "Sex in Public," 548.
24 Nzegwu, *Family Matters*, 5.
25 Povinelli, "Notes on Gridlock," 215.
26 Baker, *Modernism and the Harlem Renaissance*, 106, emphasis in original.
27 Okpewho, "Introduction," *The New African Diaspora*, xi, xiv.
28 I thank Sangeeta Ray for this formulation.

29 Edwards, "Langston Hughes and the Futures of Diaspora."

30 Blyden, *African Life and Customs*, n.p.

31 A vibrant, broadly conceived newspaper culture existed in the nineteenth cen-
    tury: black people across Africa and Afro-diaspora were reading and responding
    to each other primarily through newspapers. But I would argue that it is only
    in the twentieth century, as different groups assemble in Paris and London and
    Accra and Kampala and Dar es Salaam, that we truly see richly representative
    exchanges.

32 I take this account from Lynch, *Edward Wilmot Blyden*.

33 Blyden, *African Life and Customs*, 10.

34 Blyden, *African Life and Customs*, 11, emphasis in original.

35 Long, *History of Jamaica*, 3:383.

36 Duty has a strong presence in contemporary African philosophy. For instance,
    Nigerian philosopher Ifeanyi Menkiti writes, "African societies tend to be
    organized around the requirements of duty while Western societies tend to be
    organized around the postulation of individual rights" ("Person and Commu-
    nity," 182).

37 Blyden, *African Life and Customs*, 24. On urban women in European modernity,
    see Walkowitz, *City of Dreadful Delight* and Showalter, *Sexual Anarchy*.

38 Blyden, *African Life and Customs*, 24–25.

39 Blyden, *African Life and Customs*, 25.

40 Blyden, *African Life and Customs*, 21.

41 Blyden, *African Life and Customs*, 13, emphasis in original.

42 Mbiti, *Introduction to African Religion*, 110.

43 Wiredu, "The Moral Foundations of an African Culture," 205.

44 Menkiti, "On the Normative Conception of a Person," 326.

45 For instance, Menkiti was born in Nigeria, completed his BA (Pomona)
    through PhD (Harvard) in the United States, and, until his retirement, was
    on faculty at Wellesley College. Born in Ghana, Kwasi Wiredu was educated
    in Ghana (University of Ghana, Legon) and England (Oxford), taught at the
    University of Ghana for twenty-three years, and then from 1987, taught at
    the University of South Florida in Tampa. Perhaps the most famous African
    philosophers in the United States, Valentin Mudimbe and Kwame Appiah, are
    associated with Duke and Princeton, respectively. Among African women phi-
    losophers, Nkiru Nzegwu is at SUNY Binghamton and Oyèrónkẹ́ Oyěwùmí is at
    SUNY Stony Brook.

46 Walcott, "Outside in Black Studies," 97.

47 See Edwards, *The Practice of Diaspora*.

48 See Carby, "'On the Threshold of Woman's Era.'"

49 Hall, "New Ethnicities," 441.

50 Hall, "New Ethnicities," 441.

51 Hall, "New Ethnicities," 444.

52 Hall, "New Ethnicities," 445.

53 Hall, New Ethnicities," 447.

54 See Nyong'o, *The Amalgamation Waltz*.

55 Gilroy, *Black Atlantic*, 2.

56 Gilroy, *Black Atlantic*, 2, 99, 85, 194.

57 Gilroy, *Black Atlantic*, 101.

58 Gilroy, *Black Atlantic*, 91–92.

59 Gilroy, *Black Atlantic*, 101.

60 For examples of this influence, see Jaji, *Africa in Stereo* and Ntarangwi, *East African Hip Hop*.

61 See Browne, *Dark Matters*.

62 For a powerful argument on this, see Nunes, *Cannibal Democracy*.

63 Lorde, *Sister Outsider*, 22.

64 Césaire, *Discourse on Colonialism*, 42.

65 Spillers, "Mama's Baby, Papa's Maybe," 67, emphasis in original.

66 Snorton, *Black on Both Sides*, 57.

67 Oyěwùmí, *Invention of Women*, ix.

68 Oyěwùmí, *Invention of Women*, ix–x.

69 For an extraordinary exception, see Musangi, "Homing with My Mother."

70 Tinsley, "Black Atlantic, Queer Atlantic," 192, emphasis in original.

71 Robinson ends his preface to the second edition of *Black Marxisim*: "In short, as a scholar, it was never my intention to exhaust the subject, only to suggest that it was there" (xxxii).

CHAPTER 1. FRANTZ FANON'S HOMOSEXUAL TERRITORIES

1 Fanon, *Black Skin, White Masks* (trans. Markmann), 155, 156, 177, 180, 183. Cited hereafter as *BSWM*. I alternate between the Markmann and Philcox translations in this chapter.

2 See Edelman, *Homographesis*, ch. 3 and Fuss, "Interior Colonies."

3 Mercer, "Decolonisation," 128.

4 Moten, "The Case of Blackness," 182.

5 Fanon, *BSWM* (trans. Markmann), 12.

6 For such a claim, see Gordon, "Through the Zone of Nonbeing," 22–24.

7 I take "identity-constituting" and "identify-fracturing" from Sedgwick, "Queer and Now," 9.

8 For this account, I rely on Macey, *Frantz Fanon*, Kindle edition.

9 Sharpe, *In the Wake*, 30.

10 Fanon, *BSWM* (trans. Philcox), xv.

11 Fanon, *BSWM* (trans. Philcox), 130.

12 See Bhabha, "What Does the Black Man Want?"; Fuss, "Interior Colonies"; and Bergner, "Who Is That Masked Woman?" and "Politics and Pathologies."

13 Fanon, *BSWM* (trans. Philcox), 120.

14 Fanon, *BSWM* (trans. Philcox), 121.

15 Fanon, *BSWM* (trans. Philcox), 127.

16 Wynter, "Towards the Sociogenic Principle," 40.

17 Wynter, "Towards the Sociogenic Principle," 40, emphasis in original.

18 McKittrick, "Rebellion/Invention/Groove," 83, emphasis in original.

19 Kara Keeling writes, "Common sense contains elements that consent to dominant hegemonies, as well as to aspects that are antagonistic to them. It can be understood as a record of a group's survival, incorporating compromises to dominating and exploitative forces while retaining challenges to those forces" (*The Witch's Flight*, Kindle edition).

20 Fanon, *BSWM* (trans. Philcox), 122.

21 Fanon, *BSWM* (trans. Philcox), 118.

22 Fanon, *BSWM* (trans. Philcox), 135.

23 Fanon, *BSWM* (trans. Philcox), 137, 143, 154, 157.

24 Edelman, *No Future*, 17, emphasis in original.

25 Wynter, "Unsettling," 260.

26 Using the more economical "white and black men" presumes an equivalence that cannot exist within the phylogeny, psychoanalysis-as-ontogeny, and sociogeny triad. Hence, I use "white men and black men."

27 Fanon, *BSWM* (trans. Philcox), 132.

28 Fanon, *BSWM* (trans. Philcox), 123.

29 Qtd. in Fanon, *BSWM* (trans. Philcox), 133.

30 Fanon, *BSWM* (trans. Philcox), 133, emphasis in original.

31 Fanon, *BSWM* (trans. Markmann), 155, emphasis in original.

32 Fanon, *BSWM* (trans. Philcox), 155.

33 Fanon, *BSWM* (trans. Philcox), 135.

34 Fanon, *BSWM* (trans. Philcox), 134–35.

35 For a strong defense of Fanon's gender politics, see Sharpley-Whiting, "Fanon and Capecia."

36 Mumford, *Interzones*, 13.

37 Hodes, "The Sexualization of Reconstruction Politics," 404.

38 Macey, *Frantz Fanon*, Kindle edition.

39 Dollimore, *Sexual Dissidence*, 346.

40 Edelman, *Homographesis*, 55.

41 Fanon, *BSWM* (trans. Philcox), 165.

42 Fanon, *BSWM* (trans. Philcox), 168.

43 Fanon, *BSWM* (trans. Philcox), 168.

44 Fanon, *BSWM* (trans. Philcox), 168.

45 Fanon, *BSWM* (trans. Philcox), 126.

46 Fanon, *BSWM* (trans. Philcox), xxxiii, emphasis in original.

47 Fanon, *BSWM* (trans. Philcox), 150, emphasis in original.

48 Goldie, "Saint Fanon and 'Homosexual Territory,'" 78.

49 Reid-Pharr, *Black Gay Man*, 85.

50 For recent scholarship on homosexuality in contemporary Martinique, see Agard-Jones, "Le Jeu de Qui?" and Murray, "Between a Rock and a Hard Place."

51 Baruk, qtd. in Fanon, *BSWM* (trans. Philcox), 157–58.

52 Fanon, *BSWM* (trans. Philcox), 157–58.

53 Fanon, *Peau Noire*, 146.

54 Berlant and Warner, "Sex in Public," 548.

55 Mercer, "Decolonisation," 125.

56 Fuss, "Interior Colonies," 33.

57 Fanon, *BSWM* (trans. Philcox), xii.

58 Fanon, *BSWM* (trans. Markmann), 9, 10, 63 (emphasis in original), 72, 231, 232.

59 Fanon writes, "I seriously hope to persuade my brother, whether black or white, to tear off with all his strength the shameful livery put together by centuries of incomprehension" (*BSWM* [trans. Markmann], 12).

60 Fanon, *BSWM* (trans. Markmann), 218, emphasis in orginal.

61 Fanon, *BSWM* (trans. Philcox), 193.

62 Fanon, *Peau Noire*, 177.

63 Fanon, *BSWM* (trans. Markmann), 63; 47 on Mayotte Capecia and "lactification"; 66–69 on Jean Veneuse and his desire to marry the white Andrée Marielle; 158–59 on the prostitute who experiences climax at the thought of having sex with black men, especially the black athlete; 46, "The fact that Algerian colonists go to bed with their fourteen-year-old housemaids in no way demonstrates a lack of racial conflicts in Algeria"; 177, "There are, for instance, men who go to 'houses' in order to be beaten by Negroes; passive homosexuals who insist on black partners."

64 Bhabha, "What Does the Black Man Want?" 118, emphasis in original.

65 Bhabha, "What Does the Black Man Want?" 119.

66 Fanon, *BSWM* (trans. Philcox), 1.

67 Spillers, "All the Things You Could Be," 376.

68 Bhabha, "What Does the Black Man Want?" 121.

69 Bhabha, "What Does the Black Man Want?" 121.

70 Gordon, *What Fanon Said*, Kindle edition.

71 Hocquenghem, *Screwball Asses*, 59.

72 For thinking about queerness in this way, see Dean, *Beyond Sexuality*.

73 Holland, *Erotic Life of Racism*, Kindle edition.

74 Fanon, *BSWM* (trans. Philcox), 204, emphasis in original.

75 Fanon, *BSWM* (trans. Philcox), 206.

76 Tinsley, "Black Atlantic, Queer Atlantic," 192, emphasis in original.

77 Hartman, "Venus in Two Acts," 6.

78 Holland, *Erotic Life of Racism*, Kindle edition.

79 Gill, "In the Realm of Our Lorde," 183–84.

80 Fanon, *BSWM* (trans. Philcox), 157.

81 Berkshire Conference of Women Historians, https://berksconference.org/about/history/.

82 Bernstein, "Coming of Age," 5, 6.

83 Benson and Melosh, "Fourth Berkshire Conference," 143, 144, 148.

84 While hunting and pecking for keywords is a suspect method, I am emboldened by Fanon's own disregard for method: "It is good form to introduce a work in psychology with a statement of its methodological point of view. I shall be derelict. I leave methods to the botanists and mathematicians. There is a point at which methods devour themselves" (*BSWM* [trans. Markmann], 12).

85 Lorde, "My Words Will Be There," 161.

86 Cassandra Ellerbe-Dueck and Gloria Wekker, "Naming Ourselves as Black Women in Europe," in *The Wind Is Spirit*, ed. Joseph, 61.

87 Kraft, "Bonds of Sisterhood," in *The Wind Is Spirit*, ed. Joseph, 48.

88 Kraft, "Bonds of Sisterhood," in *The Wind Is Spirit*, ed. Joseph, 52.

89 Tinsley, "Black Atlantic, Queer Atlantic"; McKittrick, "Mathematics Black Life"; Lindsey and Johnson, "Searching for Climax."

90 Lorde, "Uses of the Erotic," in *Sister Outsider*, 53.

91 Lorde, "An Interview: Audre Lorde and Adrienne Rich," in *Sister Outsider*, 101.

92 Kraft, "Bonds of Sisterhood," in *The Wind Is Spirit*, ed. Joseph, 47.

93 Sharpe, *In the Wake*, 79.

94 Lorde, "Uses of the Erotic," 56.

95 Lorde, "Uses of the Erotic," 57.

96 Fanon, *BSWM* (trans. Markmann), 232.

97 Irigaray, "When Our Lips Speak Together" and Philip, *She Tries Her Tongue*.

98 Hemphill, "Now We Think," in *Ceremonies*, 155.

99 Califia, *Public Sex* and Delany, *Times Square Red, Times Square Blue*.

100 Delany, *Times Square Red, Times Square Blue*, 46.

101 Fanon, *BSWM* (trans. Philcox), 24.

102 Macharia, "Love," 69.

103 Fanon, *BSWM* (trans. Philcox), 24.

104 Spillers, "Mama's Baby, Papa's Maybe," 74.

105 Fanon, *BSWM* (trans. Philcox), 197.

CHAPTER 2. MOURNING THE EROTIC IN RENÉ MARAN'S *BATOUALA*

1 On Maran's influence on Harlem Renaissance writers see Ikonné, "René Maran and the New Negro"; on Negritude writers, see Kesteloot, *Black Writers in French* and Edwards, *The Practice of Diaspora*; and on Cuban writers, Miller, "Remoteness and Proximity."

2 Edwards, *The Practice of Diaspora*, 28.

3 Maran, *Batouala*, 91–92. Hereafter, page citations to this work will appear in the text.

4 See Dynes, "Homosexuality in Sub-Saharan Africa" and Zabus, *Out in Africa*.

5 Nzegwu, "Osunality," 9.

6 Crimp, "Mourning and Militancy," 11.

7 Haley, *Roots*, 679–80.

8 Hartman, *Lose Your Mother*, 41–42.

9 Pierre, *The Predicament of Blackness*, esp. ch. 5, Kindle edition.

10 The win was celebrated in the African American press: "Colored Author Wins Prize," *Savannah Tribune*, December 22, 1921; "Honor Given When Due," *The Appeal* (St. Paul, Minnesota), December 31, 1921; "Negro Wins Goncourt Prize," *Savannah Tribune*, January 5, 1922; "Literary Prize to Negro: Prix Goncourt Prize Awarded to West Indian Novelist," *Washington Bee*, January 21, 1922. When the book was translated into English, it was also widely reviewed: Review of *Batouala*, *Broad Axe* (Chicago), March 4, 1922; "The Great Novel—Batouala," *Cleveland Gazette*, July 8, 1922. The January 5, 1922, *Savannah Tribune* review was also published as "Darkest Africa: Batouala, by Rene Maran, the Negro Author, Arouses the Literary People in France," *Negro Star* (Wichita, KS), January 6, 1922.

11 Review of *Batouala*, *Cleveland Gazette*, October 22, 1922.

12 Locke, "The Colonial Literature of France," *Works*, 37–38.

13 Locke, "Negro Youth Speaks," in *Works*, 185.

14 The February 1922 issue announced, "The March *CRISIS* will print the Annual Report of the N. A. A. C. P., an article on Gandhi, the Indian leader, and our annual book review, including Maran's *Batouala*." *The Crisis* 23.4 (1922): n.p.; Fauset writes, "This is really a great novel" in "No End of Books," *The Crisis* 23.5 (1922): 208–9.

15 Fauset, "No End of Books," 208.

16 Fauset, "No End of Books," 208.

17 On modernist primitivism, see Torgovnick, *Gone Primitive*.

18 "Negro Wins Goncourt Prize," *Savannah Tribune*.

19 See Campbell, *Middle Passages*.

20 Mary White Ovington, Review of *Batouala*, *Broad Axe*, March 4, 1922.

21 Nwezeh, "René Maran," 91, 93.

22 Diabate, "René Maran's *Batouala* and Africa," 171.

23 Fanon, *BSWM* (trans. Philcox), 9–10.

24 Miller, *Blank Darkness*, 5.

25 Blyden, *Aims and Methods*, 6.

26 Blyden, *Aims and Methods*, 9.

27 Wynter, "Unsettling," 261.

28 Fanon, *BSWM* (trans. Philcox), 118.

29 Blyden, *Aims and Methods*, 17.

30 Blyden, *Aims and Methods*, 18.

31 Blyden, *African Life and Customs*, 11.

32 Fanon, *BSWM* (trans. Philcox), 91.

33 On the limits of the sex-gender system, see Oyěwùmí, *Invention of Women*; on the new possibilities opened by colonial modernity, see White, *The Comforts of Home* and Kanogo, *African Womanhood in Colonial Kenya*.

34 See Nzegwu, "Osunality."

35 See especially *Totem and Taboo*.

36 I'm thinking of Delany's *Times Square Red, Times Square Blue* and *Through the Valley of the Nest of Spiders* and Califia's *Public Sex*.

37 Fanon, *BSWM* (trans. Philcox), 191 (emphasis in original), 89.

38 Fanon, *BSWM* (trans. Philcox), 89.

39 Spillers, "Mama's Baby, Papa's Maybe," 67.

40 The 1922 translation of *Batouala* by Adele Szold Seltzer, the one that would have been available to English readers in the 1920s, renders this passage as, "Yassiguindja wore an emblem that indicated the role she was to play in the dance." Jessie Fauset and Alain Locke, both champions of Maran, were fluent in French and probably read the French and English versions of the book. Would English-language readers of the book have understood "emblem" and "role" as euphemisms for "wooden phallus"? Did those readers who understood French guide English-language readers? I am unable to pursue these questions here, but I mark them as ways of thinking about translation as textual and oral, circulating in ways that focusing solely on textual translation misses.

41 Spillers, "Mama's Baby, Papa's Maybe," 67.

42 Oyěwùmí, *Invention of Women*, ix.

43 Alexander, "Erotic Autonomy as a Politics of Decolonization," 64.

44 Williams, *Marxism and Literature*, 121–27.

45 Yee, "*Batouala*, the First 'Roman Nègre,' and Dialogism," 53.

46 Ikonné, "René Maran, 1887–1960," 14, 13.

47 Herdeck, Introduction to *Batouala*, 2.

48 Alloula, *Colonial Harem*, 39.

49 Török, "Illness of Mourning."

CHAPTER 3. ETHNICITY AS FROTTAGE IN JOMO KENYATTA'S *FACING MOUNT KENYA*

1 For these viewpoints, see Berman, "Ethnography as Politics"; Shaw, *Colonial Inscriptions*; and Owusu, "On Indigenous Anthropology."

2 See Desai, *Subject to Colonialism* and Gikandi, "Cultural Translation and the African Self" and "Pan-Africanism and Cosmopolitanism."

3 I follow Kenyan scholar Joyce Nyairo's practice that "Kikuyu" is appropriate when writing in English. However, I retain Kenyatta's own use of "Gikuyu." See Nyairo, *Kenya @ 50*.

4 Kenyatta, *Facing Mount Kenya*, 156.

5 Kenyatta, *Facing Mount Kenya*, 154–56.

6 Blyden, *African Life and Customs*, 13.

7 Burton, *Sotadic Zone*, 77.

8 I owe this line of thinking to Loomba, "'Delicious Traffick.'"

9 On the general trope of degeneration, see Chamberlin and Gilman, eds., *Degeneration*.

10 Krafft-Ebing, *Psychopathia Sexualis*, 4.

11 Somerville, *Queering the Color Line*, 27.

12 An East African high school textbook reads, "In [1896] alarmed at the revival of homosexuality and drunkenness at Mwanga's court and the steady increase in his personal entourage, the Christian government leaders had hundreds of young men and boys removed from the Kabaka's service" (Michael Tidy with Donald Leeming, *A History of Africa, 1840–1914* [New York: Africana Publishing, 1981], 61).

13 Hoad, *African Intimacies*, 3–7.

14 See Levine, *Prostitution, Race and Politics*, 37–59; Stoler, *Carnal Knowledge*, 101–6; and Povinelli, *Economies of Abandonment*, Kindle edition.

15 See Hansen, ed., *African Encounters with Domesticity*.

16 Oyěwùmí, *Invention of Women*, ix.

17 See Davis, "On the Sexuality of 'Town Women' in Kampala"; Akyeampong, "Sexuality and Prostitution among the Akan of the Gold Coast"; and Allman, "Rounding Up Spinsters."

18 Malinowski, *Sex and Repression*, 74–75.

19 Gikandi, "Cultural Translation and the African Self," 364.

20 See Muriuki, *A History of the Kikuyu, 1500–1900*.

21 "Minutes of the first meeting of the Kyambu Local Native Council held at Kyambu on Friday the 17th July 1925," Native Council Minutes Kiambu District 1925–1934, PC/CENT/2/1/4, Kenya National Archives, cited hereafter as KNA.

22 Murray-Brown, *Kenyatta*, 62–63.

23 *Muigwithania* 1.6 (1928): n.p.

24 Petro N. Kingondu, "Uria Tungikuria Bururi," *Muigwithania* 1.7 (1928): 7–8.

25 *Muigwithania* 1.3 (1928): 8.

26 See Bujra, "Women 'Entrepreneurs' of Early Nairobi" and White, "Bodily Fluids and Usufruct."

27 G. H. M. Kagika, "Uiguano wa Mutigaire," *Muigwithania* 1.3 (1928): 10.

28 Kagika, "Uiguano wa Mutigairie," 11.

29 For a more extended version of this argument, see Macharia, "How Does a Girl Grow into a Woman?"

30 Until 1920, present-day Kenya was called British East Africa, and what is now called Central Province, the elders' home, was termed Kenya Province. It was renamed Kikuyu Province in 1920 and, later on, Central Province. "A Short History of the Kikuyu Province from 1911–1927," PC/C.6/1/1/2, KNA.

31 M. W. H. Beech, "The Kikuyu Point of View," December 12, 1912, PC/CP/1/4/2, KNA. This record is unique in representing native voices. These voices became more available in the mid-1920s when the colonial government instituted Local Native Councils. Council members included members of the colonial administration and selected native representatives.

32 "Kwonjoritha kwa Airitu na Atumia Kwa Waru na Indu Ingi Gicuka-Nairobi Nikuo Kiambariria Kia Uura Matu," *Muigwithania* 1.8 (1928): 8.

33 Minutes: November 22, 23, 1928, Minute No. 65/28, Native Council Minutes Kiambu District, 1925–34, PC/CENT/2/1/4, box 1, KNA.

34 Tabitha Wangui wa Thomas Kamau, "Mugambo wa Mutumia," *Muigwithania* 2.1 (1929): 10. While indebted to the rich work on female genital cutting (FGC), I use the Kikuyu term *irua* because it more accurately represents the Kikuyu worldview in the period under discussion.

35 Qtd. in Wipper, "Kikuyu Women and the Harry Thuku Disturbances," 315.

36 Personal communication.

37 James, "From Touissant L'Ouverture to Fidel Castro," 300.

38 Edwards, *The Practice of Diaspora*, 8–9.

39 "Muranagia kai wi Muthungu Niki?" *Muigwithania* 1.4 (1928): 9.

40 Murray-Brown, *Kenyatta*, 133–40.

41 See McClellan, "Africans and Black Americans in the Comintern Schools."

42 McClellan, "Africans and Black Americans in the Comintern Schools," 80.

43 According to Winston James, British agents considered these "expatriate radicals" to be relatively benign, "like children at play," unable to affect "the sturdy metropolitan structure of metropolitan Britain" (*Holding Aloft the Banner of Ethiopia*, 76).

44 For an extended discussion of this group, see Polsgrove, *Ending British Rule in Africa*, esp. chs. 1–4.

45 I take the phrase "deep reserve" from Leopold Senghor, who mistakenly attributed it to Claude McKay (Edwards, *The Practice of Diaspora*, 188).

46 Edwards, "The Uses of Diaspora," 67.

47 Edwards, "The Uses of Diaspora," 54.

48 Edwards, "The Uses of 'Diaspora,'" 64.

49 James, *Black Jacobins*, 7.

50 Aaron Kamugisha writes, "One of the conundrums of thinking about C. L. R. James on gender is that his early literary work, written in Trinidad in the late 1920s, centers black women's subjectivity and thematizes gendered concerns in a manner that he would not fully return to until the end of his life" ("The Hearts of Men?" 79).

51 Qtd. in Kamugisha, "The Hearts of Men?" 80.

52 Kamugisha, "The Hearts of Men?" 82.

53 James, *Black Jacobins*, 16.

54 James, *Black Jacobins*, 21.

55 James, *Black Jacobins*, 20.

56 James, *Black Jacobins*, 40.

57 James, *Black Jacobins*, 92.

58 James, *Black Jacobins*, 90, 254.

59 In a footnote added to the revised 1962 edition, James writes that some of his observations in 1938 "were intended to use the San Domingo revolution as a forecast of the future of colonial Africa" (*Black Jacobins*, 18n12). In his final chapter, "The War of Independence," he makes explicit the contemporary stakes of his work

by posing comparisons between black people in Africa and the black people and mulattoes of San Domingo (375–77).

60 James, *Black Jacobins*, 19.
61 Edmondson, *Making Men.*
62 Kenyatta, *Facing Mount Kenya*, xvi.
63 For a critique of these concepts, see Magubane, "A Critical Look."
64 Lugard, "The International Institute of African Languages and Cultures," 3.
65 See Malinowski, "Practical Anthropology."
66 See Safran, "Diaspora in Modern Societies" and Rose, *States of Fantasy.*
67 James, "From Touissant L'Ouverture to Fidel Castro," 398.
68 Polsgrove, *Ending British Rule in Africa*, 25.
69 Qtd. in Polsgrove, *Ending British Rule in Africa*, 134.
70 Polsgrove, *Ending British Rule in Africa*, 41.
71 See Berman and Lonsdale, "The Labors of '*Muigwithania*.'"
72 See Tate, "Notes on the Kikuyu"; Hobley, "Kikuyu Medicines"; and Dundas, "Kikuyu Calendar."
73 Fabian, *Time and the Other*, 32.
74 Kenyatta, *Facing Mount Kenya*, xvi, xix.
75 Kenyatta, *Facing Mount Kenya*, 21, xix–xx.
76 Kenyatta, *Facing Mount Kenya*, xvii.
77 Nyong'o, "Unburdening Representation," 71.
78 Nyong'o, "Unburdening Representation," 77.
79 Barlow, Review of *Facing Mount Kenya*, 114.
80 Barlow, Review of *Facing Mount Kenya,* 115.
81 Barlow, Review of *Facing Mount Kenya*, 115.
82 Barlow, Review of *Facing Mount Kenya*, 114.
83 Later on, Barlow would edit the first Kikuyu-English dictionary.
84 Berman, "Ethnography as Politics," 333.
85 Gikandi, qtd. in Desai, *Subject to Colonialism*, 108–9; Desai, *Subject to Colonialism*, 108.
86 Kenyatta, *Facing Mount Kenya*, 128.
87 Kenyatta, *Facing Mount Kenya*, 149, emphasis added.
88 Kenyatta, *Facing Mount Kenya*, 151.
89 Leakey, *Southern Kikuyu before 1903*, 739.
90 Leakey, *Southern Kikuyu before 1903*, 739.
91 Leakey, *Southern Kikuyu before 1903*, 740.
92 Davison, *Voices from Mutira*, 180.
93 Davison, *Voices from Mutira*, 91.
94 Kenyatta, *Facing Mount Kenya*, 155.
95 Kenyatta, *Facing Mount Kenya*, 155–56.
96 Kenyatta, *Facing Mount Kenya*, 156.
97 Ellis, *Sexual Inversion*, 36–39.

CHAPTER 4. ANTINOMIAN INTIMACY IN CLAUDE MCKAY'S JAMAICA

1 Stoff, "Claude McKay and the Cult of Primitivism," 129.

2 Griffin, "The Road to Psychic Unity," 500.

3 See Holcomb, *Claude McKay, Code Name Sasha* and Newman, "Ephemeral Utopias."

4 Stephens, *Black Empire*, 142, 167–203.

5 McKay, *Banjo*, 326.

6 McKay, *A Long Way from Home*, 149–50, emphasis in original.

7 Cooper, *Claude McKay*, 75.

8 McKay, *A Long Way from Home*, 150.

9 Gilroy, *Black Atlantic*.

10 McKay, *Banana Bottom*, 45.

11 McKay, *Banana Bottom*, 17.

12 McKay, *Banana Bottom*, 11, 205.

13 Cooper, *Claude McKay*, 22–34; James, *A Fierce Hatred of Injustice*, 26–28. For the most convincing account of McKay's relationship to Jekyll, see Cobham, "'Jekyll and Claude.'"

14 James, *A Fierce Hatred of Injustice*, 34–35.

15 Holcomb, "Diaspora Cruises," 715.

16 Maiwald, "Race, Capitalism, and the Third-Sex Ideal."

17 Patterson, *The Sociology of Slavery*, 9.

18 For an invaluable overview of these debates, see Chevannes, "Sexual Behaviour of Jamaicans."

19 See Bush, *Slave Women in Caribbean Society*; Reddock, "Women and Slavery in the Caribbean"; and Cobham, "Women in Jamaican Literature."

20 Long, *History of Jamaica*, 2:327, emphasis in original.

21 Burnard, "'Rioting in Goatish Embraces,'" 188, 194.

22 See Burnard, "A Failed Settler Society."

23 Long, *History of Jamaica*, 2:414, emphasis in original.

24 Long, *History of Jamaica*, 2:415.

25 Kempadoo, *Sexing the Caribbean*, 1.

26 Kempadoo, *Sexing the Caribbean*, 2.

27 Spillers, "Mama's Baby, Papa's Maybe," 67, emphasis in original.

28 Spillers, "Mama's Baby, Papa's Maybe" 68, emphasis in original.

29 Paton, *No Bond but the Law*, 6, 7.

30 Qtd. in Holt, *The Problem of Freedom*, 78.

31 Holt, *The Problem of Freedom*, 45.

32 As Édouard Glissant explains, a similar situation existed in Martinique. The French counsel who issued the emancipation proclamation in 1848 announced, "married people are the most honorable and the most worthy of guaranteeing to the republic that henceforth the slaves will get married in order to be able to feed and care for an old father, a mother, a wife and children, brothers and sisters, an

entire family, because in this way everyone will have to work when everyone is free" (*Caribbean Discourse*, 34).

33   Paton, *No Bond but the Law*, 61.

34   Paton, *No Bond but the Law*, 122.

35   Paton, *No Bond but the Law*, 131.

36   Holt, *The Problem of Freedom*, 33–34.

37   Paton, *No Bond but the Law*, 140.

38   Brodber, "Afro-Jamaican Women," 45.

39   Cobham, "Women in Jamaican Literature," 195–97.

40   McKay, *My Green Hills of Jamaica*, 46, 47–48, 3.

41   McKay, *Constab Ballads*, 7.

42   McKay, *Complete Poems*, 314.

43   I take "vernacular glue" from Hart, *Nations of Nothing but Poetry*, 34.

44   McKay, *Constab Ballads*, 7. Unless otherwise noted, all subsequent poetry quotations are from this volume.

45   "To Inspector W. E. Clark," lines 1–2, p. 39.

46   "To Inspector W. E. Clark," lines 1–6, p. 39.

47   "To Inspector W. E. Clark," lines 13–18, p. 39.

48   The Jamaican constabulary was established in 1867, two years after the Morant Bay rebellion, and its primary goal at the time was to "control . . . the colonial population" (*Jamaica Constabulary Force: Manual for Community Policing Services Delivery* [Kingston: Jamaica Constabulary Force, 2008], iii).

49   McKay, "The Heart of a Constab," lines 21–24, p. 63.

50   Hansell, "Some Themes in the Jamaican Poetry of Claude McKay," 123.

51   McKay, "De Route March," lines 1–12, p. 11.

52   Hitchcock, "Decolonizing (the) English," 751.

53   Brathwaite, *History of the Voice*, 20n21.

54   Brathwaite, *History of the Voice*, 13.

55   Moten, *In the Break*, 26.

56   "De Route March," lines 21–24, p. 12.

57   "Flat-Foot Drill," line 25, p. 14.

58   In the 1922 foreword to *Harlem Shadows*, McKay explains his formal choices: "I have adhered to such of the older [poetic] traditions as I find adequate for my most lawless and revolutionary passions and moods" (*Collected Poems*, 315).

59   Sharpe, *Monstrous Intimacies*.

60   "Stubborn will" is from "Bennie's Departure," line 204, p. 22; "aimless will" is from "Consolation," line 26, p. 24; "cheery will" is from "Fire Practice," line 11, p. 26.

61   McKay, "Consolation," line 57, p. 25; "To W.G.G.," line 28, p. 77.

62   James, "Becoming the People's Poet," 31.

63   James, "Becoming the People's Poet," 31, 29.

64   My thanks to Melissa Girard for this clarification.

65   Gilroy, *Black Atlantic*, 85.

66 The character Dan also appears in "My Pretty Dan" in *Songs from Jamaica* (*Collected Poems*, 74–75), as the subject of affection for an unnamed and gender-neutral speaker. In "My Pretty Dan," the speaker is based in a rural location and has a long-distance relationship with Dan. A footnote in *Constab Ballads* identifies the poem "Disillusioned" as a sequel to "My Pretty Dan" (48).

67 McKay, "Disillusioned," lines 5–8, p. 43.

68 McKay, "The Apple-Woman's Complaint," line 32, p. 58.

69 McKay, "Disillusioned," lines 25–32, p. 44.

70 McKay, "The Apple-Woman's Complaint," lines 23–24, p. 58.

71 McKay, "Disillusioned," lines 45–48, p. 45.

72 McKay, Disillusioned, lines 21–24, p. 44.

73 McKay, Disillusioned," lines 49–52, p. 45.

74 McKay, *Banana Bottom*, 2–3. Hereafter, page citations to this work will appear in the text.

75 Karras, *Sojourners in the Sun*, 7.

76 Hall, *Civilizing Subjects*, 72.

77 Burnard, *Mastery, Tyranny, and Desire*, 228–40.

78 Glissant, *Caribbean Discourse*, 2.

79 Jay, "Hybridity," 177.

80 Long, *History of Jamaica*, 2:262–63.

81 Ramchand, *The West Indian Novel*, 238, 240, 241.

82 LeSeur, *Ten Is the Age of Darkness*, 153.

83 Griffin, "The Road to Psychic Unity," 502.

84 Moore and Johnson, *Neither Led nor Driven*, 96–136.

85 See Griffin, "Claude McKay."

86 Maxwell, "Introduction: Claude McKay—Lyric Poetry in the Age of Cataclysm," xxxix.

87 Rosenberg, *Nationalism and the Formation of Caribbean Literature*, 120.

88 Ramchand, *The West Indian Novel*, 250.

BEGINNINGS, IN SEVEN MOVEMENTS

1 Sharpe, *In the Wake*, 41.

BIBLIOGRAPHY

Agard-Jones, Vanessa. "Le Jeu de Qui? Sexual Politics at Play in the French Caribbean." *Caribbean Review of Gender Studies* 3.1 (2009): 1–19.

Akyeampong, Emmanuel. "Sexuality and Prostitution among the Akan of the Gold Coast c. 1650–1950." *Past and Present* 156 (1997): 144–73.

Alexander, M. Jacqui. "Erotic Autonomy as a Politics of Decolonization: An Anatomy of Feminist and State Practice in the Bahamas Tourist Industry." In *Feminist Genealogies, Colonial Legacies, Democratic Futures*, edited by M. Jacqui Alexander and Chandra Mohanty, 63–100. New York: Routledge, 1997.

Allman, Jean. "Rounding Up Spinsters: Gender Chaos and Unmarried Women in Colonial Asante." *Journal of African History* 37.2 (1996): 195–214.

Alloula, Malek. *The Colonial Harem*. Translated by Myrna Godzich and Wlad Godzich. Minneapolis: University of Minnesota Press, 1986.

Baker, Houston. *Modernism and the Harlem Renaissance*. Chicago: University of Chicago Press, 1989.

Barlow, A. R., Review of *Facing Mount Kenya, the Tribal Life of the Gikuyu*, by Kenyatta Jomo (1938). *Africa* 12.1 (1939): 114–16.

Benson, Sue, and Barbara Melosh. "The Fourth Berkshire Conference on the History of Women." *Radical History Review* 19 (Winter 1978–79): 143–48.

Bergner, Gwen. "Politics and Pathologies: On the Subject of Race in Psychoanalysis." In *Frantz Fanon: Critical Perspectives*, edited by Anthony C. Alessandrini, 219–35. New York: Routledge, 1999.

Bergner, Gwen. "Who Is That Masked Woman? or, The Role of Gender in Fanon's *Black Skin, White Masks*." *PMLA* 110.1 (1995): 75–88.

Berlant, Lauren, and Michael Warner. "Sex in Public." *Critical Inquiry* 24.2 (1998): 547–66.

Berman, Bruce. "Ethnography as Politics, Politics as Ethnography: Kenyatta, Malinowski, and the Making of *Facing Mount Kenya*." *Canadian Journal of African Studies* 30.3 (1996): 313–44.

Berman, Bruce J., and John M. Lonsdale. "The Labors of '*Muigwithania*': Jomo Kenyatta as Author, 1928–45." *Research in African Literatures* 29.1 (1998): 16–42.

Bernstein, Alison. "The Coming of Age of the Berkshire Conference." *Women's Studies Newsletter* 6.4 (1978): 5–7.

Bhabha, Homi. "What Does the Black Man Want?" *New Formations* 1 (1987): 118–24.

Blyden, Edward Wilmot. *African Life and Customs*. Baltimore: Black Classic Press, 1994.

Blyden, Edward Wilmot. *The Aims and Methods of a Liberal Education for Africans: Inaugural Address*. Cambridge: John Wilson and Son University Press, 1882.

Brathwaite, Edward Kamau. *History of the Voice: The Development of Nation Language in Anglophone Caribbean Poetry*. London: New Beacon, 1984.

Brodber, Erna. "Afro-Jamaican Women at the Turn of the Century." *Social and Economic Studies* 4.3 (1986): 23–50.

Browne, Simone. *Dark Matters: On the Surveillance of Blackness*. Durham, NC: Duke University Press, 2015.

Bujra, Janet M. "Women 'Entrepreneurs' of Early Nairobi." *Canadian Journal of African Studies* 9.2 (1975): 213–34.

Burnard, Trevor. "A Failed Settler Society: Marriage and Demographic Failure in Early Jamaica." *Journal of Social History* 28 (1994): 63–82.

Burnard, Trevor. *Mastery, Tyranny, and Desire: Thomas Thistlewood and His Slaves in the Anglo-Jamaican World*. Chapel Hill: University of North Carolina Press, 2003.

Burnard, Trevor. "'Rioting in Goatish Embraces': Marriage and Improvement in Early British Jamaica." *History of the Family* 11.4 (2006): 18597.

Burton, Richard. *The Sotadic Zone*. 1886. Reprint. Boston: Longwood Press, 1977.

Bush, Barbara. *Slave Women in Caribbean Society, 1650–1838*. Bloomington: Indiana University Press, 1989.

Califia, Patrick. *Public Sex: The Culture of Radical Sex*. Boston: Cleis Press, 1994.

Campbell, James. *Middle Passages: African American Journeys to Africa, 1787–2005*. New York: Penguin, 2007.

Carby, Hazel. "'On the Threshold of Woman's Era': Lynching, Empire, and Sexuality in Black Feminist Theory." *Critical Inquiry* 12.1 (1985): 262–77.

Chamberlin, J. Edward, and Sander L. Gilman, eds. *Degeneration: The Dark Side of Progress*. New York: Columbia University Press, 1985.

Chevannes, Barry. "Sexual Behaviour of Jamaicans: A Literature Review." *Social and Economic Studies* 42.1 (1993): 1–45.

Cobham, Rhonda. "'Jekyll and Claude': The Erotics of Patronage in Claude McKay's *Banana Bottom*." In *Queer Diasporas*, edited by Cindy Patton and Benigno Sanchez-Eppler, 122–53. Durham, NC: Duke University Press, 2000.

Cobham, Rhonda. "Women in Jamaican Literature 1900–1950." In *Out of the Kumbla: Caribbean Women and Literature*, edited by Carole Boyce Davies and Elaine Savory Fido, 195–222. Trenton, NJ: Africa World Press, 1990.

Cooper, Wayne F. *Claude McKay: Rebel Sojourner in the Harlem Renaissance, A Biography*. Baton Rouge: Louisiana State University Press, 1987.

Crimp, Douglas. "Mourning and Militancy." *October* 51 (1989): 3–18.

Crummell, Alexander. "The Race Problem in America." In *Civilization and Black Progress: Selected Writings of Alexander Crummell on the South*, edited by J. R. Oldfield, 163–73. Charlottesville: University of Virginia Press, 1995.

Davis, Paula Dean. "On the Sexuality of 'Town Women' in Kampala." *Africa Today* 47.3 (2000): 29–60.

Davison, Jean, with the Women of Mutira. *Voices from Mutira: Lives of Rural Gikuyu Women*. Boulder, CO: Lynne Rienner, 1989.

Dean, Tim. *Beyond Sexuality*. Chicago: University of Chicago Press, 2000.

Delany, Samuel R. *Through the Valley of the Nest of Spiders*. New York: Magnus Books, 2012.

Delany, Samuel R. *Times Square Red, Times Square Blue*. New York: New York University Press, 1999.

Desai, Gaurav. *Subject to Colonialism: African Self-Fashioning and the Colonial Library*. Durham, NC: Duke University Press, 2001.

Diabate, Naminata. "René Maran's *Batouala* and Africa: The Limits of the Alliance." In *Oral and Written Expressions of African Culture*, edited by Toyin Falola and Fallou Ngom, 165–83. Durham, NC: Carolina Academic Press, 2009.

Dollimore, Jonathan. *Sexual Dissidence: Augustine to Wilde, Freud to Foucault*. Oxford: Clarendon Press, 1991.

Dundas, Kenneth R. "Kikuyu Calendar." *Man* 9.19 (1909): 37–38.

Dynes, Wayne. "Homosexuality in Sub-Saharan Africa: An Unnecessary Controversy." *Gay Books Bulletin* 9 (1983): 20–21.

Edelman, Lee. *Homographesis: Essays in Gay Literary and Cultural Studies*. New York: Routledge, 1994.

Edelman, Lee. *No Future: Queer Theory and the Death Drive*. Durham, NC: Duke University Press, 2004.

Edmondson, Belinda. *Making Men: Gender, Literary Authority, and Women's Writing in Caribbean Narrative*. Durham, NC: Duke University Press, 1998.

Edwards, Brent Hayes. "Langston Hughes and the Futures of Diaspora." *American Literary History* 19.3 (2007): 689–711.

Edwards, Brent Hayes. *The Practice of Diaspora: Literature, Translation, and the Rise of Black Internationalism*. Cambridge, MA: Harvard University Press, 2003.

Edwards, Brent Hayes. "The Uses of Diaspora." *Social Text 66* 19.1 (2001): 45–73.

Ellis, Havelock. *Sexual Inversion*. 1901. Reprint. New York: Arno Press, 1975.

Fabian, Johannes. *Time and the Other: How Anthropology Makes Its Object*. New York: Columbia University Press, 2002.

Fanon, Frantz. *Black Skin, White Masks*. Translated by Charles Lam Markmann. New York: Grove, 1967.

Fanon, Frantz. *Black Skin, White Masks*. Translated by Richard Philcox. New York: Grove, 2008.

Fanon, Frantz. *Peau Noire, Masque Blancs*. Paris: Éditions de Seuil, 1952.

Fanon, Frantz. *The Wretched of the Earth*. Translated by Constance Farrington. New York: Penguin, 2001.

Foster, Frances Smith. *Love and Marriage in Early African America*. Boston: Northeastern University Press, 2007.

Frazier, E. Franklin. "The Negro Slave Family." *Journal of Negro History* 15.2 (1930): 198–259.

Fuss, Diana. "Interior Colonies: Frantz Fanon and the Politics of Identification." *Diacritics* 24.2/3 (1994): 19–42.

Gikandi, Simon. "Cultural Translation and the African Self: A (Post) Colonial Case Study." *Interventions* 3.3 (2001): 355–75.

Gikandi, Simon. "Pan-Africanism and Cosmopolitanism: The Case of Jomo Kenyatta." *English Studies in Africa* 43.1 (2000): 3–27.

Gill, Lydon K. "In the Realm of Our Lorde: Eros and the Poet Philosopher." *Feminist Studies* 40.1 (2014): 169–89.

Gilroy, Paul. *The Black Atlantic: Modernity and Double Consciousness.* Cambridge, MA: Harvard University Press, 1993.

Glissant, Édouard. *Caribbean Discourse: Selected Essays.* Translated by J. Michael Dash. Charlottesville: University of Virginia Press, 1989.

Goldie, Terry. "Saint Fanon and 'Homosexual Territory.'" In *Frantz Fanon: Critical Perspectives,* edited by Anthony C. Alessandrini, 77–88. New York: Routledge, 1999.

Gordon, Lewis R. "Through the Zone of Nonbeing: A Reading of *Black Skin, White Masks* in Celebration of Fanon's Eightieth Birthday." *C. L. R. James Journals* 11.1 (2005): 1–43.

Gordon, Lewis R. *What Fanon Said: A Philosophical Introduction to His Life and Thought.* New York: Fordham University Press, 2015. Kindle edition.

Griffin, Barbara J. "Claude McKay: The Evolution of a Conservative." *College Language Association Journal* 36.2 (1992): 157–70.

Griffin, Barbara J. "The Road to Psychic Unity: The Politics of Gender in Claude McKay's *Banana Bottom.*" *Callaloo* 22.2 (1999): 499–508.

Haley, Alex. *Roots.* New York: Vintage, 1991.

Hall, Catherine. *Civilizing Subjects: Metropole and Colony in the English Imagination 1830–1867.* Chicago: University of Chicago Press, 2002.

Hall, Stuart. "New Ethnicities." In *Stuart Hall: Critical Dialogues in Cultural Studies,* edited by David Morley and Kuan-Hsing Chen, 442–51. New York: Routledge, 1996.

Hanhardt, Christina B. *Safe Space: Gay Neighborhood History and the Politics of Violence.* Durham, NC: Duke University Press, 2014.

Hansell, William H. "Some Themes in the Jamaican Poetry of Claude McKay." *Phylon* 40.2 (1979): 123–39.

Hansen, Karen Tranberg, ed. *African Encounters with Domesticity.* New Brunswick, NJ: Rutgers University Press, 1992.

Hart, Matthew. *Nations of Nothing but Poetry: Modernism, Transnationalism, and Synthetic Vernacular Writing.* New York: Oxford University Press, 2010.

Hartman, Saidiya. *Lose Your Mother: A Journey Along the Atlantic Slave Route.* New York: Farrar, Strauss, and Giroux, 2007. Kindle edition.

Hemphill, Essex. *Ceremonies: Prose and Poetry.* New York: Plume, 1992.

Herskovitz, Melville J. "The Negro in the New World: The Statement of a Problem." *American Anthropologist* 32.1 (1930): 145–55.

Hitchcock, Peter. "Decolonizing (the) English." *South Atlantic Quarterly* 100.3 (2001): 749–71.

Hoad, Neville, *African Intimacies: Race, Homosexuality, and Globalization*. Minneapolis: University of Minnesota Press, 2007.

Hobley, Charles W. "54. Kikuyu Medicines." *Man* 6 (1906): 81–83.

Hocquenghem, Guy. *The Screwball Asses*. Translated by Noura Wedell. Los Angeles: Semiotext(e), 2010.

Hodes, Martha. "The Sexualization of Reconstruction Politics: White Women and Black Men in the South after the Civil War." *Journal of the History of Sexuality* 3.3 (1993): 402–17.

Holcomb, Gary E. *Claude McKay Code Name Sasha: Queer Black Marxism and the Harlem Renaissance*. Gainesville: University Press of Florida, 2007.

Holcomb, Gary E. "Diaspora Cruises: Queer Black Proletarianism in Claude McKay's *A Long Way from Home*." *Modern Fiction Studies* 49.4 (2003): 714–45.

Holland, Sharon Patricia. *The Erotic Life of Racism*. Durham, NC: Duke University Press, 2012. Kindle edition.

Holt, Thomas. *The Problem of Freedom: Race, Labor, and Politics in Jamaica and Britain, 1832–1938*. Baltimore: The Johns Hopkins University Press, 1992.

Hunter, Tera W. *Bound in Wedlock: Slave and Free Marriage in the Nineteenth Century*. Cambridge, MA: Harvard University Press, 2017.

Ikonné, Chidi. "René Maran, 1887–1960: A Black Francophone Writer between Two Worlds." *Research in African Literatures* 5.1 (1974): 5–22.

Ikonné, Chidi. "René Maran and the New Negro." *Colby Library Quarterly* 15. 4 (1979): 224–39.

Irigaray, Luce. "When Our Lips Speak Together." Translated by Carolyn Burke. *Signs* 6.1 (1980): 69–79.

Jaji, Tsitsi Ella. *Africa in Stereo: Modernism, Music, and Pan-African Solidarity*. New York: Oxford University Press, 2014.

James, C. L. R. *The Black Jacobins: Toussaint L'Ouverture and the San Domingo Revolution*. New York: Vintage, 1989.

James, C. L. R. "From Touissant L'Ouverture to Fidel Castro" [1962]. In *The Black Jacobins: Toussaint L'Ouverture and the San Domingo Revolution*, 391–418. New York: Vintage, 1989.

James, Winston. "Becoming the People's Poet: Claude McKay's Jamaican Years, 1889–1912." *Small Axe* 7.1 (2003): 17–45.

James, Winston. *A Fierce Hatred of Injustice: Claude McKay's Jamaica and His Poetry of Rebellion*. Kingston: Ian Randle, 2000.

James, Winston. *Holding Aloft the Banner of Ethiopia: Caribbean Radicalism in Early Twentieth-Century America*. London: Verso, 1998.

Jay, Paul. "Hybridity, Identity, and Cultural Commerce in Claude McKay's *Banana Bottom*." *Callaloo* 22.1 (1999): 176–94.

Joseph, Gloria I. *The Wind Is Spirit: The Life, Love, and Legacy of Audre Lorde*. New York: Villarosa Media, 2016.

Kamugisha, Aaron. "The Hearts of Men? Gender in the Late CLR James." *Small Axe* 15.1 (2011): 76–94.

Kanogo, Tabitha. *African Womanhood in Colonial Kenya, 1900–1950*. Oxford: James Currey, 2005.

Karras, Alan L. *Sojourners in the Sun: Scottish Migrants in Jamaica and the Chesapeake, 1740–1800*. Ithaca, NY: Cornell University Press, 1992.

Kazanjian, David. "Scenes of Speculation." *Social Text 125* 33.4 (2015): 77–84.

Keeling, Kara. *The Witch's Flight: The Cinematic, the Black Femme, and the Image of Common Sense*. Durham, NC: Duke University Press, 2007. Kindle edition.

Kempadoo, Kamala. *Sexing the Caribbean: Gender, Race, and Sexual Labor*. New York: Routledge, 2004.

Kenyatta, Jomo. *Facing Mount Kenya: The Tribal Life of the Agikuyu*. 1938. Reprint. New York: Vintage, 1965.

Kesteloot, Lilyan. *Black Writers in French: A Literary History of Negritude*. Translated by Ellen Conroy Kennedy. Washington, DC: Howard University Press, 1991.

Krafft-Ebing, Richard von. *Psychopathia Sexualis*. Translated by Franklin S. Klaf. New York: Arcade Publishing, 1965.

Leakey, L. S. B. *The Southern Kikuyu before 1903*. 3 vols. London: Academic Press, 1977.

LeSeur, Geta. *Ten Is the Age of Darkness: The Black Bildungsroman*. Columbia: University of Missouri Press, 1995.

Levine, Philippa. *Prostitution, Race, and Politics: Policing Venereal Disease in the British Empire*. New York: Routledge, 2003.

Lewis, Earl. "To Turn as on a Pivot: Writing African Americans into a History of Overlapping Diasporas." *American Historical Review* 100.3 (1995): 765–87.

Lindsey, Treva B., and Jessica Marie Johnson. "Searching for Climax: Black Erotic Lives in Slavery and Freedom." *Meridians* 12.2 (2014): 169–95.

Locke, Alain. *The Works of Alain Locke*. Edited by Charles Molesworth. New York: Oxford University Press, 2012.

Long, Edward. *The History of Jamaica; or, General Survey of the Antient and Modern State of That Island: With Reflections on Its Situation, Settlements, Inhabitants, Climate, Products, Commerce, Laws, and Government*. 3 vols. London, 1774.

Loomba, Ania. "'Delicious Traffick': Alterity and Exchange on Early Modern Stages." *Shakespeare Survey* 1.52 (1999): 201–14.

Lorde, Audre. "My Words Will Be There." In *I Am Your Sister: Collected and Unpublished Writings of Audre Lorde*, edited by Rudolph P. Byrd, Johnnetta Betsch Cole, and Beverly Guy-Sheftall, 160–68. New York: Oxford University Press, 2009.

Lorde, Audre. *Sister Outsider: Essays and Speeches*. Freedom, CA: Crossing Press, 1984.

Lugard, Frederick Dealtry. "The International Institute of African Languages and Cultures." *Africa* 1.1 (1928): 1–12.

Luibhéid, Eithne. *Entry Denied: Controlling Sexuality at the Border*. Minneapolis: University of Minnesota Press, 2002.

Lynch, Hollis R. *Edward Wilmot Blyden: Pan-Negro Patriot, 1832–1912*. London: Oxford University Press, 1967.

Macey, David. *Frantz Fanon: A Biography*. London: Verso, 2012. Kindle edition.

Macharia, Keguro. "'How Does a Girl Grow into a Woman?': Girlhood in Ngugi wa Thiong'o's *The River Between*." *Research in African Literatures* 43.2 (2012): 1–17.

Macharia, Keguro. "Love." *Critical Ethnic Studies* 1.1 (2015): 68–75.

Magubane, Bernard. "A Critical Look at Indices Used in the Study of Social Change in Colonial Africa." *Current Anthropology* 12.4/5 (1971): 419–45.

Maiwald, Michael. "Race, Capitalism, and the Third-Sex Ideal: Claude McKay's *Home to Harlem* and the Legacy of Edward Carpenter." *Modern Fiction Studies* 48.4 (2002): 825–57.

Malinowski, Bronislaw. "Practical Anthropology." *Africa* 2.1 (1929): 22–38.

Malinowski, Bronislaw. *Sex and Repression in Savage Society*. 1927. Reprint. New York: Routledge, 2001.

Maran, René. *Batouala*. Translated by Barbara Beck and Alexandre Mboukou. Portsmouth, NH: Heinemann, 1987.

Maxwell, William J. "Introduction: Claude McKay—Lyric Poetry in the Age of Cataclysm." In *Complete Poems: Claude McKay*, edited by William J. Maxwell, xi–xliv. Urbana: University of Illinois Press, 2004.

Mbiti, John. *Introduction to African Religion*. Nairobi: EAEP, 2003.

McClellan, Woodford. "Africans and Black Americans in the Comintern Schools, 1925–1934." *International Journal of African Historical Studies* 26.2 (1993): 371–90.

McKay, Claude. *Banana Bottom*. New York: Harcourt, 1933.

McKay, Claude. *Banjo: A Story without a Plot*. New York: Harper, 1929.

McKay, Claude. *Complete Poems*. Edited by William J. Maxwell. Urbana: University of Illinois Press, 2004.

McKay, Claude. *Constab Ballads*. London: Watts, 1912.

McKay, Claude. *A Long Way from Home*. New York: Harcourt, 1970.

McKay, Claude. *My Green Hills of Jamaica*. Kingston: Heinemann, 1979.

McKittrick, Katherine. "Mathematics Black Life." *Black Scholar* 44.2 (2014): 16–28.

McKittrick, Katherine. "Rebellion/Invention/Groove." *Small Axe* 49 (2016): 79–91.

Menkiti, Ifeanyi. "On the Normative Conception of a Person." In *A Companion to African Philosophy*, edited by Kwasi Wiredu, 324–31. Malden, MA: Blackwell Publishing, 2004.

Menkiti, Ifeanyi. "Person and Community in African Traditional Thought." In *African Philosophy, An Introduction*, edited by R. A. Wright, 171–82. Lanham, MD: University Press of America, 1984.

Mercer, Kobena. "Decolonisation and Disappointment: Reading Fanon's Sexual Politics." In *The Fact of Blackness: Frantz Fanon and Visual Representation*, edited by Alan Read, 114–31. Seattle: Bay Press, 1996.

Miller, Christopher L. *Blank Darkness: Africanist Discourse in French*. Chicago: University of Chicago Press, 1985.

Miller, Paul B. "Remoteness and Proximity: The Parallel Ethnographies of Alejo Carpentier and René Maran." *Symposium: A Quarterly Journal in Modern Literatures* 66.1 (2012): 1–15.

Mintz, Sidney W., and Richard Price. *The Birth of African-American Culture: An Anthropological Perspective*. Boston: Beacon Press, 1976.

Moore, Brian L., and Michele A. Johnson. *Neither Led nor Driven: Contesting British Cultural Imperialism in Jamaica, 1865–1920*. Mona, Jamaica: University of the West Indies Press, 2004.

Morrison, Toni. *Playing in the Dark*. Cambridge, MA: Harvard University Press, 1992.

Moten, Fred. "The Case of Blackness." *Criticism* 50.2 (2008): 177–218.

Moten, Fred. *In the Break: The Aesthetics of the Black Radical Tradition*. Minneapolis: University of Minnesota Press, 2003.

Mumford, Kevin J. *Interzones: Black/White Sex Districts in Chicago and New York in the Early Twentieth Century*. New York: Columbia University Press, 1997.

Muriuki, Godfrey. *A History of the Kikuyu 1500–1900*. Nairobi: Oxford University Press, 1974.

Murray, David A. B. "Between a Rock and a Hard Place: The Power and Powerlessness of Transnational Narratives among Gay Martinican Men." *American Anthropologist* 102.2 (2000): 261–70.

Murray-Brown, Jeremy. *Kenyatta*. New York: E. P. Dutton, 1973.

Musangi, Neo Sinoxolo. "Homing with My Mother / How Women in My Family Married Women." *Meridians* 17.2 (2018): 401–14.

Newman, Eric H. "Ephemeral Utopias: Queer Cruising, Literary Form, and Diasporic Imagination in Claude McKay's *Home to Harlem* and *Banjo*." *Callaloo* 38.1 (2015): 167–85.

Ngai, Sianne. *Ugly Feelings*. Cambridge, MA: Harvard University Press, 2005.

Ntarangwi, Mwendwa. *East African Hip Hop: Youth Culture and Globalization*. Urbana: University of Illinois Press, 2009.

Nunes, Zita. *Cannibal Democracy: Race and Representation in the Literature of the Americas*. Minneapolis: University of Minnesota Press, 2008.

Nwezeh, E. C. "René Maran: Myth and Reality." *Odu* 18 (1978): 91–105.

Nyairo, Joyce. *Kenya@50: Trends, Identities and the Politics of Belonging*. Nairobi: Contact Zones, 2015. Kindle edition.

Nyong'o, Tavia. *The Amalgamation Waltz: Race, Performance, and the Ruses of Memory*. Minneapolis: University of Minnesota Press, 2009.

Nyong'o, Tavia. "Unburdening Representation." *Black Scholar* 44.2 (2014): 70–80.

Nzegwu, Nkiru. *Family Matters: Feminist Concepts in African Philosophy of Culture*. Albany: State University of New York Press, 2012.

Nzegwu, Nkiru. "Osuality, or African Sensuality: Going beyond Eroticism." *JENdA: A Journal of Culture and African Women Studies* 16 (2010).

Okpewho, Isidore, and Nkiru Nzwegu, eds. *The New African Diaspora*. Bloomington: Indiana University Press, 2009.

Owusu, Maxwell. "On Indigenous Anthropology: A Malinowskian View." *Current Anthropology* 22.6 (1981): 709–10.

Oyěwùmí, Oyèrónkẹ́. *The Invention of Women: Making an African Sense of Western Gender Discourses*. Minneapolis: University of Minnesota Press, 1997.

Paton, Diana. *No Bond but the Law: Punishment, Race, and Gender in Jamaican State Formation. 1780–1870*. Durham, NC: Duke University Press, 2004.

Patterson, Orlando. *The Sociology of Slavery: An Analysis of the Origins, Development, and Structure of Negro Slave Society in Jamaica*. Rutherford, NJ: Fairleigh Dickinson University Press, 1967.

Philip, M. NourbeSe. *She Tries Her Tongue, Her Voice Softly Breaks*. Middletown, CT: Wesleyan University Press, 2015.

Pierre, Jemima. *The Predicament of Blackness: Postcolonial Ghana and the Politics of Race*. Chicago: University of Chicago Press, 2012. Kindle edition.

Polsgrove, Carol. *Ending British Rule in Africa: Writers in a Common Cause*. Manchester: Manchester University Press, 2009.

Povinelli, Elizabeth A. *Economies of Abandonment: Social Belonging and Endurance in Late Liberalism*. Durham, NC: Duke University Press, 2011. Kindle edition.

Povinelli, Elizabeth A. "Notes on Gridlock: Genealogy, Intimacy, Sexuality." *Public Culture* 14.1 (2002): 215–38.

Ramchand, Kenneth. *The West Indian Novel and Its Background*. Kingston: Ian Randle, 2004.

Reddock, Rhoda E. "Women and Slavery in the Caribbean: A Feminist Perspective." *Latin American Perspectives* 12.1 (1985): 63–80.

Reddy, Chandan. *Freedom with Violence: Race, Sexuality, and the US State*. Durham, NC: Duke University Press, 2011.

Reid-Pharr, Robert. *Black Gay Man: Essays*. New York: New York University Press, 2001.

Robinson, Cedric. *Black Marxism: The Making of the Black Radical Tradition*. 2nd ed. Chapel Hill: University of North Carolina Press, 2000.

Rose, Jacqueline. *States of Fantasy*. Oxford: Clarendon Press, 1998.

Rosenberg, Leah. *Nationalism and the Formation of Caribbean Literature*. New York: Palgrave, 2007.

Safran, William. "Diasporas in Modern Societies: Myths of Homeland and Return." *Diaspora: A Journal of Transnational Studies* 1.1 (1991): 83–99.

Sedgwick, Eve Kosofsky. "Queer and Now." In *Tendencies*, 1–20. Durham, NC: Duke University Press, 1993.

Sedgwick, Eve Kosofsky. *Touching Feeling: Affect, Pedagogy, Performativity*. Durham, NC: Duke University Press, 2003.

Sharpe, Christina. *In the Wake: On Blackness and Being*. Durham, NC: Duke University Press, 2016.

Sharpe, Christina. *Monstrous Intimacies: Making Post-Slavery Subjects*. Durham, NC: Duke University Press, 2010.

Sharpley-Whiting, Denean T. "Fanon and Capecia." In *Frantz Fanon: Critical Perspectives*, edited by Anthony Alessandrini, 57–74. New York: Routledge, 1996.

Shaw, Carolyn Martin. *Colonial Inscriptions: Race, Sex, and Class in Kenya*. Minneapolis: University of Minnesota Press, 1995.

Showalter, Elaine. *Sexual Anarchy: Gender and Culture at the Fin de Siècle*. New York: Penguin, 1991.

Snorton, Riley C. *Black on Both Sides: A Racial History of Trans Identity*. Minneapolis: University of Minnesota Press, 2017.

Somerville, Siobhan B. *Queering the Color Line: Race and the Invention of Homosexuality in American Culture*. Durham, NC: Duke University Press, 2000.

Spillers, Hortense. "'All the Things You Could Be by Now, If Sigmund Freud's Wife Was Your Mother': Psychoanalysis and Race." In *Black, White, and in Color: Essays on American Literature and Culture*, 376–427. Chicago: University of Chicago Press, 2003.

Spillers, Hortense. "Mama's Baby, Papa's Maybe: An American Grammar Book." *Diacritics* 17.2 (1987): 65–81.

Stephens, Michelle Ann. *Black Empire: The Masculine Global Imaginary of Caribbean Intellectuals in the United States, 1914–1962*. Durham, NC: Duke University Press, 2005.

Stoff, Michael. "Claude McKay and the Cult of Primitivism," in *The Harlem Renaissance Remembered*, edited by Arna Bontemps, 126–46. New York: Dodd, Mead, 1972.

Stoler, Ann Laura. *Carnal Knowledge and Imperial Power: Race and the Intimate in Colonial Rule*. Berkeley: University of California Press, 2002.

Tate, H. R. "Notes on the Kikuyu and Kamba Tribes of British East Africa." *Journal of the Anthropological Institute of Great Britain and Ireland* 34 (1904): 130–48.

Tinsley, Omise'eke. "Black Atlantic, Queer Atlantic: Queer Imaginings of the Middle Passage." *GLQ* 14.2/3 (2008): 191–215.

Torgovnick, Marianna. *Gone Primitive: Savage Intellects, Modern Lives*. Chicago: University of Chicago Press, 1991.

Török, Mária. "The Illness of Mourning and the Fantasy of the Exquisite Corpse." in *The Shell and the Kernel: Renewals of Psychoanalysis*, by Nicolas Abraham and Mária Török. Edited and translated by Nicholas Rand, 107–24. Chicago: University of Chicago Press, 1994.

Walcott, Rinaldo. "Outside in Black Studies." In *Black Queer Studies: An Anthology*, edited by Mae G. Henderson and E. Patrick Johnson, 90–105. Durham, NC: Duke University Press, 2001.

Walkowitz, Judith. *City of Dreadful Delight: Narratives of Sexual Dangers in Late-Victorian London*. Chicago: University of Chicago Press, 1992.

Weheliye, Alexander G. *Habeas Viscus: Racializing Assemblages, Biopolitics, and Black Feminist Theories of the Human*. Durham, NC: Duke University Press, 2013.

White, Luise. "Bodily Fluids and Usufruct: Controlling Property in Nairobi, 1917–1939." *Canadian Journal of African Studies* 24.3 (1990): 418–38.

White, Luise. *The Comforts of Home: Prostitution in Colonial Nairobi*. Chicago: University of Chicago Press, 2009.

Williams, Raymond. *Marxism and Literature*. Oxford: Oxford University Press, 1977.

Wipper, Audrey. "Kikuyu Women and the Harry Thuku Disturbances: Some Uniformities of Female Militancy." *Africa* 59.3 (1989): 300–37.

Wiredu, Kwame. "The Moral Foundations of an African Culture." In *Person and Community: Ghanaian Philosophical Studies*, edited by Kwasi Wiredu and Kwame

Gyekye, 193–206. Washington, DC: Council for Research in Values and Philosophy, 1992.

Wynter, Sylvia. "Towards the Sociogenic Principle: Fanon, Identity, the Puzzle of Conscious Experience, and What It Is Like to Be 'Black.'" In *National Identity and Sociopolitical Changes in Latin America*, edited by Mercedes F. Dúran-Cogan and Antonio Gomez-Moriana, 30–66. New York: Routledge, 2001.

Wynter, Sylvia. "Unsettling the Coloniality of Being/Power/Truth/Freedom: Towards the Human, after Man, Its Overrepresentation—An Argument." *CR: The New Centennial Review* 3.3 (2003): 257–337.

Yee, Jennifer. "*Batouala*, the First 'Roman Nègre,' and Dialogism: Writing 'Difference' or Writing 'Differently.'" *Francophone Postcolonial Studies* 2.2 (2004): 51–66.

Zabus, Chantal. *Out in Africa: Same-Sex Desire in Sub-Saharan Literatures and Cultures*. Suffolk: Boydell & Brewer Ltd., 2013.

INDEX

ABOUT THE AUTHOR

Keguro Macharia is an independent scholar from Nairobi, Kenya. He blogs at gukira.wordpress.com.

Printed and bound by CPI Group (UK) Ltd, Croydon, CR0 4YY

13/04/2025

14656574-0002